Westies
from head to tail

Ode to a Westie

W   for White as he should be
E   for Eagerness all must see
S   for Sight keen the quarry to spy
T   for Terrier spirit and never say die.

H   for the Happiness they always bring
I   for Inquisitive—doing their own thing
G   for Good measure in such a small frame
H   for Hi there, how about a game?
L   for their Laughter and love in their hearts
A   for Amenable right from the start.
N   for Not minding if Mum should look stern
D   for Delight upon her return

W   for Welcome, so warm and so nice
H   for Hunting and catching those mice
I   for Intelligence—more than most
T   for *Top Dog*— no idle boast
E   for Evermore Westies—our toast!

Anonymous.
From *Westie News*, Vol. 2, No. 3,
West Highland White Terrier Club of England.

Laird Doon MacDuff of Helmsdale owned by Vicki Beets, Heiskell, Tennessee.

To Lou, who loved them so much,
to Sheila, who bought the first one,
and to Ch. Elfinbrook Simon, who
started the whole happy hobby.

from head to tail

by Ruth Faherty

Drawings by Karol Croft
"How-to" Photographs by Michael Love

1981

 Publications, Inc., 1901 South Garfield, Loveland, Colorado

International Standard Book Number: 0-931866-08-1

VIII

Printed in the United States of America.

Contents

Preface

This book is written for the first-time owner of a Westie. Remembering when our first one came to live with us, I know that the new owner has much to learn. We were very lucky to have had a superb group of "Westie folks" in Pittsburgh, Pennsylvania, our residence at that time, who were willing to help us learn to groom and show our dogs. This book is intended to thank all of those who helped us and to pass along their kindness in the hope that it will come back to them.

I do not know it all, and I never will. My years in Westies changed me from the casual owner of pets to an avid learner about dogs—Westies in particular. The more I learn, the less I know, and the more I need to learn. I do hope to share what I have learned with those who are new to the breed so that they will take a giant step in getting off to a good start. I have tried to discuss everything that I would like the buyers of *my* puppies to know. If you are considering a Westie as your next dog, I hope that this book will help you to decide if this breed will suit your life-style.

Throughout the text, I have in most cases used one gender pronoun—the masculine. I hope that this will not be offensive to women readers. It was done merely to simplify. I know only too well that female dog owners, groomers, breeders, handlers, and judges of the world do their share of the work, if not more, and make an outstanding contribution to the world of dogs.

I wish to extend a special thanks to all those people who so kindly furnished photographs of their Westies to illustrate the charm and character of the breed, and to Mike Love and Karol Croft—their help and encouragement were invaluable. Also, to my "second best friends," Dr. Jimmy Stanford, Dr. George Scorey, and Dr. Kevin Ade, goes my deepest gratitude for their time, textbooks, and unflagging enthusiasm for this project.

Ruth Faherty
July 1980

XI

XII

Am. Can. Ch. Elfinbrook Simon in 1962 with his owner, Barbara (now Mrs. Edward Keenan) at Long Beach, California, where he was owner-handled to Best in Show. Shortly after this Simon won his 27th Best in Show award at Harbor Cities Kennel Club, then the largest show in California. Simon was retired to stud after winning more laurels than any other Westie in history. He went on to really prove his worth by siring 56 American champions and 10 or 12 in Canada. While his record of Best in Show wins has now been topped by dogs that were campaigned longer, Simon's record as a top producing and prepotent stud dog remains unchallenged in the breed. Simon was one of seven American and fourteen Canadian Best in Show winners that have been owned by Wishing Well Kennels, another unequalled record.

Ludwig photo

1 The Beginnings of the Breed

The West Highlands of Scotland were once a plateau rising from the North Atlantic. They have suffered much erosion and fairly recently, geologically speaking, have subsided into the ocean. In the coastal regions, the eroded valleys have become submerged and are now fiords, or firths, leaving the rocky eminences remaining. In this rugged, craggy countryside, small, short-legged Terriers were needed for hunting game like otters, badgers, foxes, and wildcats. These animals made their lairs in the rocks, between the rocks, and under the rocks. The dogs had to be able to follow the animal wherever it went—into narrow passages, between roots, and between rocks that could not be budged—and often totally in the dark. The dogs usually worked in packs, barking when they sighted game and bringing their quarry to ground. The small, flat-ribbed West Highland White Terriers (Westies) were ideal for this work. If a dog's ribs were too round, he could easily become lodged and not be able to move, causing him to starve or crack his ribs in the efffort to extricate himself. The dog also needed the intelligence to outwit a crafty opponent quickly and decisively.

Picture the speed, stamina, determination, and courage such a dog would need for this work and you understand the Westie. This staunch little dog is the product of generations of hardy hunters, fleet of foot and seemingly impervious to the salt spray and the icy winters of the North Atlantic coast. If necessary he could hunt his own food and survive the winter with only a little shelter. But he could be equally at home by his master's hearth, sharing the warmth of his companionship and the fire, welcoming friends, and warning away intruders.

Many present-day breeds have well-documented histories based on ancient writings, art works, and the records of enthusiastic cross-breeders and selective breeders. This is not true of the Terriers of Scotland. Their history is as misty as the Scottish Highlands from which they come and is based on rumor and conjecture.

The short-legged Terriers of today that had their origins in Scotland are the Cairns, Scotties, Dandie Dinmonts, Skyes, and the Westies. Undoubtedly, the Aberdeen Terrier (now the Scottish Terrier), the brindled and colored Cairn Terrier, and the present-day West Highland White Terrier were closely related. Each of these present-day breeds shows evidence of its mixed ancestry. The Scottish Terrier, now bred in iron grey, brindle, and wheaten as well as in black, sometimes shows a spot of white on his chest, indicating a white ancestor. The Cairn Terriers, which are bred in brindle and all colors except white, often have spots of white on the chest and paws, or under the tail, also showing a white forebear. Westies sometimes show a dorsal (center of the back) streak that is yellow or tan. It is anyone's guess which one was the progenitor of the other two.

Colonel Edward Donald Malcolm, whose family seat was Poltalloch, in Argyllshire, is generally credited with breeding the white dogs true. He has sometimes been confused with his older brother, Sir John (or Ian) Wingfield Malcolm, who served as a Member of Parliament. Edward,

being the second son, was destined for a career in the army, as that was the custom of the day. At that time, the breed ranged in color from brown to red to wheat, with some dogs being cream to near-white. Little was known about albinism or genetics in Colonel Malcolm's youth, since Mendel's theories were evolving at about the same time and were not really tested until the early 1900s.

In the mid-1800s, farmers and gamekeepers destroyed light-colored puppies, which were thought to be weak. The serious breeders considered the white dogs an embarrassment, never to see the light of day. Edward did not agree. As a boy growing to manhood, he kept a number of the lightest-colored dogs and hunted them in his own pack. When army duty summoned him abroad, his dogs worked along with those of his brother, proving themselves quite worthy and far easier to be seen in the field. One day a favorite reddish-brown dog, emerging from cover, was mistakenly shot for a fox, convincing Edward all the more that the white dogs were preferable for hunting.

Gameness in the dogs was the first consideration, since the dogs were used for hunting marauding animals that preyed on poultry and lambs, destroyed the crops, and competed with the people for game needed for food. Stories are told that the half-grown puppies were lowered on a rope into a barrel containing a badger or a couple of rats. If the dog was the winner in ten

2

Landseer's "Dignity and Impudence."

Colonel Edward Malcolm.

minutes, he was considered worth his keep. These sound like hardhearted tactics to dog lovers of today, when "survival of the fittest" is left to Mother Nature. But the Foxhunter or the Rabbitcatcher of those days saw nothing amiss with giving her a hand in weeding out the weak and the timid.

Colonel Malcolm's own selective breeding program produced a pure white strain. He is quoted as having disclaimed the credit, saying that the white dogs had been in the Highlands for a hundred years or more and that he did not invent the breed. After the death of his brother, Colonel Malcolm became the Laird of Poltalloch and used his influence to promote the white dogs for hunting. Slowly, the white dogs came to be preferred, as other breeders came to the same opinion as Colonel Malcolm. In the early 1900s, the breed became standard. Colonel Malcolm's dogs became known as White Poltallochs.

Two other breeders of white dogs must also be mentioned. One is the Duke of Argyll, whose family seat was Roseneath. Here, a desirable white strain was developed. These dogs are said to have had soft, but pure, white coats. They became known as Roseneath Terriers. Dr. Flaxman, of Fife, on the east coast of Scotland, also became interested in breeding the white dogs from a Scottish Terrier bitch that had white puppies in every litter. His dogs had what is described as "linty" white coats. They were said to have had good black pigmentation and jet

black noses. They were also reported to have had the heavier bodies and the long forefaces of the Scottish Terrier rather than the typical round heads and short muzzles of the Poltallochs. Other strains had hard coats that tended to be cream colored, a fact that still haunts Westie breeders today.

Later, the Roseneath Terriers, Dr. Flaxman's White Scottish Terriers, and Colonel Malcolm's White Poltallochs were entered at the bench shows. Colonel Malcolm and Dr. Flaxman became great rivals at the shows, the subject of proper heads being the bone of contention—no pun intended. The Poltallochs were considered to be the true type by the show judges. The breed standard of today states that the long foreface and the long head of the Scottish Terrier are serious faults.

Colonel Malcolm can certainly be credited with bringing the breed before the public at the bench shows. He can also be credited with creating better relations among the various breeders and with unifying the fancy by changing the breed name to West Highland White Terrier. The name is well chosen for both the rugged place of their origin and the rugged character of the dogs. When the breed was accepted by the English Kennel Club, the name became official, a tribute to Colonel Malcolm's persuasiveness and tact. In 1904 the West Highland White Terrier Club was formed in Scotland, with the Duke of Argyll as president. The West Highland White Terrier 3

Sir Ian Malcolm.

Club of England was formed about that same time, with the Countess of Aberdeen as president. Colonel Malcolm, who later became president, was the vice-president.

In 1907 there were classes for Westies at the famous Crufts bench show in London, and that same year the breed was entered into the English Kennel Club's stud book. A dog is entered into the stud book when he or she is registered and has sired or whelped a litter. In 1908, 141 Westies were registered.

In these early years, the Scottish dogs, which were the correct type, were doing all of the winning in the show ring. A "good one" was hard to come by, since many were being bred as White Scottish Terriers. But dedicated breeders and fanciers worked at breeding for proper type, using their dogs as working Terriers as well as exhibiting them at the bench shows. In those days, it was not unusual to see an entry at the bench shows with half an ear gone, or with some other "merit badge" earned in doing his work. The first breed standard called for a dog between eight and twelve inches tall at the withers. Realizing that these early Westies were often very small makes their working ability all the more remarkable.

In Great Britain, the years of World War I from 1914 to 1918 were difficult for kennel owners. Food was in very short supply, and dog owners were policed to be certain that the dogs were not being fed anything that could be given to people. Mrs. May Pacey, breeder of the famous Wolvey dogs, writes a few poignant lines in her book *West Highland White Terriers.* She says that in one day she put down fifteen of her dogs rather than see them starve to death, an experience which she said she would never forget. In our land of plenty, it is hard to imagine a time when we would not be allowed to feed our dogs. When peace came, few of the old kennels remained, and getting started again was difficult. But the indomitable spirit of the British rose to the challenge, and they were soon producing excellence once again.

World War II also worked great hardships on the British, kennel owners included. In those six years of food rationing and bombings, showing and breeding of dogs came to a grinding halt. Mrs. Pacey's brief account of those years is interesting. She recalled giving her own meat ration to a promising puppy, knowing that he needed meat for proper development. He was one of the few dogs that she had kept, having sent many out of England to safer homes. The British are noted for their devotion to their animals, and Mrs. Pacey was a dedicated breeder indeed. A 1935 photograph of Mrs. Pacey with five of her Wolvey Westies is still cited as depicting a fine example of correct head type for the breed.

Westies were exported to fanciers in Canada soon after the breed's acceptance by the English Kennel Club. The first Westie registered there was a Scottish import, registered in 1909. Westies were first shown in Canada in 1910 but were

4

Mrs. May Pacey with five of her Wolvey Westies.

more widely shown after World War I. While in Canada the breed has not kept up in numbers with the United States, many high-quality dogs are Canadian-bred. It is interesting to read pedigrees of American dogs and note the high percentage of top bloodlines in this country that have outstanding Canadian dogs in their foundations. The Canadian West Highland White Terrier Club was formed in 1952 with nine active members and two associate members. It has experienced steady growth from coast to coast.

Meanwhile, fanciers of the breed in America also were active. In 1906 the Westminster Kennel Club bench show had classes for the breed and in 1908 the breed was first listed in the American Kennel Club stud book. The West Highland White Terrier Club of America was formed and admitted to membership in the American Kennel Club in 1909. The first American breed standard, copied from the British standard, was accepted that same year.

Interbreeding of Westies and Cairns had continued. If you wanted a Cairn, you chose a colored puppy from the litter. If you wanted a Westie, you chose a white puppy. About 1917 the American Kennel Club decided on stern measures by refusing to register any Cairn that had a Westie in the first three generations of pedigree. The English Kennel Club quickly followed suit, and the two breeds were finally separated and made distinct. Since then the Westie has evolved into a dog of more substance, being about one inch taller and weighing about three pounds more, as comparison of the two present breed standards shows.

The records of the breed in America are filled with the names of many great imported dogs and fine home-breds. At first the breed gained slowly, as with most newly accepted breeds. In 1942 a lovely imported bitch, Ch. Wolvey Pattern of Edgerstoune, went Best in Show at the Westminster Kennel Club bench show, the

Some early English champions.

5

first Westie ever to win this coveted place. She was one of the dogs that Mrs. Pacey had sent to a safer home during World War II. Twenty years later, in 1962, 930 Westies were registered by the American Kennel Club.

The preceding year a winning Westie, Ch. Elfinbrook Simon, owned by Wishing Well Kennels, had made a large splash in the show ring by going Best in Show twelve times in America, a record that no other Westie had ever achieved. Before being shown here, Simon had won Best in Show three times in Canada. Fresh from four Best in Show wins in Florida in January 1962, Simon added further to his laurels and gained more attention of the dog fancy by going Best in Show at Westminster in February. This was his twentieth Best in Show win and was the first time that a Westie had taken this plum in twenty years. This win at the *creme de la creme* of dog shows, in which every dog entered must have previously won points, really marked Simon as one of the greats. The Best in Show judging was televised in some parts of the country, gaining further attention for the breed. The following year, 1963, Westie registrations rose to 1,136,

a gain of 22 percent over the preceding year. Since then, registrations have been on the increase. In 1973, 6,433 Westies were registered. Over the years, the quality of the breed, maintained by the serious fanciers, is reflected in the fine showing made by the American dogs in the ring and by the strong competition that the breed represents in the Terrier Group ring.

Many regional breed clubs have sprung up around the country, offshoots of the "parent" club—the West Highland White Terrier Club of America. Several of these have received recognition by the American Kennel Club and hold regularly scheduled Specialty shows. There are seven clubs in the northeastern states, one in Ohio, one in Illinois, one in Indiana, one in Michigan, one in Colorado, two in California, and two in Texas. Others are in the beginning stages of development. Their members are working hard to maintain the high quality of Westies and to help newcomers to the breed, as well as each other.

Breed clubs play a major role in maintaining the standard of the breed. Since all breed standards are written by experts for experts, the newcomer to a breed often has difficulty with interpretation. In addition, most breed standards allow some leeway for individual evaluation. True breed type is an elusive quality that can be very subtly undermined before most fanciers are aware of what is happening. Through discussions of correct type and the holding of fun matches, where a new person can see his dog in the company of a group of his dog's peers, the breed club helps the novice to recognize the qualities which make up a dog of proper type.

All members and their dogs benefit from the knowledge gained in breed club activities. If you have a Westie breed club in your area, join and become a working member, whether or not you plan to show your dog. You will be rewarded by the education in Westie care and the friendships made with others who share your interest. The secretary of the "parent" club, the West Highland White Terrier Club of America, will be glad to put you in touch with the nearest regional club. The address of the secretary is available by writing to the American Kennel Club.

In 1974 the new West Highland White Terrier Club of Western Pennsylvania was formed and held its first fun match. Many members were new to showing. By 1978 the fun match was well attended, with the ten pictured champion Westies representing some of the dogs that had been finished by members, presented in the Parade of Champions.

2 What is a Westie Really Like?

Raymond Loewy is an internationally acclaimed designer of things great and small. His contributions range from things as large as automobiles to things as small as advertising logos. His work is noted for its engaging eye appeal and its classical simplicity. I think that if Mons. Loewy were to turn his talents to designing a dog, it would look like a Westie.

On appearance alone, the Westie merits an award for design excellence. With his natty white coat and black trimmings, dark hazel eyes deep-set in a shaggy face, perky ears, and tail carried like a banner, he is a delightful small and compact package of a dog. All breeds of puppies are darling, but I believe that the Westie is the only breed which is even cuter as an adult, when he has come into his full coat. Surely this is the breed for the connoisseur of dogs.

The Westie is big enough to really be a dog but small enough to go in the car or to share your easy chair. He enjoys the outdoors, regardless of weather, but fits nicely into a small apartment. His beautiful white coat is easy to keep clean with a brush. He is virtually shedless and does not develop "doggy odor." He looks like a stuffed toy, but he is wonderfully alive. He is fine-tuned to everything around him. Nothing new escapes his interested investigation, from the new trash can in the garage to the new clock on the mantelshelf.

To me, a Westie is the A-one, first-class, triple-distilled companion dog. I admit to bias. For the past several years of owning, breeding, raising, and showing Westies, I have come to wish that I had known about these charmers much earlier in life so as to have enjoyed them longer. And I devoutly hope that the time never comes when I am unable to have at least one or two around to keep things cheery and lively.

Westie puppies are bouncing and sometimes boisterous, full of the joy of living and light-hearted impudence. These qualities carry over into adulthood. I have seen Westie senior citizens, twelve or thirteen years old, entered at Specialty shows in Veterans class, gaiting jauntily around the ring like youngsters and enjoying the day at the show site. Small wonder that so many people who own one Westie decide that two Westies would be twice the fun. Most owners who lose one through accident or death will accept no other breed as a replacement. Once you have been taken over by a Westie, nothing else will do.

Basically, the Westie disposition is sweet, loving, and loyal, but he is not at all subservient. People who want a lie-at-your-feet-type dog would not want a Westie. If a Westie wants your attention and affection, he may climb into the middle of your newspaper or poke his head under the bottom of it, wearing the pages draped over his ears. As the breed standard says, he has "no small amount of self esteem." It would never occur to him that you might be too occupied to pet him. A Westie has a great sense of personal worth, which is one of his most endearing qualities. When a guy knows he's great, it's hard to be humble.

His effervescent and fun-loving disposition and his sturdy bones and small size make him an ideal playmate for children. Women love his ease of care, his lack of "doggy odor," his smart good looks, and his infectious charm. But his pluck and stamina make him a man's dog, too. He is not a "one-man dog,"—he freely gives his affection and loyalty to his whole family. He may show some slight preference for one member, especially the last one to return after being away for a few hours.

The Westie is highly intelligent and learns very quickly. He is too intelligent to be argumentative, but he will never back off from a fight, if someone else wants to start one, no matter how large the aggressor. He is a positive thinker and has a great heart in that small body. He knows his moral rights and will always defend them. I often say that if you own a Westie, you do not

8

Donnybrook's Douglas II at age four and one half months. This dog grew up to be Ch. Donnybrook's Douglas II, shown (left) at the age of five years. "Douglas" belongs to Owen Conner, Atlanta, Georgia.

need a big dog, because a Westie thinks that he is one. He is a happy combination of powerhouse and pussycat.

The hunting instincts of his ancestors are carried on in his bones and blood. Like the hounds and the bird dogs, these instincts must be trained and reinforced if he is to be used as a working dog. Unlike the bird dogs, which worked at a man's knee, the Westies were independent hunters, charging ahead to seek and find alone. The Westie of today still feels the need to bark at the "game" he sights, which may be the neighbor's cat, a squirrel, or some loose dog beyond his fence. After all, a Westie owns the whole world.

Dog experts say that the Westie has all the good of the Terrier breeds and none of the bad. Mordecai Seigel and Matthew Margolis in their book *Good Dog, Bad Dog* list the Westie's negative qualities as "none." I was delighted to find that these two noted dog trainers agree with me! It must be stated, however, that it is difficult to generalize about any breed. Individual dogs are as different as individual people. A puppy or a person is the sum total of his genes. This could be likened to one shuffle of a deck of cards. The odds of getting the exact same arrangement with another shuffle must be astronomical.

Each individual is also the product of his environment. The first three months of a puppy's life are just as important to his potential development as are the first three years in the life of a child. Westie puppies that are well socialized with people and that have been introduced to children in these formative early weeks go to their new homes as well-adjusted family members. This would be true of any other breed of dogs, not just Westies.

I have known many people who own other breeds of dogs, especially those with the big breeds that must be kept outdoors, who decide to get a Westie as a second, live-in dog. The story is always the same. The Westie comes to rule the roost, regardless of the size of the other dog or dogs in the household. To my knowledge, this has never resulted in arguments over territorial rights. It simply becomes a tacit understanding that the Westie is the top dog.

I never advise anyone to keep two male Westies, if they are both used for stud dogs, unless the owner has facilities for housing the two dogs

"Glinda," one of the Taradink Westies belonging to Tom and Lois Drexler of North Huntingdon, Pennsylvania, looks like a stuffed toy as she shares the chair with the Drexler's granddaughter, Jessica.

These two winsome lassies, Martha Jo Anne and Briarcliff Satin Doll ("Dolly") make their home with Dr. and Mrs. Neal Dye of Concord, Tennessee. "Martha" is in Obedience classes, and "Dolly" is being shown in Conformation.

separately. Two dogs might fight, even to the death of one, over territorial dominance. I know owners of two males, kept only as pets, and the dogs live happily together and enjoy each other. One will probably dominate the other, but they work out a fine relationship. Usually a male dog and a bitch will never fight, so two Westies of different sex can be a happy choice. If you do not wish to breed them together, the dog can be neutered or the bitch spayed. Neutered animals make the best and most problem-free pets.

The Westie kept indoors should be provided with a window or door from which to see the world outside. This need to be a part of the great outdoors must be satisfied. Be certain that his vantage point is safe by taking the same precautions that you would for a toddler. An open, unscreened window could be an invitation to disaster. Let me cite you two examples, one which ended in tragedy, the other a near tragedy, which ended in the hilarity of relief.

In the first case, a young woman owned a nice Westie bitch, and they lived in an apartment on the fourth floor. The apartment had a lovely railed balcony that both tenants enjoyed. One particularly nice morning in early spring the owner decided to let her bitch enjoy the outdoors while she went to shop. When she left, she kept her Westie on the balcony. When she returned, she found her dog dead on the drive four stories below.

In the second case, a Westie puppy dog of mine went to live with a family that had several children of various ages and a cat. The cat and Rickie, the puppy, became fast friends, frolicking through the house together. It was soon time for spring cleaning, with screens to be removed and windows washed. The cat got out of the house and was gone for several days, while Rickie moped and hunted for his companion cat. On Sunday morning, while the family was at breakfast, the cat returned. The two animals were overjoyed to see each other and began their favorite game of tag. The cat bounded up the stairs to the bedrooms, with Rickie in hot pursuit. Then came a rending, crashing sound from outdoors, which brought the family from the table to rush out to see what had happened.

At the foot of a huge holly tree sat Rickie, dazed but unhurt. A forgotten open and unscreened window was just above the treetop. The rumpled bedspread in the bedroom verified the facts. The cat had dashed up the stairs, into the room, onto the bed, onto a desk in front of the window, and out to the tree, where he had climbed down. Rickie had done the same, following the cat out of the window and crashing down through the thickly branched tree. How lucky that it had been a bushy holly tree! Rickie's fine double coat had protected him from getting even a scratch. So we all had a good chuckle, enjoying the animated cartoon overtones of the escapade and the relief of knowing that Rickie was unhurt. It was so "typically Westie" that Rickie had not questioned his own ability to do anything that the cat could do. There's a whole lot of Clark Kent in every Westie.

10

Ch. Kortni of Windy Hill, an appealing young bitch, is one of the Westies at Kilkerran. She was bred by Ann M. Frinks, Selkirk, New York, and is owned by Wayne and Kathy Kompare of Katonah, New York.

3 The Westie Standard

THE OFFICIAL AMERICAN
BREED STANDARD (AS AMENDED IN 1968)

1. **General Appearance** of the West Highland White Terrier is that of a small, game, well-balanced, hardy-looking Terrier exhibiting good showmanship, possessed with no small amount of self-esteem, strongly built, deep in chest and back ribs, straight back and powerful hindquarters on muscular legs, and exhibiting in a marked degree a great combination of strength and activity. The coat should be about two inches long, white in color, hard, with plenty of soft undercoat. The dog should be neatly presented. Considerable hair should be left around the head to act as a frame for the face to yield a typical Westie expression.

2. **Color and Pigmentation**—Coat should be white, as defined by the breed's name. Nose should be black. Black pigmentation is most desirable on lips, eye-rims, pads of feet, nails and skin.

   Faults: Any coat color other than white and nose color other than black are serious faults.

3. **Coat**—Very important, and seldom seen to perfection; must be double coated. The outer coat consists of straight hard hair, about two inches long, with shorter coat on neck and shoulders, properly blended.

   Faults: Any silkiness or tendency to curl is a serious fault, as is an open or single coat.

4. **Size**—Dogs should measure about 11 inches at the withers, bitches about 1 inch less.

   Faults: Any specimens much over or under height limits are objectionable.

5. **Skull**—Should be fairly broad, being in proportion to his powerful jaw, not too long, slightly domed, and gradually tapering to the eyes. There should be a defined stop, eyebrows heavy.

Faults: Too long or too narrow skull.

6. **Muzzle**—Should be slightly shorter than the skull, powerful and gradually tapering to the nose, which should be large. The jaws should be level and powerful, the teeth well set and large for the size of the dog. There shall be six incisor teeth between the canines of both lower and upper jaws. A tight scissors bite with upper incisors slightly overlapping the lower incisors or level mouth are equally acceptable.

Faults: Muzzle longer than skull. Teeth much undershot or overshot are a serious fault as are teeth defective or missing.

7. **Ears**—Small, carried tightly erect, set wide apart and terminating in a sharp point. They must never be cropped. The hair on the ears should be short, smooth and velvety, and trimmed free of fringe at the tips.

Faults: Round-pointed, drop, broad and large ears are very objectionable, as are mule-ears, ears set too closely together or not held tightly erect.

8. **Eyes**—Widely set apart, medium in size, dark in color, slightly sunk in the head, sharp and intelligent. Looking from under heavy eyebrows, they give a piercing look.

Faults: Too small, too full or light colored eyes are very objectionable.

9. **Neck**—Muscular and nicely set on sloping shoulders.

Faults: Short neck or too long neck.

12

Ch. Hilltop's Foxy Lady, daughter of top-producing dam, Ch. Charlain's Holly-Go-Love-Leah. Foxy was bred and is owned by Frank and Carol Boatwright, Charlain's Westies, Downers Grove, Illinois.

Worline photo

10. **Chest**—Very deep and extending at least to the elbows with breadth in proportion to the size of the dog.

   Faults: Shallow chest.

11. **Body**—Compact and of good substance, level back, ribs deep and well arched in the upper half of the rib, presenting a flattish side appearance, loins broad and strong, hindquarters strong, muscular, and wide across the top.

   Faults: Long or weak back, barrel ribs; high rump.

12. **Legs and Feet**—Both fore legs and hind legs should be muscular and relatively short, but with sufficient length to set the dog up so as not to be too close to the ground. The shoulder blades should be well laid back and well-knit at the back bone. The chest should be relatively broad and the front legs spaced apart accordingly. The front legs should be set in under the shoulder blades with definite body overhang before them. The front legs should be reasonably straight and thickly covered with short hard hair. The hind legs should be short and sinewy; the thighs very muscular and not set wide apart, with hocks well bent. The fore feet are larger than the hind ones, are round, proportionate in size, strong, thickly padded, and covered with short hard hair; they may properly be turned out a slight amount. The hind feet are smaller and thickly padded.

   Faults: Steep shoulders, loaded shoulders, or out at the elbows. Too light bone. Cowhocks, weak hocks and lack of angulation. A "fiddle-front" is a serious fault.

13. **Tail**—Relatively short, when standing erect it should never extend above the top of the skull. It should be covered with hard hairs, no feather, as straight as possible, carried gaily but not curled over the back. The tail should be set on high enough so that the spine does not slope down to it. The tail must never be docked.

   Faults: Tail set too low; tail too long or carried at half mast or over back.

14. **Movement**—Should be free, straight and easy all around. In front, the leg should be freely extended forward by the shoulder. The hind movement should be free, strong and fairly close. The hocks should be freely flexed and drawn close under the body; so that when moving off the foot the body is thrown or pushed forward with some force.

   Faults: Stiff, stilty or too wide movement behind. Lack of reach in front, and/or drive behind.

15. **Temperament**—Must be alert, gay, courageous and self-reliant, but friendly.

   Faults: Excess timidity or excess pugnacity.

THE BRITISH BREED STANDARD

General Appearance. The general appearance of the West Highland White Terrier is that of a small, game, hardy-looking Terrier, possessed of no small amount of self esteem with a varminty appearance, strongly built, deep in the chest and back ribs, level back and powerful quarters on muscular legs, and exhibiting in a marked degree a great combination of strength and activity. Movement should be free, straight and easy all around. In front, the legs should be freely extended forward by the shoulder. The hind movement should be freely flexed and drawn close in under the body, so that when moving off the foot the body is pushed forward with some force. Stiff, stilted movement behind is very objectionable.

Head and Skull. The skull should be slightly domed and when gripped across the forehead should present a smooth contour. There should be only a very slight tapering from the skull at the level of the ears to the eyes. The distance from the occiput to the eyes should be slightly greater than the length of the foreface. The head should be thickly coated with hair and carried at a right angle or less to the axis of the neck. On no account should the head be carried in the extended position. The foreface should gradually

13

taper from the eye to the muzzle. There should be a distinct stop formed by heavy, bony ridges, immediately above and slightly overhanging the eye, and a slight indentation between the eyes. The foreface should not dish or fall away quickly below the eyes where it should be well made up. The jaws should be strong and level. The nose must be black, should be fairly large, and forming a smooth contour with the rest of the muzzle. The nose must not project forward giving rise to a snipy appearance.

Eyes. Should be widely set apart, medium in size, as dark as possible in colour, slightly sunk in the head, sharp and intelligent, which, looking from under the heavy eyebrows, imparts a piercing look. Full or light coloured eyes are objectionable.

Ears. Small, erect and carried firmly, terminating in a sharp point. The hair on them should be short, smooth (velvety) and should not be cut. The ears should be free from any fringe at the top. Round pointed, broad, large and thick ears are very objectionable, also ears too heavily coated with hair.

Mouth. Should be as broad between the canine teeth as is consistent with the sharp varminty expression required. The teeth should be large for the size of the dog, and should articulate in the following manner: the lower canines should lock in front of the upper canines. There should be six teeth between the canines of the upper and lower incisors. The upper incisors should slightly overlap the lower incisors, the inner side of the upper incisors being in contact with the outer side of the lower incisors. There should be no appreciable space between the incisors when the mouth is closed, ensuring a keen bite; a dead level mouth is not a fault.

Neck. Should be sufficiently long to allow the proper set on of head required, muscular and gradually thickening towards the base, allowing the neck to merge into nicely sloping shoulders, thus giving freedom of movement.

Forequarters. The shoulders should be sloped backwards. The shoulder blades should be broad and lie close to the chest wall. The joint formed by the shoulder blade and upper arm should be

placed forward, on account of the obliquity of the shoulder blades, bringing the elbows well in, and allowing the foreleg to move freely, parallel to the axis of the body, like the pendulum of a clock. Forelegs should be short and muscular, straight and thickly covered with short hard hair.

Body. Compact. Back level, loins broad and strong. The chest should be deep and the ribs well arched in the upper half, presenting a flattish side appearance. The back ribs should be of considerable depth and the distance from the last rib of the quarters as short as is compatible with the free movement of the body.

Hindquarters. Strong, muscular and wide across the top. Legs should be short, muscular and not too wide apart. The hocks bent and well set under the body so as to be fairly close to each other when standing, walking or trotting. Cow hocks detract from the general appearance. Straight or weak hocks are undesirable and are a fault.

Feet. The forefeet are larger than the hind ones, are round, proportionate in size, strong, thickly padded and covered with short hard hair. The hind feet are smaller and thickly padded. The under-surface of the pads of the feet and all nails should be preferably black.

Tail. 5-6 in. (13-15 cm.) long, covered with hard hair, no feather, as straight as possible, carried

Ch. Arnholme Dove, an English import owned by Mrs. Anita Becky, B. J.'s Westies, Denver, Colorado. "Jill" finished her title at five consecutive shows and is the dam of a finished litter of four (see page 34).

jauntily, not gay or carried over the back. A long tail is objectionable and on no account should tails be docked.

Coat. Colour pure white, must be double coated. The outer coat consists of hard hair, about 2 in. (5 cm.) long, free from any curl. The undercoat, which resembles fur, is short, soft and close. Open coats are objectionable.

Colour. Pure white.

Size. About 11 in. (28 cm.) at the withers.

Note. Male animals should have two apparently normal testicles fully descended in the scrotum.

STANDARD FOR THE WEST HIGHLAND WHITE TERRIER (APPROVED BY THE CANADIAN KENNEL CLUB, EFFECTIVE JANUARY 1, 1976)

1. **Origin and Purpose.** The "Westie" or "Highlander" as he is sometimes called is a smallish dog stemming from the basic branch of the Terrier family. He has great agility and is quick in movement with tremendous stamina and courage, attributes which he needed as a hunter of fox and otter in his native Scotland, where rocks and crags and generally rough terrain made ease and quickness of movement vital. By selection and interbreeding, the white colour was purposely bred so that the dog could be easily distinguished from his foe during the hunt, while his double coat gave necessary protection against the teeth of his foe and the climate. The West Highlander is not an argumentative terrier but is a plucky individual who will not back down and who will stand against a larger animal in matters of moral rights; yet he is fun loving and a devoted companion.

2. **General Appearance** of the West Highland White Terrier is that of a small, game, well-balanced, hardy-looking Terrier exhibiting great showmanship, possessed with no small amount of self-esteem, strongly built, deep in chest and back ribs, straight back and powerful hindquarters on muscular legs, and exhibiting in a marked degree a great combination of strength and activity. The coat should be about two inches long, white in colour, hard with plenty of soft undercoat. The dog should be neatly presented. The ruff of hair around the head should act as a frame for the face to yield the typical Westie expression.

3. **Temperament**—Must be alert, gay, courageous and self-reliant, and friendly.

   Faults: Excess timidity or excess pugnacity.

4. **Size**—Dogs should measure 11 inches at the withers, bitches 1 inch less.

   Faults: Any specimens as much as one inch over or under the height standard are very objectionable.

5. **Coat and Colour**
   (a) Coat: Very important, and seldom seen to perfection, must be double-coated. The outer coat consists of straight, hard hair, at least two inches long on the body of mature dogs, with proper blending of the shorter coat on neck and shoulders.

   Faults: Any silkiness or tendency to curl is a serious fault, as is an open or single coat.

   (b) Colour and Pigmentation: Coat must be white, as defined in the breed's name. Nose must be black. Black pigmentation is most desirable on lips, eye-rims, pads of feet, nails and skin.

   Faults: Any coat colour other than white and nose colour other than black are serious faults.

6. **Skull**—Should be fairly broad, being in proportion to the powerful jaw, not too long, slightly domed, and gradually tapering to the eyes. There should be a defined stop, eyebrows heavy.

   Faults: A too long or too narrow skull.

7. **Muzzle**—Should be slightly shorter than the skull, powerful and gradually tapering to the nose, which should be large. The jaw should

15

be level and powerful, the teeth well set and large for the size of the dog. There shall be six incisor teeth between the canines of both upper and lower jaws. A tight scissors bite with the upper incisors slightly overlapping the lower incisors or level mouth are equally acceptable.

Faults: Muzzle longer than the skull. Teeth much undershot or overshot are a serious fault as are teeth defective or missing.

8. **Eyes**—Widely set apart, medium in size, dark in colour, slightly sunk in the head, sharp and intelligent. Looking from under heavy eyebrows, they give a piercing look.

   Faults: Too small, too full or light-coloured eyes are very objectionable.

9. **Ears**—Small, carried tightly erect, set wide apart and terminating in a sharp point. They must never be cropped. The hair on the ears should be short, smooth and velvety. Ears should be free of fringe on the tips.

   Faults: Round-pointed, drop, broad and large ears are very objectionable, as are mule-ears, ears set too closely together or not held tightly erect.

10. **Neck**—Should be sufficiently long to allow the proper set-on of head required, muscular and gradually thickening toward the base, allowing the neck to merge into nicely sloping shoulders.

    Faults: Short neck or too long neck, thus upsetting the overall balance.

11. **Forequarters**—Forelegs should be muscular and relatively short, but with sufficient length to set the dog up so as not to be too close to the ground. Height from the highest point of the withers to the ground should be approximately equal to the length from the withers to the set-on of tail; height from elbow to withers and elbow to the ground should be approximately equal. The shoulder blades should be well laid back and well-knit at the backbone. The chest should be relatively broad and the front legs spaced apart accordingly. The front legs should be set in under the shoulder blades with a definite body overhang before them, and should be reasonably straight and covered with short, hard hair. The forefeet are larger than the hind ones, are round, proportionate in size, and strong, thickly padded, and covered with short, hard hair; they may properly be turned out a slight amount.

    Faults: Steep shoulders, loaded shoulders, or out at the elbows. Too light bone, a "fiddle-front" is a serious fault.

12. **Chest and Body**—Chest very deep and extending at least to the elbows with breadth in proportion to the size of the dog. Body compact and of good substance, level back, ribs deep, and well-arched in the upper half of rib, presenting a flattish side appearance; loins broad and strong, hindquarters strong and muscular, and wide across the top.

    Faults: Shallow chest, long or weak back, barrel ribs, high rump.

13. **Hindquarters**—Should be muscular, the hind legs relatively short and sinewy, the thighs very muscular, well angulated, and not set wide apart. The hocks well bent and parallel viewed from the rear. The hindfeet are smaller than the forefeet, and thickly padded.

    Faults: Too light bone, cowhocks, weak hocks, lack of angulation.

14. **Tail**—Relatively short, when standing erect it should be approximately level with the top of the skull thus maintaining a balanced appearance. It should be covered with hard hairs, no feather, as straight as possible, carried gaily but not curled over the back. The tail should be set on high enough so that the spine does not slope down to it. The tail must never be docked.

    Faults: Tail set too low; tail too long or carried at half mast over the back.

15. **Movement**—Should be free, straight and easy all around. In front, the leg should be freely extended forward by the shoulder. The

hind movement should be free, strong and fairly close, the hocks should be freely flexed and drawn close under the body; so that when moving off the foot the body is thrown or pushed forward with some force.

Faults: Stiff, stilted or too wide movement behind. Lack of reach in front, and/or drive behind.

Summary of Faults: Excess timidity or excess pugnacity; any specimens as much as one inch over or under the height standard; silky or curling coat, open or single coat; any coat colour other than white, or nose colour other than black; skull too long or too narrow; muzzle longer than skull; undershot or overshot bite, missing or defective teeth; eyes too small, too full or light-coloured; ears round-pointed, drop, broad and large, mule-ears, ears set too close, or not held tightly erect; neck too short or too long; steep shoulders, loaded shoulders, out at elbows, too light bone in forelegs, fiddle-front; shallow chest; long or weak back, barrel ribs, high rump; cowhocks, weak hocks, too light bone in hind legs, lack of angulation; tail set too low, tail too long, carried at half mast or over back; stiff stilted movement, too wide movement behind, lack of reach in front and/or drive behind.

This photograph shows four Of the Rouge Westies, Pickering, Ontario, Canada, three of which later finished their titles. They are, left to right, Am. Can. Ch. Mercury of the Rouge, dog; Can. Ch. Philomel of the Rouge, bitch; Herald of the Rouge, dog, at age six months; and Am. Can. Ch. Gallant Lad of the Rouge, dog. A study of current Westies from this outstanding Canadian kennel will reveal that this carefully planned breeding program has established correct and definite "type," with these later dogs strongly resembling the four in this 1963 photograph. These dogs were bred by Mrs. Dorothea Daniell-Jenkins.

E. L. Taylor photo

This gorgeous head study is a favorite of everyone in the world of Westies. Am. Mex. Ch. Merryhart Aspen Able is one of the many fine dogs owned by Jim and Neoma Eberhart of Merryhart Kennels, Santa Ana, California. "Able" was sired by Am. Can. Mex. Ch. Dreamland's Councillor, Canada's third top stud dog. His grandsire was Can. Ch. Dreamland's Cyclone, one of Canada's top producing studs. His dam, Merryhart Bon Bon, was one of the thoughtfully bred Merryhart bitches. In addition to the sheer pleasure that the picture gives the viewer, it represents an excellent example of perfection in heads and in head trimming. "Able" now lives with Don and Lillian Palmer, Sault Ste. Marie, Ontario, Canada. *Ludwig photo*

4 Translating the Breed Standard

The breed standards were written for breeders and dog judges. The standard is the description of the various parts and qualities of an adult dog, which combine to make a total of perfection. Each standard also lists the various faults that are commonly seen in the breed. The standards are used as guidelines for evaluation of the breeds and allow some latitude for individual interpretation. This often presents a problem when the newcomer to a breed attempts to understand the fine points.

Most purebred dogs were developed by man for a specific purpose. Each of these breeds needed certain physical characteristics in order to do the work it was developed to perform. When the standard is read with this in mind, it becomes easier to understand. The Westie was developed for hunting small game among the rocks and boulders. Each part of his body was important in his functioning well as a working dog. If we compare the written standard to the physical qualities that the dog needed for doing his work, we understand what is meant by a dog of "correct type." It is this "typey" dog that all serious breeders are trying to maintain, striving always to breed for individuals that correctly resemble the standard of the typical Westie, well equipped to do his work. Eyes and ear-set are also important, in that they lend to the dog the typical expression that uniquely belongs to the Westie. In addition, the Westie should present the appearance of great strength and activity, along with the self-assurance that is a prerequisite for doing his work.

THE TYPICAL HEAD

The adult Westie's head is covered with a long, thick coat of hair forming a full, round ruff. The overhanging eyebrows gave protection for his eyes. His small, pricked ears presented a small target, especially when set down into the full head furnishings. Like the ears of a cat, Westie ears can turn like radar, picking up every sound and identifying the direction. The thick hair on the sides of the cheeks and chin protected these areas from the teeth of the quarry.

The skull under the hair is shaped rather like a little skullcap, or half a grapefruit rind, being rounded both from back to front and side to side, forming a small dome. The ears should be set on the outer edges of the skull and should sit up straight. The ears should be small and sharply pointed, and they are *never cropped*. They should not be set on the top of the skull, as are the ears of the Scottish Terrier. Neither should the ears be set on the sides of the head and stick out at the sides. These are termed "mule ears." Ear linings that have grey pigmentation are highly desirable, but pink ear linings are acceptable. From the level of the ears to the level of the eyes, the skull should not taper in from the sides. The skull should be fairly broad. If the skull is too narrow, even correctly placed ears will appear to be set too closely together.

The front curve of the skull drops down to meet the flat plane of the muzzle. This juncture is called the "stop," and it should be well defined. If the front of the skull is not well rounded but is flattish, there will not be a well-defined stop. This flattish skull, similar to that of the Scottish Terrier, can usually be found on a Westie with an overlong foreface and a skull that is too narrow. This doubtless harks back to an old White Scottish Terrier ancestor.

The eyes are set at the level of the stop. Above the eye socket is a slightly projecting bony ridge. The eyes in the correctly broad skull will be widely spaced. If the skull is narrow, the eyes will be set together too closely. The eyes are medium in size. A large, full eye gives too soft an expression. An eye that is too small appears beady, and it usually accompanies a skull that is too narrow. The eyes of the Westie are his whole expression, sometimes appearing sharply penetrating and inquiring and the next second filled with lighthearted good humor. The eyes should be dark in color. They are not black, but are dark hazel. Light-colored eyes are a fault. Under the bony ridge of the eye socket and the overhanging eyebrows, the eyes appear deep-set, sharp, and intelligent, giving a "piercing" look.

The muzzle is short with powerful and punishing jaws, the teeth being large for the size of the dog. The muzzle should taper in enough from the sides so as not to present a "bullish" appearance. The nose should be large, but it should form a smooth contour with the muzzle. The projecting nose of the Scottish Terrier is not typical for the Westie and is usually combined with a long and narrow jaw. The nose should be solid black. Some Westies do lose some pigmentation in the nose in the winter months. The nose will sometimes fade to dark charcoal grey or dark brown. This is known as "winter nose" or "snow nose" and may be due to lack of sunshine in the winter months or the absence of some of the trace minerals in the diet.

The length of the muzzle from the nose to the stop should be shorter than the length of the skull from the stop to the back of the head when

Incorrect ears, set too wide; these are termed "mule ears."

Incorrect ears, set too close together and on top of the head.

Well-defined stop and flat-planed head that lacks definition.

the head is viewed in profile. In the early days, when the breed was first being exhibited at the bench shows, self-styled critics termed the Westies "baby faced," saying that this short muzzle made the breed no good for its work. Colonel Malcolm contended that the breed's short muzzle gave the dogs a distinct advantage in a fight. The power of the jaw muscles and teeth could be concentrated in a shorter span. A long foreface is not typical for the "baby faced" Westie.

Both eye rims and lips should be black. The roof of the mouth may be black or mottled pink and black. Skin under the hair around the nose may be very dark. The more pigmentation, the better. Some breeds of dogs that are dominant for a color but are bred to white through a recessive gene tend to go blind and/or deaf due to a lack of pigmentation. The white coat color in Westies is dominant, which has great bearing on the dogs' sight and hearing. A well-pigmented Westie will have dark grey skin on his belly as well as on the skin of the ear linings.

The Westie's teeth are large for the size of the dog. In each jaw, at the center front, should be six small incisors with a canine tooth on either side of them. The incisors of the upper jaw may slightly overlap those in the lower jaw for a tight "scissors" bite. (The word "bite" refers to the meeting of the front incisors and canines.) The upper incisors may meet the lowers, end to end, for a "level" bite. Either of these two bites is

Tight "scissors" bite, with six incisors and two canines in each jaw.

Left to right: "level" bite; "overshot" bite; and "undershot" bite.

acceptable in the adult dog. The canines should properly "mesh" with the lower ones coming up into the space provided in the upper jaw. Thus, when the mouth is closed, the lower canines are in front of and next to the upper canines.

If the lower incisors are set at a slight angle and protrude slightly, this bite is not heavily penalized in the show ring as long as the two jaws are the same length. If the upper jaw is longer, causing an "overshot" mouth, or if the lower jaw is longer, causing an "undershot" mouth, these are considered serious faults. The standard states: "Teeth much undershot or overshot are serious faults, as are teeth defective or missing." Many judges fault any Terrier that has a faulty bite to any small degree, feeling that it renders the dog unfit for doing his work.

The breed standard does not mention the balance of dentition in the Westie. Nor do the British and Canadian standards discuss the premolars and molars. This has puzzled me for years. Then a recent "Westie News," sent to members by the West Highland White Terrier Club of England, arrived with an article about dentition, which answers the question. The article, written by Julie E. B. Sills, stresses the fact that the British standard was the *original standard from the country of the origin of the breed*, and therefore should be accepted worldwide and not be changed—certainly not in the matter of dentition. Ms. Sills says that, in order to breed for the correct shortness of foreface and to breed out the "dish face," some of the premolars have had to be sacrificed. The article further states that breeding from two Westies with complete dentition does not ensure puppies that have four premolars in each jaw. The lack of premolars follows no particular pattern. Since these teeth erupt at different times, they are sometimes lacking at twelve months of age. At times a puppy may have a full set of premolars in the milk teeth, may shed those, and may never cut any permanent premolars. In X-rays, the "buds" of the permanent teeth may sometimes be seen, never having cut through the gums.

I own a bitch that had premolars as a puppy. At fifteen months of age, she began to shed them. I found the teeth on the floor. She did not cut new ones for such a long time that I gave up watching for replacements. After her first litter,

21

at age three years, I was amazed to discover that the premolars were there, all but two on one side of the lower jaw, which are still absent. A "Westie friend" told me that one of her bitches finally cut premolars at the age of five.

The article also states that wild dogs, who depended on their hunting prowess to live, had no premolars, proving that dogs do not need premolars to be successful hunters. It further says that the better the "expression" and conformation to the breed standard, the more likely the Westie is to be missing his premolars, and that many of the best British dogs simply do not have them.

In continental Europe, judges are "fussy, fussy" in regard to full dentition for every breed. The British sell many of their excellent dogs overseas, only to have great disappointment when a really good dog is severely penalized in

the show ring because he is missing his premolars, which are not even written into the British "book." The article cited the case of one dog that had gotten by the judges with only four of the necessary six incisors in the continental zeal for counting premolars. Please note that missing incisors are a fault. The British feel that excellence of conformation, not premolars, should come first.

THE TYPICAL BODY

In order to do his work, the Westie needed to cover the ground very quickly to follow the quarry, and his body had to be properly structured for speed, stamina, and maneuverability. The dog's front legs needed great reach and thrust. His hindquarters needed great power for driving his body forward. These well-muscled rear legs served another important function. They were vital to his ability to dispatch the adversary. All of the leverage of a dog's bite comes from his back legs. In a fight, a dog plants his hind legs as firmly as he can every time he tries to close his jaws in a firm bite.

The flat-sided rib cage allowed the Westie to maneuver his body between rocks and boulders and other tight places better than the round-ribbed dog. The rib cage, springing well from the spine, formed ample width across the chest, which, combined with depth dropping down deeper than his elbows, provided ample room for his heart and great lung capacity. This depth of rib allowed him to rest his body on his chest and still be able to use his forelegs for digging or propelling himself forward in a tight situation. A round rib cage provides no depth, and a narrow rib cage has too little room for the required lung capacity. Neither of these two structures is typical for a Westie. The correct ribs spring out from the spine, dropping into flattish sides, and are rounded at the bottom in the shape of a heart.

The Important Angulation

Only the proper skeletal structure could provide the Westie with all of the physical attributes needed for doing his work. This is brought about by the correct angulation of the bones in relation to one another. "Angulation" is a word often heard in dog circles but seldom understood by the novice. I have known Westie owners who

22

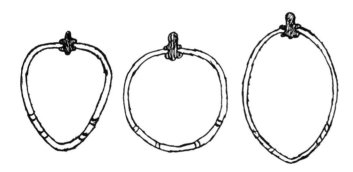

Left: correct heart-shaped ribs, well-sprung from the spine; middle, too round rib; has no depth; right, too narrow; lacks space for lungs and heart.

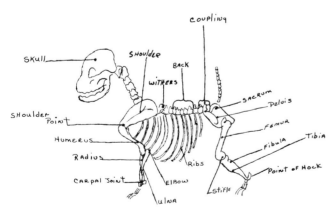

Only the proper skeletal structure could provide the Westie with the physical attributes that he needed for doing his work.

had their dogs for several years but never really knew what was meant by angulation. Even if you flunked Anatomy 101, all you need to know to understand angulation is the little song about "the neck bone's connected to the shoulder bone." It is really very simple. Angulation refers to the size of the angle formed when two bones meet each other and form a joint. Correct angulation is vital to the dog's ability to move with the greatest efficiency and the least fatigue. The most important angles in the dog involve the largest bones—the shoulder blades (scapula, plural scapulae) and the pelvis.

The "Laid Back Shoulder"

Regardless of breed, every dog needs a "well laid back" scapula. This means that the upper end of this broad bone connects to the dog's spine at a backward slant. This causes the lower end of the scapula to automatically slope diagonally downward and forward to the chest, where it connects to the upper foreleg bone (the humerus). The positioning of the scapula on the spine is often referred to as a forty-five-degree angle, formed with the dog's level back. Actually, the size of this angle becomes a matter of where the angle is to be measured. If an imaginary line were to be drawn through the exact center (or "spine") of the scapula to the point of the shoulder, the

angle would be narrower than forty-five degrees. It would more nearly approximate a thirty degree angle in relation to the dog's level spine. However, if the line were drawn from the topmost point of the scapula, where it joins the spine, to the top of the joint formed with the humerus (the point of the shoulder), the angle formed would be the approximate forty-five degrees that is most often referred to in dog circles.

At the point of the shoulder, the lower end of the scapula connects with the humerus at an approximate ninety-degree angle. This is like one corner of a square, or an "L" tipped on its side, the corner being the point of the shoulder. The long side of the "L" is the scapula connected to the spine at a forty-five-degree angle. The shorter bottom of the "L" is the humerus. The humerus angles downward and backward. Its lower end is connected to the two lower leg bones (the radius and the ulna) at the elbow. From the elbow, the radius and ulna drop straight down to the foot.

This correctly angled front structure causes the foreleg to be set back under the dog. As the breed standard says, "The front legs should be set in under the shoulder blades, *with a definite body overhang before them.*" The only way that a Westie can have his legs set under the shoulders with a definite body overhang before them is if he has the right angulation in the forequarters. Without this he does not meet the breed standard.

23

The Relation Between the Scapula and the Neck, Head, and Back

Everything is cause and effect. The laid back scapula automatically creates a good length of neck due to the location on the spine. In turn, the

The correctly angled front structure causes the foreleg to be set back underneath the dog, with a definite body overhang.

good length of neck makes for good carriage of the head at a ninety-degree angle or less. The laid back scapula also provides shortness of the back, since the rib cage begins well back on the spine. This makes the lower end of the rib cage come well back, with the balance of the spine being short. This creates a "short coupled" or "cobby" Westie.

The Overlay of the Muscles

The scapulae are joined at the spine and to the ribs only by two layers of muscles. The Westie standard states that the shoulders should be "well knit." This means that the muscles at the spine should be strong and close so that no shifting of the scapulae occurs at the withers when the dog moves. If the muscles are not well knit, the shifting scapulae give the dog an undesirable loose-jointed appearance when he moves. The laid back scapula requires a broad sheath of long muscles to hold it in place. The scapulae attach the entire front of the dog to the rest of the body, and they act as the anchor. These broad muscles over and under the scapulae, where they join the neck, contribute to the description in the standard, which states, "Neck: Should be muscular and nicely set on sloping shoulders." "Sloping shoulders" are the backward sloping scapulae.

24

The "upright" shoulder has shallow angulation and provides no body overhang. This creates a short neck and a longer back.

The Faulty "Upright" (Or "Steep") Shoulder

This structure is so called because the upper end of the scapula is joined to the spine in an upright position, moving the scapula closer to the head. The upright position makes the lower end of the scapula automatically drop downward, rather than slope diagonally forward as it does in the laid back shoulder. The humerus connects to the lower end of the scapula in a wider angle than the correct "L." The radius and ulna connect to the elbow, bringing the leg into a more forward position. The dog with this wide-angled shoulder structure still may have his legs "under the shoulder blades," but the shallow angulation provides for no body overhang. This dog is said to "lack angulation." This dog should never be used for breeding.

Special Note to Future Westie Breeders: The shoulder assembly on the dog is the most complex part of the anatomy. For breeders, correct lay back of shoulder is the hardest thing to get and to keep in breeding stock. Correct shoulders should *never* be bred away from, in the effort to improve heads or tails or any other part of the anatomy. Faulty shoulder structure, once bred into a line, will be nearly impossible to breed out of the line.

The "Upright" Shoulder Related To Neck, Head, and Back

This upright shoulder automatically creates a short neck. The withers are flat, and the neck does not join the body "nicely set on sloping shoulders." Rather, it forms an abrupt angle. The set of the neck causes the head to be carried in an extended fashion. The rib cage joins this upright shoulder at a more forward position on the spine. The back coupling is longer. Combined with the flatness of the withers, the back seems much longer than the correctly structured back. Due to the shallow angulation, which drops the humerus down lower, this dog will often have short legs, making him seem too close to the ground.

The Overlay of the Upright Shoulder Muscles

The upright shoulder structure needs a narrower sheath of muscles of shorter length to anchor the scapula to the spine, ribs, and neck. This structure lacks substance, due not only to the narrow band of muscles. The dog with this structure will probably have lighter and narrower bones.

The Faulty "Loaded" Shoulder

The muscles of the scapulae lie both on top of and underneath the bones. As one muscle expands, the other contracts, so they are alike in size. When these muscles are heavy and coarse, those underneath the scapulae will push the bone outward and too far away from the rib cage. Together with the overlying coarse muscles, this gives the dog what is termed "loaded shoulders." This also creates a dog that is "out at the elbows," since his shoulder blades have forced the elbow joint outward. This dog should never be used for breeding.

The Front Legs and Feet

The Westie, as a digging dog, should have front feet that toe out slightly, in order to do his work. If his feet were perfectly straight and he were digging, the displaced soil would be thrown underneath his body and eventually behind him as he worked forward. He would be "digging himself in." If his feet toe out, he will throw the soil to the right and left of his body as he digs. Straight legs and flat elbows are a must. Crooked legs, protruding elbows, and legs that curve outward and back in at the feet (fiddle front) all are faults. A straight column supports more weight than a curved one. All of these faults require the dog to use muscles to help support his weight, when the weight should be supported by the bones.

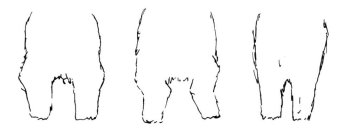

Left, "out at the elbow;" center, "fiddle front;" right, "too narrow."

Length of leg is a debatable subject. The standard says that the legs should be "relatively short, but with sufficient length to set the dog up so as not to be too close to the ground." Admittedly, this leaves the breeder or judge some latitude, and the novice puzzled. I can only write my own observations, as a guide. The Westie should *not* be set low to the ground, as is the Scottish Terrier. In viewing the dog in profile, the depth of chest is a factor. The leg can appear to start from the chest down. By measuring many dogs, I have found that the length of foreleg that best meets the description in the standard, to my own eye, is when the height of the elbow is one half the height of the dog at the withers.

Thus, an eleven inch dog would measure five and one-half inches from the top of the elbow to the floor. This ratio seems about right so that the dog is not "too close to the ground." My own preference is a foreleg about one-half inch longer than that. I find that a foreleg much longer makes the dog appear "too up on leg." A leg much shorter than half the height makes the dog "too low on leg," and the dog appears cloddy, to my eye.

Good tight feet are a must to give leverage as the dog moves. Splayed toes lack rigidity and do not give sufficient leverage. The dog's pads are so called because of their function. They act as "pads" to cushion impact and protect the bones. A Westie's pads should be thick and preferably black. Some Westies have pads that show some pink and some black. I have never seen a judge who inspected pads for color. All-black pads indicate good overall pigmentation and are the preferred color. All-black claws also are preferred but are not required. A Westie may have all-white claws or some of each color on the same foot.

The Back and Top Line

The back should be level from behind the shoulder to the set of the tail. Technically speaking, a dog's back begins at the last rib and extends forward about five ribs. The section between the last rib and the pelvis is called the "coupling." The entire back is referred to as the "top line," which should be level. There should be no upward arching, called "roaching," in the

25

spine. The muscles should give strong enough support so that the back does not sag downward, making a "sway back." There should be no rise over the pelvis, making the dog high in the rump. The tail should be set on high enough so that the back does not slope down to it. It is a fault if the back curves down to the tail, a condition called a "low set" tail.

Length of back should be relatively short. Usually dogs are shorter in the back than are bitches. The bitch can be forgiven a *little* length of back since she will need space in which to carry a litter. An overlong back in either sex is a fault. Westies with this fault, or with the roach back, the sway back, the high rump, or the low set tail, should never be used for breeding.

What Makes a "Good Rear"

This end of the dog, too, is a matter of correct angulation, where the bones meet one another. The "rear end assembly" consists of the pelvis, the upper thighbone (the femur), the lower leg or "second thighbones" (the fibula and tibia), and the heel (hock). From the hock, the bones of the foot continue to the floor.

The pelvis is a broad bone which is fastened firmly to the spine at the sacrum. A line through the center of the pelvis should meet the level spine at about a thirty-degree angle. The pelvis has the hip socket, and the upper end of the femur fits into this ball joint. If the pelvis is correctly angled, the femur will conect to it at about a ninety-degree angle. Instead of the tipped "L" of the shoulder, these two bones connect in a tipped "7." The short top of the "7" is the angled pelvis. The corner is the "point of the hip." The long side of the "7" is the femur, positioned downward and diagonally forward. The lower end of the femur connects to the second thighbones, forming the knee (stifle).

The ninety-degree angle between the pelvis and the femur creates a "well-bent" stifle. From the stifle, the fibula and tibia angle backward and downward to the hock. Like the correct front structure, this correct rear angulation appears broad when viewed from the side. It requires a broad span of muscles to cover it. This correct rear angulation is considered a necessity for every running dog.

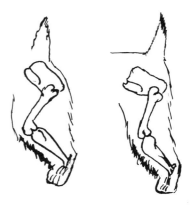

The correctly angled rear forms a well-bent stifle. The flat pelvis provides little bend at the stifle.

26

Back should be level, with the tail set on high enough so that the back does not slope down to it.

Low tail set.

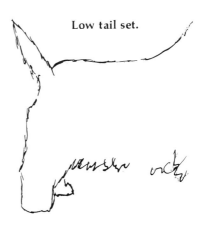

The Faulty "Straight Stifled" Dog

This dog has a flat pelvis that joins the spine at a narrower angle than the ideal thirty degrees. This drops the femur down straighter, forming a wider, more shallow angle. As a result, there is very little bend in the stifle. As in the front, this shallow angulation appears narrower. It requires a narrower band of shorter muscles to support it. The bones, too, may be lighter and narrower.

The Hocks and Rear Feet

The standard calls for hocks that are "well bent." The dog with good angulation at the stifle, combined with relative length of the second thighbones, will have a well-bent hock short in length from heel to toes. While the standard does not say that the dog should have hocks that are "well let down," it implies that since a well-bent hock is also well let down. This expression refers

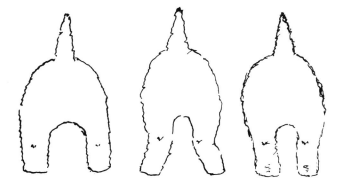

Left, rear too wide; center, "cow hocks"; right, correct rear, short, straight hocks.

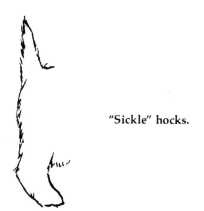

"Sickle" hocks.

to the length of the hock in relation to the length of the second thighbones. The hocks should be relatively short because short hocks give the dog stamina. Shorter thighbones and longer hocks make for speed in the short stretches. As an example, for short distances the long-hocked bunny rabbit will have great speed. But the dog with the short hock will have the advantage of staying power. In the long run, the short-hocked dog will catch the bunny rabbit.

Hocks also should be straight. They should not "sickle," which means to angle forward underneath the dog, thus resembling the blade of a sickle. These hocks provide no rear propulsion and cause a shuffling rear gait. Hocks should not slant inward at the heels, a condition called "cow hocks" due to the resemblance of the hocks to those of a cow. This causes the dog to "toe out" in the rear, which is very objectionable.

Rear feet are slightly smaller than front feet. Like the front feet, they should be good and tight, with no splaying of the toes, so that this rigidity provides good leverage in movement.

The Front Movement

The "front end assembly" of the dog is vital to his movement. The dog with the correct lay-back of scapula is able to swing his front legs forward with great reach and thrust, extending out ahead of his body in a long flat arc. Because the leg also is able to swing well back, it propels the body forward rather than upward, causing less fatigue. The dog with the steep shoulder has a much shorter front stride. He cannot cover the ground, as does the other dog, which has two and one-half times the ability to propel himself forward. The steep-shouldered dog is forced to take many more steps because he is hampered by the limited swing of his upper arm and the narrow span of muscles which control his movement. The first dog meets the standard with movement that is "free, straight, and easy." The steep-shouldered dog exhibits a stilted, choppy gait, devoid of freedom of movement.

The Rear Movement

The dog with the well-angled rear structure is able to swing his knee forward like a compressed spring that can burst into full power as

27

the leg extends backward. The largest part of a dog's drive comes from this backward sweep of the leg aided by the longer muscles that support his bones. The straight-stifled dog has very little bend in the knee. He is unable to swing his knee forward and extend his leg backward like the first dog due to lack of angulation and the shorter muscles. Like the steep front, the rear gait is stilted rather than free and easy. The lack of angulation causes this dog to move wide in the rear.

The Combined Good Front and Good Rear

This is the ideal arrangement for perfection. Since the Westie was developed to be a running dog, built for speed, he must have a laid back shoulder and a well-angulated rear. This dog moves with maximum power and efficiency. At the fast gait, his front feet stride out with full front thrust. His hind feet come forward and nearly trace the steps of the front feet, meeting no interference. Thus, the Westie with the correct angulation is like the old description of the hunter (horse), "short in the back, but standing over a lot of ground."

The Combination of Body Structure

A dog can have correct front structure combined with a straight-stifled rear. This dog moves well in front because he relies on his forward momentum for balance, but he lacks rear drive. The rear movement is stilted and wide. Conversely, a dog can have a steep shoulder with a well-angulated rear. This dog has difficulty keeping his front feet out of the way of his harder driving rear feet. He has to compensate for this in some way. He may gait at the trot with an over-reaching of the front legs to try to avoid the collision of front and rear feet. He may overwork his elbow muscles as he moves his front feet in an extra high and very tiring action, trying to lift his front feet out of the way. He may take on a spiritless rear movement, compensating in the easiest way by reducing his rear propulsion to better agree with his front stride and avoid conflict of feet. The gait in the front is bouncy and rapid. The dog with both faults has a stilted and bouncy gait, both fore and aft. His movement cannot be

"free, straight, and easy" due to the limitations imposed by his body structure.

Size and Balance

The American standard says that dogs should measure "about eleven inches at the withers, bitches being about one inch less." The British standard reads "eleven inches" for either a dog or a bitch. No approximate weight is given for either sex. Under "Faults," anything much under or over the stated heights is objectionable. Here again, we are permitted some leeway for individual interpretation. In the reality of the show ring, a Westie that is a little above the standard for its sex will do better than one that is under the standard height. Many exhibitors insist that a larger Westie makes a better "Group" dog. This means that as the only Westie being shown in the Terrier Group judging, along

In correct movement, front feet stride out. Hind feet come forward and nearly trace the steps of the front feet.

The dog with both faults has a stilted and bouncy gait.

28

with an assortment of various other Terrier breeds, the larger Westie will stand a better chance of attracting the attention of the judge.

Actually, the key word to a good dog is "balance." This is a matter of proportions—of length to height, neck length to tail length, depth of chest to leg length, and head size to body size. A dog being shown in a correct two inches of coat will appear taller than the dog stripped down to one-half inch of coat, so this must be taken into account. Any exhibitor who has shown several dogs through to their titles will attest to the fact that a dog slightly under the standard is harder to "finish" (show to his title) in competition with dogs at or slightly over the standard. So, as exhibitors, it behooves us to remember that any deviation of size from the standard must be a question of degree.

A good reason why no specific weight is recommended in the standard is because bone accounts for part of the weight that is registered on a scale. A heavily boned dog could weigh a pound or so more than his lighter-boned counterpart. A good rule of thumb is that a dog of correct weight and that is eleven inches tall at the withers will weigh between seventeen and eighteen pounds.

Balance in movement is equally important to balance in body proportions. The dog's angulation must be equal, front and rear, for balance. The steep-shouldered dog with the well-angulated rear is not in balance, with his short steps in front trying to avoid his rear feet. The well laid back dog with a steep rear is not in balance. He overworks his front while his rear gait is stilted, wide, and choppy. The dog with the steep shoulders and the straight stifle may be in balance, but the quality of movement is poor.

The Variation of the Angles

The preceding paragraphs have explained the differences between correct angulation and the "lack of angulation." It must be understood that, as in most other things, angulation is not all "black and white," but various shades of grey. The lay-back of the scapulae can range from the ideal forty-five degrees to a steep shoulder that is almost perpendicular to the spine. The angulation also can be narrower, moving the top of the

scapulae further toward the rear of the dog. As wide angulation gives the dog a neck that is too short, narrower angulation makes a longer neck. This dog appears shorter in the back. However, a neck that is too long is just as much a fault as one that is too short. In the same way, the rear angulation can vary, being very good, very poor, or anything in between.

Examining the Angulation of a Dog

The dog that has good angulation, or that lacks it, should be easy to spot when the dog is seen in motion if the viewer has a well-trained eye. But even the judge at the dog show sees

Top: use the side of your hand to easily see the angle at which the blade joins the spine.

Bottom: your hands can tell you if this is a square corner, between the scapula and the humerus.

29

every Westie on the table for closer examination. Here the dog is further checked for teeth, coat texture, testicles, and structure. Everyone can learn to check the body structure, even though the correct movement may be harder to see.

Put the dog into the "show stack," positioning the rear feet a little toward the back and the front feet underneath his shoulder. The dog's front pad should be directly under the center of the top of the shoulder blade where the blade connects to the spine. Locate the blade with your hands, gently feeling the bone from the spine to the point of the shoulder. By using the side of your hand as a guide, it is easy to see the angle at which the blade joins the spine.

At the point of the shoulder, the lower end of the shoulder connects to the humerus. This

Top: check the angle of the pelvis to the spine.

Bottom: right angle of femur and pelvis.

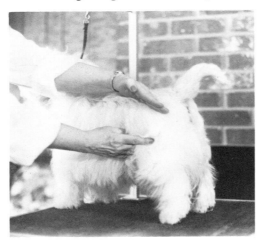

joint is easy to feel, as is the humerus. Your hands can tell you if this is a square corner or if the angle is wider than the ideal ninety degrees. Since the angles are approximate, there is no need for any measuring instrument. All you need is a pair of gentle hands.

The rear of the dog is also easy to feel with your fingers. Find the center of the pelvis. It starts at the spine and should angle backward, ending below the level of the tail. Locate the ball joint of the hip socket and trace the line of the femur to the stifle. You can tell if the pelvis and the femur form a square corner or if the angle is wider. You can feel the bend of the stifle or the lack of it as you trace the length of the second thighbones to the heel. And with your eyes you can see if the dog has short, straight hocks.

TAILS

Westie tails are short and are never docked. The standard states that, when carried erectly, the tail should not be longer than the top of the skull. In practice, many good dogs have tails that are about the same height as the head ruff, which is slightly longer than the skull level. It becomes a matter of balance of tail length to the overall dog. Tails should be as short as possible and should be trimmed free of feather. The tail is an extension of the bones of the spinal column. It is completely sheathed in muscles. Certain muscles pull the tail backward and draw it between the back legs. Other muscles move the tail from side to side and make the tail wag. A broad sheath of muscles, located on the back and continuing to the tip of the tail, pull the tail erect. All of these muscles, plus the size of the underlying bones, make up the circumference of the tail. Coarse muscles and heavy bone make a thicker tail.

Tail carriage should be as straight and erect as possible. The standard says that the tail should be carried "gaily." The *A.K.C. Complete Dog Book* defines a gay tail as one which is carried upright. The standard also says that the tail should not be "curled over the back." I have seen dogs in the ring, during the excitement of showing, gaiting with the tail pulled forward and parallel to the back. This includes a famous, top-producing champion stud dog. I also remember a dog winning in strong competition that gaited with his tail "squirreled" over his back in the ring. When stacked for the judge, however, the tails of these dogs were straightly erect. In these cases, the judges must have forgiven the temporary lapse of tail carriage due to the overall excellence and balance of the dogs.

THE COAT

The perfect Westie coat is double with a straight, hard outer coat about two inches in length and a soft undercoat. The dog needed such a coat for protection from the elements and adversaries. Any tendency to curl or any silkiness are serious faults. An "open" coat is one that lacks the soft undercoat. Without the undercoat, the hard outer coat shows gaps, making the coat appear open. A "single" coat could either lack undercoat or consist only of soft undercoat. Either of these two conditions is a fault. The coat should be white, of course.

The standard says that the coat is "very important and seldom seen to perfection." This, in my opinion, places emphasis on the coat, which is all too frequently misunderstood. The British standard reads, "Colour pure white, must be double coated. The outer coat consists of hard hair, about 2 in. long, free from any curl. The undercoat, which resembles fur, is short, soft and close. Open coats are objectionable." This puts the coat in better perspective.

I know that the writers of the American breed standard were well intentioned, and the coat is, indeed, important. The correct coat on a Westie, double and white, is uniquely his. Certainly every show dog in every breed should have a proper coat for that breed, blooming with health and cleanliness. In practice, however, the words "seldom seen to perfection" too often are interpreted in a way that I do not believe was intended by the writers of the standard. I am sure that every Westie exhibitor has been beaten in the ring by a swaybacked dog with a good coat, by a steep-shouldered dog with a good coat, or by a dog that gaited with his tail drawn between his back legs but that had a good coat. We have also been beaten by dogs in pure white soft coats, when our own entry had a correct hard coat showing a trace of color. On these occasions, the emphasis on coat written in the standard stayed in the judge's memory. The placements in the ring clearly showed that the judge decided that the coat was more important than structure.

Given a choice between two dogs of equal quality, one in a soft white coat and one in a hard double coat with a trace of color, a judge who really knows Westies will consider the hard coat to be the lesser of two faults. This judge knows that the coat is "seldom seen to perfection." Some dogs have inherited a trace of color in the dorsal streak; other dogs have some temporary color due to being heavily stripped or being discolored by the sun. If a dog is otherwise excellent, a trace of color in his coat is a minor flaw, since this coat is invariably hard. The pure white soft coat should be rejected, since this is not a typical coat.

By all means, every breeder should strive for white, double-coated dogs. There are so many of them around that it is obvious that the white coat color can be bred. For the benefit of future Westie breeding programs everywhere, however, the first consideration must be the skeleton under the coat. This is what gives the dog his movement, balance, soundness, size, and substance. If a Westie lacks these qualities, the best coat on the planet cannot make up for their absence. Since the coat is, indeed, "seldom seen to perfection," judges should look beyond coat for the dog underneath. Winning show dogs become future breeding stock. Let us not lose sight of the fact that coat is variable with the seasons, while skeletal faults, once bred in, will go on forever. The entire cake should be judged, not just the frosting.

31

Ch. Kortni of Windy Hill is one of the Westies at Kilkerran. Here she is a puppy, age about seven months.

THE PERFECT WESTIE

This is a dog that measures eleven inches at the withers and weighs eighteen pounds. The dog has a beautiful head covered with full furnishings in proportion to his size. He has a well-defined stop and a short muzzle, dark hazel, deep-set eyes rimmed with black, and small ears well set on the side edges of the skull. The ear linings are grey. He has a good tight scissors bite and a full complement of gleaming teeth behind the black rims of his lips.

His coat consists of two inches of hard outer coat with profuse soft undercoat. It is the silvery white of snow. He has a good reach of neck, which blends beautifully into his sloping shoulders. His forelegs are set well under the front overhang of his chest. The front legs are straight with flat elbows. His chest has the good breadth that his well-sprung ribs have provided, and his ribs drop deeper than his elbows. His back is short-coupled, is perfectly level in top line, and ends in a good high tail set. The tail is short, straight, and carried erectly. His hindquarters are well angulated and have well let down hocks for close-in rear movement. His forefeet are a little larger than his rear feet. All feet have tight toes and thick black pads. All the claws are black.

This dog moves like a dream. His front feet swing forward in a long, low arc, barely off the floor. Watch the withers. There is no bounce. His rear moves in perfect coordination with his front, his backward stroking rear feet lending propulsion and a jaunty spring to his gait. As a matter of balance, his feet, both front and back, move toward the center of his body. The dog seems to sail along, his back staying level with the floor, his back feet nearly tracing the steps of his front feet. This dog is a showman, gaiting with a smile on his face, his neck extended for propulsion, his head up.

Now where do we find this dog? Only in the dreams of the dedicated breeder. The truth is, he does not exist. It is well said that every dog has at least three faults, if you know where to look. Knowing this does not deter the knowledgeable breeder whose planned breeding programs are all directed toward his goal of producing Westies of correct type and soundness. This is the breeder who studies pedigrees, individual dogs, and individual grandparents, selecting breeding partners for the ancestors and their individual attributes. Who knows? Some fine day that absolutely perfect Westie may be one that comes from this breeder's well-laid plans and from his whelping box, and he will never give up trying to produce such a dog. Here's to all such breeders—clink!

This beautiful "blocky" head belongs to Briarwood Bit o' Bonnie Brier, about six months old here. She was bred by Bettina King, Sebring, Florida, and is co-owned by Christine Swingle of North Canton, Connecticut.

5 Evaluating Westie Puppies

Many people who are seeking a pet have said to me, "If you ever have one with a spot on it, or something, I would love to have it!" A spotted puppy would not be a purebred Westie. A "pet quality" Westie is one which falls short of the breed standard or short of perfection in his "conformation," or bone structure. He may have a poor head, an overlong back, an overlong tail, a low tail set, an undershot mouth, an overshot mouth, or any combination of these and other structural faults—faults that would spoil his chances for becoming a real contender in the show ring. Since perfection is unattainable in any breed, every litter will have pet quality puppies in it. The two finest show dogs bred together probably will not yield an entire litter of show quality offspring. If it happens, send off the rockets and break out the champagne when the last one gets his title! Depending on the size of the litter, a breeder is very lucky to have two littermates which have been shown to their championships in the ring.

WATCHING THE PUPPIES DEVELOP

Westie puppies are born with pink noses and pink pads on their feet. These very quickly darken, and in a few days—sometimes even hours—the area around the nose will be grey and the nose black. Black is the only acceptable color for Westie noses. A partly black, partly pink nose, known as a "butterfly nose," is a serious fault. Pads may take longer to turn black, and some pads may never be black. A Westie can have some pink pads, some grey-pink, some black and pink. Claws may turn black or remain their original white or even be both colors on the same foot. At birth the puppies have very short muzzles and round heads like little tennis balls. They have small, pointed ears that are never cropped and that are sealed shut for nineteen to twenty-one days. The tails are short and pointed and are never docked. At about three days of age, the puppies should be taken to the veterinarian to have their little dewclaws surgically removed, weather and circumstances permitting. Since the dogs do not need these extra claws on the inside of the forelegs, it is best to have them removed before they become attached to the leg bones.

Teeth

The puppy's teeth begin to erupt at about three to four weeks of age; the canines are usually the first to appear. These are the long, fanglike teeth in the side front of the mouth, both in the upper and lower jaws. Later the small teeth between the canines in the center of the mouth will appear. These are the incisors. This is the usual pattern, but I have had puppies cutting their premolars and molars—the teeth on the sides of the mouth—before the incisors. Muzzles begin to lengthen when the teeth begin to erupt and the jaws grow longer to accommodate them.

In the upper jaw will be six small incisors in the center of the mouth. Then there will be a space, and then the upper canines. Behind these will be the premolars and molars. In the center of the lower jaw will be six small incisors, with the canines immediately following and no space.

These lower canines fit into the space provided in the upper jaw between the upper incisors and the upper canines so that when the mouth is closed the canines can properly "mesh." The sides of the lower jaw also will have premolars and molars.

The small upper incisors may slightly overlap the lowers for a "scissors" bite. The upper and lower incisors may meet together, end to end, for a "level" bite. In the breed standard, these two bites are equally acceptable. The lower jaw may be a little longer than the upper jaw and project outward. This is called an "undershot" bite. Conversely, if the upper jaw is longer and protrudes, this creates an "overshot" bite. Neither of these two conditions is acceptable in the show ring or in breeding stock. The best bite for a puppy is the scissors bite. If the puppy has a scissors bite after the canines and incisors have erupted, the probability is 90 percent that the mouth will stay that way. That is not 100 percent, but it is very good

34

The radiant smile on the face of Anita Becky, B.J.'s Westies, Denver, Colorado, reflects the pleasure she feels as she hugs her Ch. B.J.'s Sir Becket after a Group placement. Like a dream-come-true, "Becket" is one of four littermates, all of which are finished champions. The other three "children" are Ch. B.J.'s Sir Ballot, Ch. B.J.'s Sir Brevit, and litter sister, Ch. B.J.'s Baby Grand.

The sire of this litter was Eng. Am. Ch. Ardenrun 'Andsome of Purston, imported and owned by Dr. Alvaro Hunt (see page 132). The dam was Ch. Arnholme Dove, another English import, owned by Anita Becky (see page 14).

When Anita Becky presided over the whelping box to assist with the delivery of this lovely group, she had no way of knowing that each and every one of the puppies would grow up to be champions. In addition to their fine showing in the ring, these Westies now have champion children of their own, and Becket is the sire of ten champions. A truly outstanding group. Dedicated fanciers like Dr. Hunt and Mrs. Becky do the whole breed a true service in importing excellent dogs, which often go from being top winners to becoming top producers, adding luster to American breeding programs.

Gilbert photo

odds. If at the same stage of development the puppy has a level bite, this is a questionable bite. The mouth could mature with the same level bite, become a scissors bite, or become overshot or undershot. If the upper jaw is a little long and the bite is overshot, the lower jaw has a fair chance of growing longer and eventually matching the upper jaw. The mouth with an undershot bite has very little chance of correcting itself.

To better understand how the jaws mature, it is necessary to know that the upper jaw, the maxilla, is all one with the skull. The lower jaw, the mandible, is separate and is hinged to the upper jaw. The two jaws grow independently of each other. To further complicate matters, there are four separate genes for the two jaws, one for each quadrant. It is possible that the puppy could inherit all four genes from one parent, or two from one and two from the other, or three from one and one from the other. This is true of all breeds and explains mismatched jaw lengths, wry mouths, and other forms of malocclusion. However, it is estimated that about 50 percent of all malocclusions will correct themselves and are not genetic in nature.

Puppies with overshot bites can be helped by the owner. Daily games of tug-of-war with a piece of knotted cotton sash cord or with an old terry towel can work wonders. This should be started at about three months of age, when it has been pretty well established that the puppy's mouth is staying overshot. In getting a good grip on the towel or rope, the puppy's lower jaw and the hinge are forced slightly forward. The masseter muscle firms and strengthens, which helps to keep the mandible forward. The lower jaw will gradually approach the length of the upper jaw. This game should not be played as the give-and-take of one puppy playing with another. It should be played hard, with the owner getting a good grip and getting the puppy to pull as firmly as possible. Let the puppy be the winner after a time. This will encourage him to play the game. This method has improved the bites of my own puppies and those of puppies belonging to friends. Recently a "Borzoi friend" was expressing her disappointment that a young bitch that she had hoped to show had "gone overshot." I told her about the games of tug. Later she told me that the puppy's mouth was so improved that

even her veterinarian was astonished. The bitch is presently winning in the show ring.

Nothing I know of will help the undershot jaw, since there is no way to persuade the skull bone, of which the maxilla is a part, to move out into place with the lower jaw. Games of tug would only make it worse. One method that can be tried is to extract the milk canine teeth in the hope that the permanent canines will have a better chance of erupting in the correct "mesh." This involves taking the puppy to the veterinarian, who will anesthetize the puppy and pull the teeth. After that, about all you can do is hope and pray a lot. The puppy with the good scissors bite or the level bite should *never* be allowed to play tug, at least until he has finished growing. This could cause an undershot mouth. I have known this to happen, too.

The Head

After about ten to twelve weeks of age, the puppy's head shape and proportionate size will remain the same. He will have to grow his head furnishings, but otherwise this shape will be that of his adult head. If he does not have a good head at this age, it will never be good. A good head should have some width across the crown and not taper in from the sides to the level of the eyes. The muzzle should be shorter in length than the length of the skull. The muzzle should have a little width at the nose so as not to be too pointed. The front of the crown of the head should curve down to the flat plane of the muzzle to form a well-defined "stop." The ears should be set on the outer edges of the skull and should set up straight. They should not be set on the sides of the head and stick out at the sides. A

35

Young puppies often look very large in the ears. Six-week-old Fairtee Chortle Checkmate, C. D., soberly regards the camera.

skinny head, a long foreface, or a shallow or non-existent stop will never mature into a nicely rounded skull with a short foreface and a well-defined stop. If the head is narrow, the ears will look as if they are set too close, and the eyes will be too close together.

Young puppies often look very "large in the ears." Usually this is because the head hair is lacking, and the puppy will seem to "grow into his ears." Some puppies get their ears up very early, at four and one-half to five weeks of age. Other puppies get their ears up, then drop the tips again as they are cutting teeth. Some puppies will not have their ears fully up at two and one-half months and may need a little help, especially if the ears are very large. This help consists of taping the ears and is described in the chapter on puppy grooming.

The Body

The rest of the puppy, neck to tail, will be a miniature of the adult dog minus the coat which he will develop later. An examination of his bone structure with your hands, as described in the chapter on the breed standard for the adult, will tell you what you need to know about his skeleton. His length of back should be relatively short, and his tail should be short and well set at the end of his level spine. An upward curve in the spine ("roaching") will not improve. On the contrary, this condition will worsen as the puppy matures.

The puppy's tail should be put into the "up" position to check its proportions. It should not extend much above the top of the skull. An overlong tail and an overlong back are said to go

1

A nicely uniform litter of Fairtee puppies, stacked for evaluation. All of the puppies have well laid back shoulders, and all have well-bent stifles, except one. Can you pick the straight-stifled puppy? It is puppy #5. While this camera angle is slightly above and looking downward, you can still envision the square (1) the top of the back, from inside the tail set to the shoulder; (2) from the shoulder, down the front leg; (3) the table-top; and (4) up the back leg to the tail set. Tail lengths are short, not extending above the top of the skull.

2

3

4

5

together. Puppy bitches, like the adults, are usually a little longer in the back than puppy dogs. An acceptable amount of length of back must be a question of degree. If you will look at the puppy in profile, you should be able to imagine a square. Its four sides will be (1) the top of the back from inside the tail set to the shoulder; (2) from the shoulder down the front leg; (3) the floor or the table top; and (4) up the back leg to the tail set. The puppy dog that is a little shorter in the back than a square is very, very good. The puppy bitch that is a *little* longer than the square is acceptable.

Going over the puppy gently with your hands is the surest way to determine the underlying bone structure, which is what makes the dog. This is especially true of the young puppy in the eight- to ten-week age bracket. This fellow is too frisky and may be a trifle wobbly in the rear. Watching him move will not tell you what you need to know about the skeleton. Even at this early age the positioning of the bones is evident, and positioning will never change. If the puppy lacks angulation, the adult will lack it. The bones also should be sturdy and of good substance. Of course, you will want to watch the puppy run about and play, but only your hands will be able to judge the structure. Check also for the proportionate width of chest, which will be evident if the puppy has the correct heart-shaped ribs. The depth of ribs should reach at least to the point of the elbows.

Westie puppies come in two types of coat, and often a litter will have two types. Some coats are soft and fluffy, and some are hard and straight. The soft-coated puppy, seeming prettier and more puppylike, is very appealing to the newcomer to the breed. This coat will require work to bring it into the desired hardness. The straight, hard coat requires much less work and will stand the dog in good stead all of his life. The skin under the coat should be clean, pink, and healthy, with no trace of scaling, "dandruff," rash, or irritation.

Good pigmentation also should be evident. This shows in the solid black of the nose, the dark grey skin around it, the black eye rims, and the grey or grey-pink belly. Dark grey ear linings

Good substance is evident in Fairtee Perspi Kassidy, along with straight, hard coat.

"Iona," "Ivy," and "Ingrid," three Taradink Westies belonging to Tom and Lois Drexler, North Huntingdon, Pennsylvania, are ten weeks old and ready to have their puppy fluff removed.

are a special bonus as are all-black claws and pads on the feet. The more pigmentation in these areas, the better. All serious breeders are trying to maintain it.

Good substance, mentioned before, is hard to define, but it is very important. It means correct bones coupled with the broad muscles that support the skeleton. A Westie should not have the light bones of the Cairn or the heavier bones of the Scottie. A comparison of the three breed standards helps to clarify this. The Scottie standard calls for a ten-inch dog weighing between eighteen and twenty-one pounds, and the Cairn standard calls for a ten-inch dog weighing fourteen pounds. The Westie standard calls for a dog "about eleven inches" and does not specify weight. However, it is generally acknowledged that a properly balanced Westie that is eleven inches at the withers should weigh seventeen to eighteen pounds. We are talking about the ideal, when discussing weight, which automatically rules out the overweight dog. The differences, then, are a result of the substance of the bones. The shorter Scottie has heavier bone, while the shorter Cairn has much lighter bone than the Westie.

Temperament, too, is important in a puppy. Some puppies are bold and devil-may-care, and others are more reserved. The bold one will be the hardest to train, but he should make a good showman if his conformation is good. The reserved one should not be overlooked, however, since he may just be looking you over. If one puppy seems a little shy, he may have been the underdog in his litter. However, he may blossom into a fine pet and companion once he leaves the litter.

Much can depend on the quartering of the littermates as they develop. For the best individual development, Westie puppies should be housed separately from adult Westies, except for the dam. In this way, none of the adults can boss the little ones around. After the age of seven weeks, if one puppy is lording it over his littermates, or if one always seems to be at the bottom of the pile, it is better to break the litter into two groups so that the "know-it-all" cannot impose his will on smaller littermates. This gives all the puppies the best chance to develop their individual potential.

At the age of three months, a puppy dog should have two testicles properly descended in the scrotum. Ideally, both testicles should be located in the scrotum at birth, but this is not always the case. While their descent to the scrotum after three months of age is possible, it is chancy. To be eligible in the show ring, a dog must be equipped with two testicles in the scrotum. This is referred to as being "entire." The subject of "chryptorchidism" (hidden testicle) is discussed in the chapter on defects. But if you are planning to show the dog, do not wait any longer for the testicles to descend than about three months of age.

A Westie puppy grows "up" and, having finished that, grows "down." He will attain most of his height by about seven months of age. The upward growth will slow at about six months, and after seven months he will grow very little taller. During this period of rapid growth, the rump can look high and will actually measure as much as one-half inch taller than the height at the withers. Then the shoulder end of the puppy grows, and the back levels out again. A young puppy, age ten to twelve weeks, with a level back should mature into a level-backed adult. After the upward growth, the puppy begins to get his depth. This is hard to describe since it is impossible to measure with a tapeline. The chest deepens, and the whole dog seems to gain more substance.

The six-month-old Westie can look like a teenager. Breeders say that a puppy whose overall appearance does not change from the nest to the adult is sure to be a good one. However, I believe that a Westie can look a little gangling due to various reasons. He could be a self-limiting eater and be a little underweight due to rapid growth. He could be a winter puppy, slow at coming into coat in the summer, and the lack of it could make him appear leggy. He could simply be a little slower in developing. Some Westies that are well-developed very young have finished their titles in the ring before their first birthday. Others need to be two years old before they are any real competition in the show ring. The same method for judging the very young puppy must be applied. If the bones in the dog are correctly positioned, the dog will mature into a good one.

Whether you are considering a show dog or

a companion dog, remember that each dog has his faults. In evaluating an entire litter of any breed, it is best to sort the puppies by sex. Westie litters are small, but the purpose is to select the best puppy in each sex. First, select the male with the most faults, the one with the second most faults, and so on. Then follow the same procedure with the female puppies. In this way, by the process of elimination, you can determine which puppy has the fewest faults in each sex.

If you are a breeder, there has undoubtedly been one puppy in the litter to which your eye has been constantly attracted from the beginning. As the litter develops, each puppy becomes a little individual, and certainly each one has his virtues. *It is in learning to see the faults that the honest breeder keeps himself from being "kennel blind"— seeing nothing but the virtues.* I have heard of breeders who claim that they choose the best of the litter at birth, before the puppies are barely dry. The wisdom of this method escapes me, since so many changes can occur as the puppies grow. To me, only learning to evaluate the faults, in spite of the virtues, can bring improvement to a breeding program. Faults cannot be eliminated in a kennel that fails to recognize them.

These precious five-week-old tykes are two of the P. J.'s Westies, bred by John and Pat Baldwin of McKeesport, Pennsylvania.

Four generations of quality Westie bitches pose with their dedicated breeder, Mrs. Dorothea Daniell-Jenkins, Of the Rouge Kennels, Pickering, Ontario, Canada, founded in 1947. From left to right they are youngest to eldest: Joy of the Rouge, at age four months; her dam, Can. Ch. Vigil of the Rouge; her dam, Can. Ch. Wendy of the Rouge; and her dam, Can. Ch. Fanfare of the Rouge, age eleven years. This photo was taken in 1963, but devotion to selective line-breeding has continued over the years. This is evidenced by the many Westies of correct type and temperament that continue to bear the Of the Rouge name, registered in perpetuity by the Canadian Kennel Club. Mrs. Daniell-Jenkins is also licensed by the American Kennel Club to judge Hounds, Terriers, Toys, and Non-Sporting breeds.

Bob Dorsey photo

6 Buying a Westie Puppy

Acquiring any puppy should be regarded as serious business, even approaching the same level as child adoption. With any luck, the dog will become a long-time member of the family. Acquiring a Westie puppy will be more difficult than locating a more common breed of dog. Those of us who love Westies are grateful that they are not one of the "popular" breeds being bred in "puppy mills," sold to dog wholesalers, and winding up in a pet store for sale. The ratio of registered Westie individuals to registered litters is about two and one-half dogs per litter. Average litter size, then, is three or four puppies. This small litter size is a blessing, since the average owner of a puppy mill prefers to breed those dogs that give a higher yield per litter.

Certainly no serious breeder, regardless of breed, would sell whole litters in wholesale lots, to be sorted out and shipped to pet stores. These puppies are taken away from their dams, usually too soon, and are crated for shipment around the country by the wholesaler of dogs. The wholesaler pays a ridiculously low price for the puppies. Most likely, these puppies have missed their immunization shots, since the "puppy miller" wants to make some profit. Health certificates are often falsified.

Even if the sellers and the pet shop owners are competent, these puppies have missed so many meals and have been through so many hands that they have not gotten off to a very good start in life. The price for the puppy, at the point of sale, is exorbitant, particularly in view of the usually poor quality of the puppies, whatever their breed. The pet store cannot really guarantee that the puppies are purebred, since they have no certain knowledge. I am always amazed that the pet store puppy buyer never stops to wonder how the puppy came to be there.

A serious breeder, on the other hand, takes very good care of his adults and puppies. The dam has been properly fed and maintained during her pregnancy for optimum results at whelping time. When the litter is young, the breeder has no certain way of knowing which puppies will be future show dogs or which one will eventually be his own "keeper." Even if he did, he would still give all the puppies the same care, food, veterinary attention, and immunizations simply because he cares about the well-being of all of his dogs.

The breeder will give you any help you need in learning to care for the puppy. Usually a bag of the food that the puppy has been eating will be sent home along with his feeding schedule. You will be given his record of visits to the veterinarian and a record of his worm checks and shots. You will get a pedigree that you can trust to be correct and the puppy's application for registration with the American Kennel Club. You will pay less for the puppy from the breeder. If nothing else, you will be eliminating the middleman.

You will be able to see the dam and perhaps the sire, if the breeder owns him. Often bitches are bred to stud dogs miles away, so the sire is not always on the premises. The dam may be looking a little thin, especially if she has been feeding a large litter, and she will probably be "out of coat," since most bitches lose coat after whelping. These two factors must be taken into account. Nobody can be Miss America while tending a family of demanding babies.

The buyer of a puppy should never decide that he must have it by December 24, or the first two weeks of May, or any other arbitrary date. The time to buy a puppy is when the breed you want in the sex you prefer is available from a reliable breeder, *even if you have to wait several months.* The gestation period for puppies is about two months (nine weeks), so if a bitch has just been bred, it will be four to five months before the puppies will be ready to go. People adopting children sometimes must wait years before the one that they want is available for adoption. The point is that no one should buy any dog on impulse. Dog ownership is a responsibility that should never be undertaken without due consideration. If you wait until you can get the dog that you really want, you will be happy with your choice.

WHERE TO LOOK

Locating a breeder is not always easy and may take some diligent work, depending on the area in which you live. The most obvious place to

42

This appealing group, bred at Bonnie Brier by Christine Swingle, clearly shows the care and attention that has been given to their well-being.

look is in the classified section of the local newspapers. Reading the ads under "Pets" two or three times a week can sometimes be rewarding. However, many breeders never advertise their puppies for sale. The next best place to look is in the telephone book for the listing of the veterinarians in your city. Inquire if they see any Westies as patients and if they know of any litters. The local kennel club would know if any of their members breed Westies. If you do not know how to contact the kennel club, again the veterinarian is a source of information. These people know which of their clients have show dogs and belong to the kennel club. The kennel club holds dog shows, and each show has a catalogue that lists all the breeds at the show, the individual dogs, and their owners. The catalogue can be another source of information on Westie owners, and possibly Westie breeders.

Dog magazines carry ads for breeders that have puppies. If you do not find these on the newsstand, check your local library or the waiting room at the veterinarian's office. You also can write a letter to the American Kennel Club requesting the name and address of the secretary of the West Highland White Terrier Club of America. That person can put you in touch with the nearest regional breed club. The parent club also publishes a litter listing for members, and you could request a copy.

It is hoped that you can see the puppy, his dam, and his littermates before you buy him. Seeing the entire litter can be important, since overall quality of a litter makes a big difference. You will be better off with the poorest puppy from a really good litter than with the only good puppy in an otherwise poor litter. Meeting the dam also is important. Great stress is placed on the value of a fine stud dog, while too little emphasis is given to the value of a good bitch. She contributes 50 percent of the genes in the puppies, and she is equally to be credited with a lovely litter. In fact, in a breeding program, one fine-quality bitch is equal to two quality stud dogs. I have read many ads for stud services of dogs that are "siring champions," "throwing good heads," "passing on his substance and hard white coat," and I always want to ask the owner, "Out of which bitch?"

While disposition is inherited, it is really in the "paws" of the dam. In this, she is the most influential creature with which the litter will come in contact. As she rears her young in the nest, she will pass along all of her attitudes. While she may be protective of a very young litter where strangers are concerned, or with other

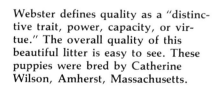

Webster defines quality as a "distinctive trait, power, capacity, or virtue." The overall quality of this beautiful litter is easy to see. These puppies were bred by Catherine Wilson, Amherst, Massachusetts.

dogs, she is not "spooked" by her owner. She also will discipline her puppies with small sounds and growls and sometimes be rough with them if she feel the occasion demands it.

Acquaint yourself with the breed standard. In fact, memorize it. Attend dog shows, if possible, and see the Westies being shown. If you are unable to do that, a good educational source is a magazine published for Terrier breeds, composed almost totally of pictures of winning dogs—all of the breeds recognized by the American Kennel Club. This is *Terrier Type*, sold only on subscription (address in back of book). There will be many photographs of Westies, in some issues more than others. The pictures are the next best thing to seeing a lot of dogs in the ring. In some ways they are better, since the pictures will be of dogs that are being selected by the judges at the shows, many as Best of Breed and Group placement winners, and you will have the pictures to study. You will soon develop an eye for a "good one." You may be surprised to find that you will also develop an eye for a "good one" in the other Terrier breeds.

Any good breeder knows the standard well, is fully conversant in it, and should be able to fault his own puppies. Of course, you will always find the breeder who is "kennel blind." All of his puppies are faultless and gorgeous. This breeder literally does not see the shortcomings of his

dogs. If the dog or bitch is said to be a "blue ribbon winner," this does not necessarily mean a top-quality dog. The dog could have won first in his class as the only entry in that class at the show and may have won several blue ribbons. Remember, too, that "purebred" and "AKC registered" do not automatically equal "quality." As long as the parents are registered, the puppies are eligible for registration, and the AKC can make no judgements as to the quality of any individual dog.

It is not always possible to visit the breeder, since he may be a long distance away. Many people buy dogs and puppies by having them shipped by air. This is perfectly satisfactory if the buyer has return privileges. In this case, it is most important to know the breed standard so that you can evaluate the dog that is shipped to you. If possible, find someone who knows the breed to accompany you when you pick up the dog. Wherever he comes from the dog should be taken to your veterinarian as soon as possible along with the health certificate and any record of immunization that you have received from the seller.

It is a very difficult thing for most people who love dogs to return a small, insecure animal to a shipping crate and have it sent back to the seller. You must also deal with your own disappointment. But if the puppy is not everything that you have been led to believe, harden your

44

A puppy owned by Coreley Plasek, Darien, Illinois.

heart and return it to the seller. As the buyer, you will be sent the puppy at your expense—that is, you will pay for the shipping and the crate in which the puppy is shipped, in addition to the purchase price of the dog. You and the seller should agree in advance who pays the return freight in the event that the dog is to be returned for any reason. All of these arrangements are best made by letter so that all mutually agreed terms of purchase are in writing.

All of these measures are suggested as protection for the buyer. While unethical dog breeders are in the minority, as in all other fields, they do exist. You have decided to enrich your life with a nice companion dog or a future champion, and a great deal of sentiment is involved in your decision. But, like any other purchase, the business aspect must enter into it. Just use the same good judgement that you would use in buying a car or anything else. You will probably be expected to pay for the dog before shipment, and the breeder may wish to keep the registration until your check has cleared. If so, request the litter registration number and the registered names of the sire and dam, if the registration slip is held up for any reason. You should also request a copy of the puppy's pedigree.

Do not be surprised if you are given a screening by the breeder. Serious breeders are highly interested in the homes that their puppies will have. The dedicated breeder may have slept on the floor by the whelping box for several nights to make certain that the puppies got off to a good start. He wants to know that this dog has a run or a fenced yard, will be walked on a leash, and will be properly maintained as a good citizen in the neighborhood and for the dog's own safety. He wants to know that you are not a "puppy miller," interested only in breeding dogs as fast as Mother Nature can produce them, and that his lovely little bitch will not be dead in three years from overbreeding. There are unethical dog buyers, too—people who should never be allowed to own a dog.

WHAT AGE IS BEST?

How old should the puppy be? An honest breeder has two choices when selling puppies. He can sell them as youngsters, with no guarantee as to the final quality at maturity and promising only that the puppy is healthy at the time he is sold. Or he can keep the entire litter until they are five to six months old and evaluate them at that time, selling some as pets and some as "show quality." To be sure, long-time breeders with much experience can and do sell "show prospects" as young puppies. But *no one,* however informed and experienced, can guarantee that a young "show prospect" will indeed grow up to be a show specimen. The seller can only make an educated guess. He may be able to guarantee a replacement, but this is not always satisfactory. If you have fallen in love with the dog, you may not wish to have it replaced. Beware of the seller who claims that his puppy is a guaranteed "show dog" at age three months. You could be buying a big disappointment and paying too much for the "privilege."

Every breeder in the world would love a "show home" for every really good puppy he sells. He would be so happy to see every puppy with his kennel name in the show ring. But his first consideration should be a good home and the right home. Show homes are about 10 percent of the market, at most. The average buyer is seeking a nice pet. The show home is not necessarily the right home, either. Many fine dogs live in kennels, are groomed and trained for the show ring, are used for breeding, and never really enjoy the opportunity of bestowing all the affection that they have to give. They never receive it, either, which is sad.

Seven weeks of age is the time in the puppy's growth when he is ready to form attachments for humans and is a logical time for him to be separated from his dam and his littermates. *But*—the next five weeks, the period from seven to twelve weeks, is very important in his future development. He can "learn to learn" before seven weeks, but real learning begins after that, in the next five weeks. He needs to learn that learning is fun and brings approval and that humans are kind and are to love. This period is crucial to his development to his fullest potential. What he learns now, he will never forget. It is extremely important for him to learn the right things and with no restraints or harsh punishments. Unless the buyer of a young puppy knows the importance of this early training, the puppy should not go to a new home until he is three months old. Then he is far less likely to be ruined by the bad handling that he could receive from his well-meaning but uninformed new owners.

Westie breeders often keep their puppies long enough to get them stripped of their soft coats so that the buyer will have a dog coming into hard coat by the time the dog leaves for his new home. Depending on the season of the year, stripping cannot be started before about eight weeks of age. If it is winter, the coat may not be ready to pluck easily at eight weeks. Between eight and ten weeks of age is the time in his life when the puppy can be imprinted with fear. Knowing this, the wise breeder goes slowly when working at the grooming table. He prefers to take whatever time is necessary to bring in the hard coat as an extra service to the buyer, who will find the hard-coated puppy easier to keep clean. The new owner will not understand how to strip the puppy, so it is best done before the puppy goes to his new home.

If the dog that is virtually assured of finishing his title in the ring is what you are seeking, buy an older puppy or dog. Five or six months of age would be about right, but even a two-year-old dog is not old; in fact, he has just reached maturity. By five months of age he should have most of his permanent teeth, and you can be reasonably sure that he will keep a good bite. Some of the premolars and molars may still not be permanent ones, and their proper eruption may still be in question. A puppy dog will be sure to be entire by five to six months, if he is ever going to be. The quality of the coat will be evident, even though the dog is not fully "furnished out" at this age. His mature size can be evaluated, since he will probably grow only one to one and one-half inches taller. His overall balance will be evident. So will his movement, which is so important in the show ring.

You will pay more for this older puppy or dog. The breeder has kept him, groomed him, given him all of his shots, and taken the chance on how he will shape up. The puppy should certainly be priced accordingly. A prime consideration is how this older puppy or dog has been kept at the breeder's home or kennel. If he has had plenty of human socialization from the beginning, he will adjust to his new owner, given a couple of weeks and gentle, understanding treatment. If he has been kept as a "kennel dog," he may never adjust. I am inclined to think that older dogs and puppies being kept for future show homes have been well socialized. The show dog needs an outgoing disposition, a head-up-tail-up attitude that is so important to a successful ring career. Even so, ask questions, visit if possible, and request return privileges.

Often, older show puppies and dogs are sold on a co-ownership basis. This means that the dog is registered in both your name and that of the breeder. You may be sold a dog on these terms so that the breeder may have future access to the dog's free stud services or may have a "say" in the choice of bitches to which the dog will be bred. You may be sold a bitch with the understanding that the breeder will select the future breeding partners or will be given a return puppy when she is bred, or one-half the litter, or other "breeder's terms." In these cases, the dog in question should be sold to you at a substantially reduced price, depending on the terms.

If you decide to accept the breeder's terms, there are certain things you should know. The AKC issues only one registration slip per dog and issues it to the person whose name appears in

Four-and-one-half-month-old Westray's Fancy Clancey, bred by Mr. and Mrs. Ed Chappell, Jr., Signal Mountain, Tennessee, shows potential as a real contender in the show ring.

46

the "Owner" section of the application. The "Co-owner" can and should request a duplicate of the registration, which costs a nominal extra fee. Any agreement between buyer and seller should be in writing *at the time of the purchase,* with all terms clearly defined and with both parties having a copy. Are all expenses for the dog—that is, feeding, veterinarian bills, dog show expenses, and/or handler's fees—to be shared equally? Which person houses, grooms, shows, and breeds the dog? Showing a dog to his title can be a lengthy, time-consuming, expensive activity. All of these questions should be settled at the time of purchase, including the disposition of the dog in the event of the death of either party. If one owner dies, the AKC requires a sworn statement that the deceased did not will all of his worldly goods to someone else. The co-ownership also should have a time limit so that at some designated future date the dog will become the sole property of the buyer.

Many co-ownerships have been very rewarding, with the buyer being given a fine start in Westies and learning much from the breeder. The other side of the coin is often unpleasant. Many bitter disagreements have been brought about by the co-ownership of a dog, and even the best of friends may no longer be speaking to one another. It is unbelievable how emotional two people can become when a cherished dog is involved. This makes it very important that each party fully understands what will be expected of him, in writing, and has a copy of the agreement.

Which Sex Do You Want?

Which sex should you buy? Ah, that is a difficult question. Many people believe that a bitch is naturally more gentle and sweet, more of a stay-at-home, and easier to train. This is not true. Some Westie puppy bitches are rowdy tomboys, just as hell-for-leather as the puppy dogs. Frankly, I can never make up my mind which sex is better. Owning a bitch can be a problem when she is in heat and must be kept isolated for twenty-one days to prevent unwanted puppies by some unknown philanderer. Dogs do not have this problem, and I have found them to be just as affectionate as the bitches. Your own preference will have to be your guide. Many people decide

on a bitch, planning to breed her and recover the purchase price by selling the puppies. Believe me when I tell you that there is no way to get rich breeding one bitch, if you do it right. You will be lucky to break even. At best, you will earn about twenty-five cents per hour for your time and effort. Buying a bitch for future recovery of her purchase price is an *extremely* poor reason. Only the uninitiated would consider such a rationale.

If becoming a serious breeder is of interest to you, buy the best bitch that anyone is willing to sell you. This bitch will be all-important to your plans. Good bitches for sale are very hard to find, since many breeders keep them for their own breeding programs. The small "hobby breeder" will be more likely to sell you a good bitch than a large kennel, where the owner has adequate facilities for keeping as many dogs as he wants.

Prices for Westie puppies vary from one part of the country to another. Large kennels, which are well known for the number of champions bearing their kennel name, will ask more for their puppies. Their best puppies are not usually for sale except to guaranteed show homes. But a Westie, whatever its price, will give you back so much! As one friend said to me, "I've paid lots more than that for a piece of furniture, and it never gave me anything in return!"

An eight- to nine-week-old puppy owned by Coreley Plasek of Darien, Illinois.

48

A puppy bred by Christine Swingle, North Canton, Connecticut.

7 Bringing the New Puppy Home

The appointed day is here at last, and the puppy for which you have waited has materialized. The breeder should urge you, if not insist, that you take the puppy to your veterinarian, or even to his veterinarian, for a checkup within twenty-four hours. This is in your own best interest, since you should assure yourself that you have a healthy puppy. This gets you off to a good start. Take along any records of shots or other veterinarian care that the puppy has received. If you do not have a veterinarian, this is a good time to become acquainted with one.

Any puppy leaving his former home to go to a new place needs time to adjust. Not only will he have to get to know new people, he will also have to learn a new group of sights, sounds, and scents. He will no longer be able to play with his littermates and dam. He will not be competing for food, and eating alone is another new experience. He used to have a spot in which to relieve himself, and now he does not know where it is. He should not be given the run of the house. He should be confined to one area, one with a floor that you can mop in case of an accident. Doorway gates are available in children's departments of most stores. One of these can be set up, without hardware, to confine the puppy to the kitchen or the utility room. He should be kept there whenever you cannot give him your undivided attention.

Chances are good that the puppy was paper trained by his breeder. Puppies will paper train themselves at the age of three weeks, when they get up on all fours and never crawl again. If allowed out of the whelping box, they will walk to papers spread in front of it to relieve themselves and to exercise their natural instinct for keeping their nest clean. The newspapers also present a challenge, since the surface is slick after the softer surface in the whelping box. The puppies learn how to cope with a new surface and how to be clean in their habits. They become accustomed to the newspapers under their feet in just a few days.

If your puppy was paper trained, spread a generous area—even the entire floor—with papers. The puppy should be praised when he has used his papers. When picking up the soiled ones, keep one piece that has his scent on it to help him find the right spot the next time. He may have a preferred area in spite of that and will teach you where it is. This will serve nicely until he is old enough to go outdoors.

A young puppy that has not had his "permanent" shot for distemper should not be taken out of doors where other dogs have been. Many dog trainers believe that paper training is the best for the entire life of the dog, since it is one way of preventing the world from being fouled with dog droppings. Certainly a paper trained bitch is easier to keep indoors during her seasons. For the first few days, the puppy does not know how to get outdoors anyway. A young puppy will not stay dry overnight since his bladder is not large enough. No puppy should be expected to remain continent for more than two hours during the day until he is at least twelve weeks of age. But at eight weeks of age he can be trained to use a specific toilet area. He must have a place where he can relieve himself without the trauma of being scolded or punished.

The puppy that is twelve weeks of age or older can be directly housebroken if that is what you want and your living quarters permit it. The puppy should be confined to a limited area of the house and be taken out frequently, about every hour in the beginning, and on a leash, always to the same spot. These should be "business trips"—no play allowed. If the puppy relieves himself, praise him enthusiastically with an "Okay!" or a "Good boy!" and return him to the house. If he does not relieve himself, keep a careful eye on him. If he soils the floor, mildly scold him and take him back to the yard to his spot. If you cannot watch him every minute, tie him on a short length of rope to some heavy object, like the refrigerator door handle, with papers on the floor. He will be reluctant to soil an area in which he has to stay. Take him out frequently to his spot. In about two weeks the housebreaking will be done. *The puppy should not be tied and left for long periods while you are gone from the house.* But confining him during training is the kindest way for the puppy. He will soon learn what you want and will stay in the good graces of the family. I never expect a puppy to be truly reliable until he is past five months of age. He will want to relieve himself sometime after each meal and in between.

THE PUPPY'S CRATE

People who know dogs advocate the purchase of a crate. This is my recommendation to every puppy buyer. If your puppy came by air, he already has a crate. If not, crates are available from pet supply houses and from national catalogue stores under "Pet Supplies." The crate should be of sturdy wire and have a good latch and a removable pan in the bottom. It will fold flat to go in the car trunk if you wish. This crate is not to be confused with the cages in which dogs are kept in pet stores, or in which the animals are kept in the zoo.

The puppy is not going to live in it. He is going to sleep in it at night. It is the bed that he cannot chew up, as he certainly will do to one of those lovely baskets. He is going to stay in it when you cannot watch him every minute, such as when you need to shop or go to church. He will be perfectly safe until you return. He will be unable to chew any lamp cord and electrocute himself. Nor will he be chewing up the sofa skirt or ruining a thousand dollars worth of carpet. Those are the plusses for you.

50

Doorway gates are available in children's departments of most stores. These can be set up without hardware. Older dogs, like "Duffy" and "Piper," are also safer, since they cannot go bounding out of the front door when it is opened.

For the puppy there are many advantages. A dog likes his crate and soon comes to think of it as "His Place." If you have young children, it is especially important that your dog have a place where he can rest undisturbed. A dog spends more time sleeping than any other activity. If kept without sleep for a week, he would die. The children should also know that the crate is "His Place." They must not be allowed to reach in and pull him out, but must coax him to come of his own volition. He will ride in the car in his crate; this is the safest way to transport him. The local fire chief tells me that dogs are much like children and will hide under beds and in closets during a fire. They will also often run back into the house after being rescued. He says that crated dogs are therefore the easiest to rescue in a fire.

People who object to crates would not hesitate to put a toddler in a crib and raise the side for his safety during naps and at night. Nor is a young child in a playpen, for keeping him out of danger and mischief, viewed with dismay. These people fail to recognize that a dog is nothing more than a toddler in a furry coat, and he needs confinement on occasion as well as a place to nap and sleep that is his very own.

The correct size crate should be large enough to hold the adult dog. In the case of a Westie, this would be twenty-four inches long by eighteen inches wide and eighteen inches high. A taller twenty-one-inch crate would also work. The eighteen-inch is fine, however, and fits into the car better. In the beginning, you should leave the door open so that if the puppy needs to relieve himself he can get out. He can have his meals in his crate and have a toy or two. If you are paper training, do not put papers in the bottom of the crate. Do not leave a blanket or pillow in the crate if the puppy is going to chew them. My own dogs like the cool metal pan underneath their tummies and do not like anything that covers it.

For the first nights the door should be left open. If you have to leave for a short time, latch the door to keep the puppy confined. Keep the time short, gradually lengthening the time when he is kept confined with the door latched. Soon he will learn that you will be back to let him out. It should go without saying that no dog should be left crated for hours on end, except for overnight, especially a young puppy.

When you are ready for serious housebreaking, the puppy should be kept in his crate for about one hour at a time. He should be praised if he relieves himself when taken outdoors. Return to the house and allow the puppy to have a short romp before being returned to his crate for another hour. If he does not relieve himself when taken to the yard, he should be returned to the crate immediately and taken out again in a short while. This way you prevent the puppy from relieving himself anywhere but outdoors. He will not soil his crate unless he is absolutely desperate. In about two weeks time, you will have a housebroken dog. When it comes to housebreaking aids, a crate has no peer.

If you plan to show your dog, you will need a crate in which to take him to the shows. The type sold by the airlines is made of hard plastic and is used by many exhibitors. The only problem with this type of crate is that the floor is made of hardboard with small holes. The floor is held up from the bottom at the four corners. If the dog is sick or urinates in transit, liquid will run through the holes and away from the dog. The hardboard bottom is removable for cleaning. I never feel that I can keep this board as clean as the metal pan of the wire crates, which is nonporous and can be scrubbed and disinfected.

FEEDING THE PUPPY

The person who sells you the puppy will probably send the dog home with some of the food he has been eating or give you the name of it. If this is one of the popular puppy chows, it will be easy to keep him on the same food. If for any reason you prefer to change his food, do it gradually. Add one-fourth new food to three-fourths old for several days. Then increase the amount of new food to one-half, with one-half old. Continue this method until he has been transferred to all new food. A sudden change of diet can cause digestive upsets in any dog. With the puppy, which has had the stimulus of his littermates' competition at mealtimes, you may see a temporarily lagging appetite, anyway, and sticking with the familiar is best in the beginning.

Try to serve his meals by the clock. A dog's digestive juices begin flowing at the same time every day. If he is not fed on time, he may vomit some of this digestive juice, which is yellow with a little foam on the top, indicating that his tummy is empty. The seller should give you a feeding schedule. Depending on the age of the puppy, he will be eating three or four meals a day at first. Later, he will get down to two and perhaps eventually to one. My own adult dogs are far happier with two meals a day, breakfast and dinner, but you can see what best fits your dog and your schedule. Feed the puppy before your own meals, if possible. This is a good way to discourage a dog from begging at the table. He has already eaten. And, since he should never be fed one bite from the table, it also helps you to be firm if you know that the dog has already been fed.

Americans are prone to think that bigger is better. They think that adding calcium to build bigger bone and adding vitamin D to absorb the calcium will make a better dog faster. Not true. Recent studies show that growing larger bones before the muscles are ready to support them does more harm than good. Large breeds, which are prone to hip dysplasia, can be induced to develop it, even if they do not show the tendency in the first place. In the chapter on nutrition, the danger of adding one mineral to the diet is discussed, as well as the high calcium content of dry dog foods. If you have to add something, let it be a multivitamin, like *Pet Tabs.*® Steady growth makes the best and healthiest adult. Your dog is going to be the size that his genes entitle him to be, whether overfed as a puppy or underfed—so long as you do not confuse "underfed" with "undernourished."

Very good puppy chows are available at the supermarket. These are well-balanced diets with all the nutrients that the puppy's growing bones and muscles need. While they say that a dog thrives on monotony, he certainly does enjoy some variety. In the chapter on nutrition, you will find a list of various supplements that may be added to your puppy's diet. Use these as flavorings, in small amounts, on his basic dry puppy chow.

Put the puppy's food in his crate or on the floor and give him twenty minutes to eat it. If he has not eaten it by then, take it away and serve it for the next meal, holding it in the refrigerator. If you are housebreaking the puppy, this is very important. A dog will want to relieve himself after he has eaten. Exactly when depends on the individual, but it is easy to check by the clock for a few days. If you leave food for the puppy to eat whenever he pleases, you will never know when he needs to go outside. Many veterinarians recommend leaving food at all times, and self-feeders are available. These are fine for kennel situations or for the adult dog, but if the owner is trying to housebreak the puppy, they complicate the training.

How much to feed is a question that is always asked. Basically, a growing puppy should have all the food that he wants. His stomach is about the same size as his skull. Like everything else, there are exceptions. My first Westie was an overeater. If he had been served a washtub of food, he would have seriously devoted himself to eating it at one meal. If you raise an overweight puppy, you will have an overweight dog that will need to diet. Your puppy should be well-covered in the ribs but not be allowed to become grossly fat. I have had dogs that were self-limiting eaters, too, and that were a little on the thin side. So try feeding him all he will eat in twenty minutes. If he gets too pudgy, reduce the size of his meals.

If your puppy skips a meal, do not worry. It probably means that he is ready to reduce his number of daily meals. Usually this will be the middle meal, and he will still want his breakfast and dinner. If he skips meals for more than one day, have him checked by your veterinarian.

ITEMS YOU WILL NEED

One of the most useful items to own is a rectal thermometer. If you are concerned about your dog's well-being, taking his temperature is often reassuring. A dog's body temperature is normally higher than that of a human. The normal temperature for a dog is about 101 or 101.5 degrees. I have one bitch whose normal temperature is 100.5. Anything above 102 degrees should be considered a fever and should be checked by your veterinarian. Anything in the 99-degree area should also be checked as soon as possible. This low temperature can be very serious, indicating shock or a sudden drop in the blood sugar level.

Taking your dog's temperature is easy. Generously lubricate the tip of the thermometer with petroleum jelly, and insert the tip gently into the dog's rectum. This is easiest to do if the dog is on a table. Talk to him and pet him while you wait. I always wait five minutes, just to be sure. Remove the thermometer and wipe the petroleum jelly from it. Once you have assured yourself that his temperature is normal, you will feel better. If you think that the dog should be seen by your veterinarian, be sure to tell him the dog's temperature.

A supply of fresh drinking water should be made available for your puppy, especially if he is on dry food. If he is a water paddler, who thinks that the water bowl is really intended for a swimming pool, he will soon make your floor into a lake. You will have to put water down after meals and take it up after he has had a drink. This makes it harder to remember, but do see that he has plenty of water, especially in hot weather. If he does not play in the water, it should always be available to him in the same place.

"Amos," bred by Barbara Adams of Jackson, Mississippi, loves to enjoy a dip in the water, even though the "pool" is not of Olympic proportions.

Buying the puppy some toys and a leash will be next on the agenda and fun for everybody. The pet stores always have such darling little soft rubber toys, straight out of Disney, in charming poses and with squeakers inside. These are not for Westies. Leave them there for the Toy Poodles of the world and their owners. Westies have very large teeth and powerful jaws. They make short work of soft rubber and latex toys. Save your money and save your Westie from the possibly serious consequences of a swallowed piece of latex or rubber and/or the squeaker. Dogs have died from just one small piece of swallowed toy.

Hard rubber toys are for Westies—objects like hard rubber bones, rings, and balls. A small ball can be an aggravation, always being under a large piece of furniture, so buy one large enough to see and fish out with the broom. If it is temporarily too large to carry in your puppy's mouth, he will still have fun rolling it about. Another good item is a leather bone. I send one home with every puppy. But the only kind I ever have is called *Rawbone,*® which comes in a plastic bubble package. It is made in St. Louis, Missouri. I stress this because a warning from the American Dog Owners Association has stated that some rawhide items being imported from the Orient are being cured with arsenic. Those rawhide "chewies" are not 100 percent digestible for every dog. A *Rawbone,*® is made for chewing only and should last a long time. The leather in it is tough enough to hold up under the onslaught of Westie teeth and jaws. It has a large knot at each end. If your dog gets it untied and chewed into a soft whiteness, get the scissors and cut off the soft end and throw it away. Your dog will still have more than half of it left for chewing.

On the subject of bones, natural bones are a no-no. For all dogs, chicken bones and chop bones (like those from T-bone and club steaks or pork chops) are very brittle and can have sharp ends that can puncture intestines. Any bone that your dog *eats* is potential trouble. If eaten, the bone tends to gather inside the intestine and assume its original shape, which can cause a serious obstruction. Dog books often advise you to cook a lovely knucklebone for your dog. As long as the dog only *chews* on the bone, all is well. But you may not always be standing ready to take away this prize before he starts to eat it. Unless you are willing to watch carefully while he enjoys chewing his bone, do not give one to your dog.

Pet stores also have a large assortment of fancy dog collars—every color of the rainbow, rhinestone-studded, classy camel leather, and even Scottish plaid. These, too, should be left for the other breeds. Westies do not wear collars, generally speaking. The collar wears off the hair of the neck in a band. No potential show Westie should wear a collar every day. If you buy one with a buckle and leave it loose enough so as not to choke the dog, he will feel it as it pulls up behind his ears. With one lightning-fast backward snap of his head, the collar will pull right off over his small ears. There he goes after the neighbor's cat, while you are wondering why you are holding the empty collar and lead. Still, if I had to recommend any collar for everyday wear, it would be a rolled leather one, which would wear off less hair on the neck than any other variety.

The safest collar is the slip collar, often misnamed the choke collar. It is only a "choke" collar if put on the dog incorrectly by someone who does not know what he is doing. It starts out as one long strip with a ring on each end. The collar is dropped through one of the rings and becomes a circle. If the collar is held over the left hand, one ring will be up, and the collar will drop down and circle underneath your hand. As the collar comes up and crosses over the top of your hand, the other ring will pull to the right. The leash fastens to the ring pulling to the right. This is the correct way to put it on the dog. Substitute his head for your left hand. The upward ring goes under his right ear, and the collar goes down under his chin, then up across the back of his neck, where the loose end threads upward through the ring behind his ear. When the loose end is pulled, the collar tightens. If it is relaxed, the ring under the ear instantly drops down, and the collar loosens. This collar should always be used, with a leash, when the dog goes away from home.

This collar is available in washable nylon cord or in chain. If you use chain, the links should be medium-sized. Small links can cut into the neck. The rings provide a place to attach the dog's license and rabies tags. You could also get a tag with your name and address. It does not need the dog's name, since that only gives someone more control over your dog if he is lost or stolen and the person decides not to return him. *This is not a collar to be worn every day.* It can be dangerous if the dog gets it caught on something. But for leaving home, with the owner holding the leash, no collar is safer. An adult Westie will need one about sixteen inches long. This is a little long for a puppy, but it can be used.

A good first collar for a puppy is a martingale, which is a collar and leash combined. It, too, is a straight strip with two rings. It is made of

54

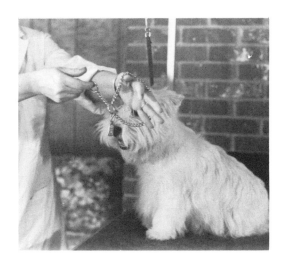

The slip collar, correctly worn, will not choke the dog and is the safest collar when going away from home.

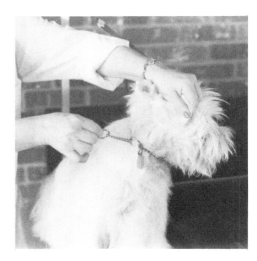

washable nylon cord. A second piece of cord is the leash, which has a wrist loop at the top and a loop through the two collar rings at the bottom. Like the slip collar, if the leash is pulled, the collar pulls up tight around the dog's neck. The leash is forty-eight inches long, and a puppy will need an eight-inch neck size. These come in several colors. This makes an excellent training collar for a puppy. It is light and easy on him and makes no jingle to distract him. A show prospect puppy is helped to get his ears up when the collar is pulled up behind his ears.

The best lead for the slip collar is made of six-foot-long flat webbing or leather. This is the type used in Obedience training. It should have a good hasp. A leather leash would be about one-half inch wide. My personal preference is the webbing leash, about three-fourths inch wide and with a single thickness. This type is lightweight but strong and is easy on the hands of the handler. It folds easily into the palm. For training, it will give six feet of space between you and the dog. This lead comes in both cotton and nylon.

When traveling in the car, your puppy will be safest in a crate. If not crated, he should always ride in the back seat. If you have him in the front seat and have to stop suddenly, he could go through the windshield. In some European countries it is the law that pets must ride in the back seat. No matter how much he seems to like it, he should never be allowed to ride in the car with his head out of the window. He could be seriously injured if any object were to fly up from the road. Whether crated or loose, he should always wear a collar and leash in the car. If he needs to be exercised en route, he will be equipped to go. If he is loose and decides to bound out of the car when the door is opened, you will have a much better chance of catching the trailing leash. This small dog is easy to catch, right? Wrong! People who are new to Westies are usually totally unprepared for the speed and maneuverability of the dog.

Children, especially young children, should never be permitted to carry any puppy. A puppy is a play*mate*, not a play*thing*. Children should be taught to sit on the floor and play with the puppy. A Westie, even a puppy, has surprising muscular strength. If the children are allowed to carry him and the puppy decides to jump, he could break his bones. I recall one very sad incident in which a three-year-old child was carrying a Westie puppy. At the top of the basement stairs, the puppy jumped or fell, all the way to the bottom. His four legs were so shattered that he had to be destroyed. It is a fact that every dog loves someone who will get down to his level. The puppy and the children will develop a fine relationship in playing on the floor together.

All puppies are chewers. Like children, they examine everything with their mouths. When puppies are cutting teeth, the chewing helps to get the teeth through the gums. Do not complain that the puppy has chewed up your new—or old—shoes. Pick up your shoes from the floor. Provide your puppy with other objects for gnawing. Ice cubes are nice and feel good on sore gums. Of course, you cannot move out the furniture. My method for stopping the chewing of chair legs, sofa skirts, kitchen cabinets, and other furniture is a quick, light tap on the puppy's rear with a plastic flyswatter. I keep three swatters in strategic locations where they are easy to reach in a second. The chewing puppy soon discovers that chewing on furniture makes his seat sting. I give a firm "*No*" as I swat. It only takes a light tap

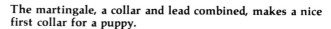

The martingale, a collar and lead combined, makes a nice first collar for a puppy.

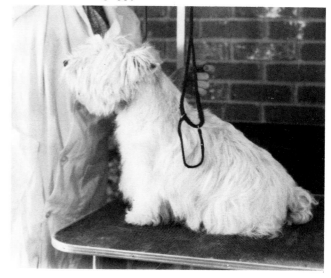

with the swatter, but it gives just enough sting-
ing shock to make the puppy cease and desist.
This has a double benefit. It also teaches him
what the word "No" means. This word should be
used for all infractions and is the most important
word that you can teach your dog.

TRAINING THE PUPPY

Leash training should be started very early
in the house. At age seven weeks a puppy has an
adult-sized brain. He can be taught anything that
an adult dog can learn. Obviously, he will have
the physical limitations that are related to his
smaller size. Like young children, puppies have
short attention spans, so short periods of training, repeated often, will produce the best results.
A puppy will never forget what he learns in the
first three months of his life. Without early training, he will never be as good a dog as he might
be. Do not miss the opportunity to teach him by
thinking that he is "just a puppy" and cannot
learn.

The attitude of the trainer is very important.
Correction should be given instantly but gently
when needed. Praise must be instant and exuberant when it is earned. Without praise, the dog
will never know what is expected. A Westie loves
to please, and he needs to be told when he has
done what you want. The dog should be trained
with patience, consistency, love, and praise.

For his early training indoors, a light show
lead or martingale lead can be used. Many trainers advise allowing the puppy to trail the lead so
that he can become accustomed to it. This is fine
if the puppy is not going to develop the bad habit
of chewing the lead. I have had great success
with simply putting the martingale collar on the
puppy and persuading the puppy to follow me
about the room. When I have litters, I start leash
training at five weeks of age with this method.
Just get the puppy to come with you, and to you,
with gentle tugs and persuasive words and tone
of voice. Daily sessions of five minutes will soon
accustom the puppy to the leash. Two daily sessions of five minutes each will teach him faster.
Gradually, the sessions can be lengthened as he
becomes old enough to be taken outdoors for
training.

The martingale leash is fine for this, provided the collar size is correct. If the collar is
loose, the puppy could conceivably extricate his
head. The slip collar, in chain or cord, plus a webbing leash, can be used. On his first trips into the
big world, the puppy may seem a little skittish. If
you have been taking him on a leash to the yard
to relieve himself, those trips have been more
casual, with plenty of time for smelling about.
Now he is going to learn a different type of leash
training—that of accompanying you along the
street or sidewalk. Keep him on your left side
and go only a short distance. Go a little further
each day.

Learn to fold the leash into your palm, keeping enough length of lead between your hand
and the collar to keep the puppy walking in a
straight line by your left foot. His head should be
straight down from your hip so that he can see
your feet. In this way he can learn to follow your
feet, wherever they go. If he is ahead of you, he
will not be able to see your feet. After your walk,
no matter how short, always praise him if he did
well.

After a few days, carry the puppy a distance
from home. How far must depend on the
weather. On hot and sunny days, a blacktop road
can feel very hot to his unaccustomed feet. Put
the puppy on the ground, on your left side, and
begin walking home. He will come right along
with you, not wishing to be left behind in strange
territory. Keep some tidbits in your pocket.
These should be quite small, something that the
puppy can swallow in a gulp. Bend down and
give him one now and then. Do not allow him to
jump up on you for his treat.

Now and then, take two treats out of your
pocket. Drop one on the ground and forbid him
to pick it up. Instantly offer him one from your
hand. In this way you will teach him not to pick
up anything from the ground. This is good training for any dog being walked in strange territory
and is important for the show dog. Handlers
before you in the show ring may have dropped
pieces of bait in baiting their dogs. Your dog
must learn to gait, head up, and not nose along
on the mats or grass of the show ring, smelling
for dropped bait.

Take every opportunity to put the puppy in
the car and take him somewhere. It must be

stressed that in hot weather a car becomes an oven in a matter of a few minutes. Your dog or puppy cannot be left in the car in the summer. I am appalled at the number of unthinking people who lock their dogs in the cars at dog shows. These are people who should know better. Even though you only intend to stay a few minutes, a chance encounter could divert you and make you forget the time and the dog. Just develop the good habit of never leaving the dog in the car, at any time. That way he will not die of heat stroke or be stolen from your car.

Every trip in the car will be of value, however short. Soon the dog will become a seasoned traveler. He will come to enjoy his outings with his master. If you never take him in the car, except to the veterinarian for checkups and shots, he will never enjoy going in the car.

This lovely bitch, Twickenham Holly Tara, was bred by Mary G. Allen, Huntsville, Alabama. The bitch is a daughter of the top winning Ch. Ardenrun 'Andsome of Purston x Ch. Twickenham Torey O' the Ridge.

Bonnie Wee Maggie at six weeks. Owner Sheila Turner, Edinburg, Indiana.

West-Bairn Independence, with her beautiful—and un-usually large!—litter of seven, sired by Int. Ch. Monsieur aus der Flerage and owned by Jacklyn Maupin, San Mateo, California.

Worline photo

8 Grooming the Westie Puppy

Early grooming of the puppy will have been started by the breeder. Some short periods of gentle brushing with a soft bristle brush can be started at about four weeks of age. Nails need to be trimmed of their sharp points at about one week of age for the comfort of the dam when the puppies are nursing. The nails will need weekly trimming with the scissors. This is easiest to do if the puppy has been asleep and you can get a few nails trimmed before he is fully awake. All work should be done gently to accustom the puppy to being handled.

Westie puppies being paper trained will pick up newspaper ink on their coats. They must be cleaned so as not to look "tattletale grey." A light dampening of the coat with a spray bottle of water followed by a light dusting of cornstarch will quickly have the puppy clean. When the cornstarch is brushed out, the soil will come with it.

Cleaning the puppy on a table is the best practice, but always be sure that he is secure. A rubber sink mat will provide nonslip footing for the puppy. Most young dogs feel afraid of heights in the beginning. Never swoop down from above the puppy and quickly pick him up. Stoop down by him and give some reassuring sounds or words. Then lift him slowly and firmly onto the table. The puppy should have some short sessions on the table every day so that he comes to accept his grooming as a necessary part of his day. When you are finished, hold him firmly in your arms and stoop or bend to place him steadily on his feet on the floor. During the period from eight to ten weeks, it is easy to imprint the puppy with fear. Care should be administered only with gentleness and reassurance during this critical period.

Train the puppy to lie on his back or side to have his belly brushed, the earlier the better. Lying on his back is an act of total submission to a dog. It will be difficult, if not impossible, to teach an adult Westie to "roll over and say Uncle," which is what it represents to him, in order to be groomed, no matter how much he loves you. Always praise the puppy when you are finished working on him.

STRIPPING

If the puppy is soft coated, this fluffy coat will need to be removed to allow the hard coat to come in. The breeder may have done some of this early stripping before you bought the puppy,

depending on the puppy's age. This is not usually started before eight weeks. If it is midwinter, the coat may not pluck readily until the puppy is older. By twelve weeks of age, the hard coat should be coming in, particularly on the back near the tail. Once in a while a soft-coated dog stays soft coated all of his life. This is rare and is due to heredity. Even so, all efforts should be made to bring the puppy into hard coat with stripping.

Stripping is different than brushing, to the puppy. For one thing, it requires longer sessions on the table. It is started at an age when the puppy would much rather be frolicking on the floor or wrestling with his littermates. All puppies will resist to some degree. The puppy must be made to understand that the work is going to

Fairtee Imp Prudence learns about being on a matted table at five weeks of age.

Fairtee Jolly Good Chappie is an old hand at the grooming business at eleven weeks of age.

60

Chappie has had his coat heavily stripped. "My word, you've RUINED him," a friend said. He is fifteen weeks old here.

Chappie at seven months of age, finally beginning to grow some coat but looking very gangling.

be done. Use the same tactics that his dam would use. Give him a shake and a stern "No" when he resists. He will settle down and let you work on him eventually. When he does, let him know that he has pleased you greatly.

Make these sessions short, no more than twenty minutes. This way the puppy will soon learn that it does not last forever and that his good behavior brings praise. Offer him a small treat before you put him down so that he will associate the treat with being on the table. Remember that what a puppy learns when he is between seven and twelve weeks of age he will never forget, so teach him what you want him to learn with love, patience, and gentleness.

Some people strip Westie puppies all the way down "to the pink," meaning their little pink skins, including the head hair and the leg furnishings. I decided to try this once, but never again. I thought that the puppy would *never* come back

into coat, and when he did, he was lacking the important undercoat. I live in the warm South, which may be a factor. But he was a July puppy and should have been coming into winter coat much faster. Since then, my practice has been to remove the soft fluff from the back, neck, and the sides. From the head and legs I remove only the longest hairs, as I would on an adult. I am sure that some breeders would disagree with me.

Finger stripping is easiest to do on puppies, and the method is described in the grooming chapter. Remove the coat in the direction in which you want the new coat to lie, since you will be training this new coat to grow in the correct direction.

EARS

If your puppy does not have his ears up in full pricked position, you can help. Trimming the

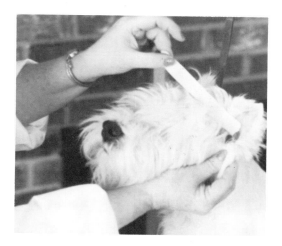

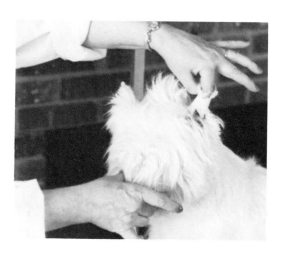

Above, left: Place one end of the tape in the front center of the ear. Take the tape to the front inside edge of the ear, where it joins the skull.

Left: Continue the tape across the back of the ear, to the outside edge. Place your finger into the ear opening.

Above, right: Roll the outside ear edge over your finger, continuing the tape across your finger and back over the tape already applied.

hair from the back of the ear tip and from the ear edges will often help the ear tips to stand. It is hard to believe that this trifling amount of weight can make a difference, but it can. Further help can be given by taping the ears. I do not like adhesive tape, supports of toothpicks, or other elaborate headgear for this purpose. These measures are not really necessary, and they always are in need of replacement. When a Westie puppy is happy—and what Westie puppy is not?—he lays his ears back. The adhesive tape, which does not stick very well, soon comes loose. Also, if the puppy crawls under a low object, he will drag his superstructure away as he emerges.

A much simpler and equally effective method was shown to me by my veterinarian when I had my first Westie, who had enormous ears. The dog's ear has a natural fold in it that runs vertically down the center from the tip to the base. Due to the curvature of a Westie's skull, the inside ear edge—the one closest to the center of the head—emerges from the head in a higher position than the outside ear edge. Paper masking tape adheres much better to the coat than does adhesive tape. You will need some one-inch-wide masking tape. With the puppy facing you, take a strip of tape about six inches long and place one end of the tape in the front center of the ear. Take the tape to the front inside edge of the ear, where the ear joins the skull. Continue the tape across the back of the ear to the outside edge. Place your forefinger vertically into the ear opening. Roll the outside ear edge over your finger, continuing the tape across your finger and back over the tape already applied. You are pulling the outside ear edge toward the center edge and will finish up on the back of the now folded or rolled ear. Because the outer edge joins the skull at a lower position, there will be an ample gap between the tape and the ear opening to allow for circulation of air into the ear.

The masking tape is so lightweight that the puppy will never know that he is wearing it. There is no need to run a horizontal tape between the two ears to get them to "work together." This treatment allows the puppy to wag and smile, all that a happy puppy should do, without disturbing the tape. Often, only twenty-four hours are needed to get the ears up. Large ears may take a little longer. Sometimes the ears will stand when the tape is first removed, then drop again in a few hours. If this happens, just retape the ears for another day or two. If this is one puppy in a litter, you will need to watch to be sure that the littermates are not unduly interested in removing the tape.

TEETH

Careful attention must be paid to the eruption of the puppy's teeth. The logical time and place for this is during grooming on the table. In the chapter on puppy evaluation, the subject of teeth and their anomalies in relation to the development of the puppy is discussed. If you have bought a very young puppy, you must remember to monitor the shedding of the milk teeth for proper replacement by the adult teeth. Sometimes in the course of events, the puppy may fail to resorb the roots of his milk teeth before the adult replacements erupt. The canine teeth are most often a problem. When the incisors are cut, the mouth should be checked to make certain that the canines are correctly meshing. If they are not, ask your veterinarian about having them pulled, in the hope of giving the permanent canines a better chance to erupt in their proper place. The milk teeth should be pulled if they are not out when the adult teeth erupt. Each adult tooth is surrounded by a ligament and is held in place by it. The ligament develops in the first month after tooth eruption. If the milk and adult teeth are side by side, the ligament will surround the base of both teeth. Then, if the milk tooth has to be pulled later, the ligament will not give proper support to the adult tooth. Familiarize yourself with your puppy's teeth so that you will recognize any changes that occur. Seemingly they can occur almost overnight.

9

Keeping Your Westie in the Pink

Many factors must be taken into account to maintain any dog in top condition—housing and exercise, the control of parasites, grooming, and proper diet. Each of these factors is integral to maintaining the others. Like the proverbial chain, none of the links can be weak. Actually, all of these elements are simple to provide. They require only an understanding of the basics and a little thought.

HOUSING AND EXERCISE

The Westie is a breed that thrives in all climates. The breed's double coat makes the dog underneath it very nearly weatherproof. Westies also thrive as house dogs and apartment dwellers, being out-of-doors for short periods and indoors most of the time. But the breed was developed for hunting, and the dog is a natural-born investigator of new sights and scents. If you want to keep your Westie at home, you will need to provide a fenced yard or run. This should be provided for every dog, regardless of breed. The day when a dog could run loose with safety went out with the horse and buggy. Now there are too many cars, too many garbage cans at the curbs, too many dog haters (due to too many free-running dogs), and too many dognappers.

Every serious owner-breeder of dogs is aware of the problems created by the irresponsible dog owners. These are the people who open the door in the morning and let their dogs out to become nuisances in the neighborhood. These people care little for their neighbor's property. They are entirely unconcerned about what their dog is doing while he is out on his own. This attitude is resulting in restrictive legislation in communities everywhere. I refer not only to leash laws. Many communities also limit the number of dogs that can be owned and the number of litters that can be bred.

What is sad for the responsible dog owner is that he is not guilty of allowing his dogs to run loose. He has too much concern for his dogs' safety. Yet, all restrictive legislation automatically affects his rights to own dogs. People who know dogs know that even the largest breeds do not need ten acres on which to run. A properly sized fenced run will give the dog all the space he needs for exercise. So join the ranks of responsible and knowledgeable dog owners and keep your Westie at home. Apart from being a good neighbor, the many other benefits will become clear as this chapter progresses.

Fencing a whole yard is expensive and may be impractical due to terrain. While a fenced yard is ideal, it is not an absolute necessity. As a small breed, a Westie does not need a lot of space out-of-doors. A run about four feet wide and twelve feet long is adequate. A run twenty feet long is even better, since the extra length allows the dog to extend himself when running. The fencing need not be high if the puppy is started in a run when he is young. As a youngster, he will come to recognize and respect the barrier. Clarence Pfaffenberger's book, *The New Knowledge of Dog Behavior*, says that even a large breed like a German Shepherd dog can be kept in turkey wire if started in the run as a puppy. You will need ever higher and stronger wire to keep the dog in if you wait to build a run until he is grown. Chain link fencing is not required for a young Westie. Although it is very nice, a roll of galvanized wire, thirty-six inches high, with posts at intervals, will do nicely. The fencing need not be rigid. In fact, I believe that the lack of rigidity discourages climbing. If the fence gives slightly with the puppy's weight, he feels unsure that it will support him.

Pea gravel makes a nice surface if it is put in at least six inches deep. This depth helps to keep the surface clean by allowing urine and rainwater to drain away. Also, water from the garden hose and disinfectants will quickly settle to the bottom. The gravel rolls under the dog's pads, making the pads strong and tight. The drawbacks are that some of the gravel will inevitably be thrown into any surrounding lawn, and puppies may ingest pieces of the gravel. Also, gravel is not as easy to keep free of snow and/or dog droppings as a cement surface.

The large breeds of dogs do not do well on cement if kept there all the time. The weight of the dog on such a hard surface can break down the feet. A Westie does not have this problem, since he is not a large and heavy dog. The Westie's heavy claws are worn off on a cement surface, helping the dog to gait on his toes. Less trimming and filing of the claws is needed. Cement is easy to keep clean and odor-free. A bucket of water with a little Clorox® will remove odors and keep the surface disinfected. A Westie will also stay a little cleaner on cement than on gravel.

But you did not want a large cement mixer to drive across your lawn? Hired cement finishers are expensive, especially to come for such a small job. If you are a do-it-yourself type, you do not need either one. The best surface we ever had for a dog run was made of two-by-two-foot cement stepping stones from the garden supply shop. These were laid over six inches of well-tamped sand. The cement squares were tightly butted together. The surface was sloped to have drainage of one-fourth inch of fall per foot, the same amount the plumbers allow for drainpipes. The slope was provided in two directions, both length and width.

Water from the garden hose, rain, and melting snow readily ran off, in two directions and into the cracks between the cement squares. The six inches of sand underneath kept the surface from heaving, even in the cold winters of Pennsylvania. Snow was easy to remove, and the surface of the run was clean and dry in no time. The cement squares are heavy, but my do-it-yourself husband laid them himself—with my moral support, of course. If you do not wish to do it yourself, you can get the help of a landscaper. Smaller squares of cement are also available.

Not one blade of grass ever grew in the cracks, due to frequent cleanings with Clorox,® which killed the weed and grass seeds before they had a chance to take root. The run was twelve feet by twenty-four feet and had room for the four Westies we had at that time. One of the dogs was a digger before we put in the cement stepping stones. "Digger Duffy" had never dug out of the fence, but he was busy making foxholes for everyone in the event of World

War III. This is another advantage of a cement surface. It cures digging.

Obviously, any dog run should be situated where some shade is available all day. If the run is large enough, a square or rectangular platform can be built for the center, one that the dog can get underneath to get himself out of the sun and rain. Or he can sit or lie on the top and be "King of the Hill." A Westie loves to be "King of the Hill." When building a run, do not overlook the possibility that you may want to keep more than one Westie at some later date. Plan ahead. If possible, make the run with a door to the house. This makes it simple to let the dog in and out. If one wall of the house forms one side of the run, less fencing will be required.

Your Westie should not be left in the fenced yard or run when you are away from home. The threat of dognappers is very real and is one that no owner of a valuable and beloved dog should dismiss. Neither is it a good idea to tie the dog in the yard. The dog will be at the mercy of any other dogs that may be running loose and may decide to come and pick a fight. Use the simple precaution of putting your dog in the house before leaving home.

If you are an apartment dweller and a Westie owner, you will need to exercise the dog on a leash. Roadwork is also important for the dog kept in a run, especially for the dog being shown, the stud dog, and the pregnant bitch. These activities require stamina and well-toned muscles. Your Westie will like nothing better than a brisk walk with his owner. Your dog loves the attention; it is very good for his ego. It is very good for the master, too. Unless your dog is slowly conditioned to jogging or running, as any human needs to be, take him only for short distances. The dog may run four times as far as you do if his path is zigzag. Remember that a dog does not sweat through his pores as you do. The dog sweats through panting and takes much longer to release his body heat. Keep this in mind during hot weather exercise and see that your dog gets plenty of cool water to drink.

PARASITES

The most important reason for a cleanable surface on which to keep your dog is to control parasites. Parasites are the most common affliction of all dogs. More time and effort are spent on parasites than on any other aspect of dog care. My dogs and puppies are kept worm-free and flea-free by the simple application of preventive measures. I am viewed with wonder and respect at my veterinarian's office because of this, and I love it. But the important thing is that my dogs are healthy and happy. I also know that if my dogs contract any type of infection, their chances of a speedy recovery are considerably enhanced if they are not infested with parasites, especially worms.

65

The best surface we ever had for a dog run was made of two-by-two-foot cement stepping stones laid over six inches of well-tamped sand. Fencing need not be chain link if the puppies are started in a run as youngsters. This fencing is thirty-six-inch plastic coated wire, with posts at intervals. Access to the run was through a door opening into the laundry of the house.

Internal Parasites

Five types of worms are found in dogs—heart worms, roundworms, hookworms, whipworms, and tapeworms.

Heart Worms — These worms are spread by mosquitoes. Once they were confined to the southeast coastal areas, but now they are seen widely in many parts of the country. The mosquito feeds on a dog with heart worms, picking up microfilariae (microscopic larvae) with the dog's blood. The microfilariae develop within the mosquito and, within three weeks, move to the mosquito's mouth parts. The mosquito feeds on a healthy dog and deposits the infective larvae on the dog's skin. The larvae burrow into the dog's tissues and live there three or four months. Soon they are in the veins and circulate to the dog's heart, where they mature into adult worms within about five months.

Mature worms in the heart are a very serious problem because they retard the circulation of blood and oxygen to vital organs. Medication is given to kill the worms. This must be followed by about one month of recuperative confinement for the dog. The dog must be kept from any strenuous exercise that would result in an increased heart and respiration rate. The dead worms in the heart could float free into the bloodstream and travel to the lungs and other vital organs, obstructing the arteries. It is very hard for the dog to understand why he must remain inactive for such a long period, and it is difficult for the owner, who cannot explain it to his dog.

Fortunately, preventive medication is available from your veterinarian. Given daily, it will keep your dog from having heart worms. A chewable type is available that 80 percent of dogs will accept readily as a treat. Other forms are tablets and liquid. Your veterinarian will know if the dogs in your area need to be on the medication. An interesting sidelight is that more than 100 cases of heart worms have been diagnosed in humans. Some were thought to have lung cancer until the worms were found in surgery. The human victims, too, have gotten it from mosquitoes, not from dogs. In my area, we have what is termed "epidemic heart worms," and my dogs are on daily medication twelve months a year. This has a side benefit: the medication inhibits roundworms.

Round Worms — These worms are the most common type found in dogs. Sometimes they are seen in the stool looking like strands of spaghetti. But your dog can have worms without your ever seeing them. The adult worms produce eggs that pass into the feces. The eggs also hibernate in the tissues of the dog. In the pregnant bitch, they pass into the mammary glands and through the placenta, where they infect the fetus. The puppy is born with worms, and he gets a double dose when he nurses his dam. Because the eggs can hibernate for long periods in the tissues, it is said that if a bitch has ever had roundworms, her puppies will have them. Due to the heart worm medication being given my dogs, my puppies never have worms. I know because I have them checked for worms at the age of four weeks. Signs of infection are diarrhea, poor growth, and potbellies in puppies and the microscopic evidence of eggs in the feces. Roundworm eggs have a hard crust that is impervious to heat, cold, and to insecticide. They will *live in the soil for years.*

Hookworms — These worms are very dangerous parasites, especially in young puppies. As the name indicates, the worm has hooks that attach to the wall of the upper intestine, where the worm sucks the victim's blood. Adult dogs pick up the larvae *from soil or feces.* Any larvae that penetrate the lower legs and feet of dogs can cause dermatitis. The larvae travel to the intestine and grow to be adults. In the pregnant bitch, they may lie dormant in the uterus and mammary glands, as do roundworms. Therefore, puppies of a bitch infested with hookworms will have worms before they are born. Adult worms in young puppies cause severe anemia, diarrhea, and death.

Whipworms — These worms are much like hookworms, but they attack the large intestine. They have a long incubation period of one to three months, making them difficult to cure. The mature worm deposits microscopic eggs in the feces. These can survive *for long periods in the soil.* They do not transmigrate from mother to puppies, so the puppies seldom have them. They cause bleeding in the large bowel and anemia in adult dogs.

The Roundworm, Hookworm, Whipworm Solution — We have seen how the dog gets each of these three types of worm. It is not "because the mailman feeds him candy," as the owner of a Saint Bernard confidently told me. Dogs get worms from picking up the eggs or larvae on their feet, from other dogs' droppings, or even from their own droppings. When a worm-infested dog defecates, the feces lie on the ground. The rain comes, the wind blows, and the sun shines. The feces disappear, but the eggs or larvae live on in the soil. Along comes a worm-free dog and unsuspectingly steps on the infested soil. In a short time this dog has adult worms. Then their eggs are deposited on the ground as this dog infests the soil with his own droppings. This poor dog is able to continually reinfest himself with his own worms, and his puzzled owner wonders why the dog has worms again.

To keep your dog worm-free, pick up the droppings. In a cement run this is easy to do. I keep a large spoon and a plastic pan, one that is not harmed by frequent cleanings with Clorox.® I pick up all droppings, carry them to the nearest toilet, and flush them away. For the grassy yard, learn to use the pooper-scooper. One type comes with a toothed pusher, which makes lifting droppings from the grass very easy. Keep a supply of plastic bags in which to put the droppings in case you get any blades of grass. Tie the bag shut and drop it into the garbage. All droppings should be promptly found and thrown away. You will have a healthier dog and a cleaner environment with just a few minutes' work.

It is also easy to check your dog for worms. All you need is a microscopic examination of the dog's stool by your veterinarian. It is not even necessary to take the dog, if all he needs is a worm check. The best specimen for examination is the first dropping from the first stool in the morning. Select a day when an errand or appointment will take you out of the house early in the morning. Accompany your dog to the yard, armed with a piece of plastic wrap and a plastic bag. When your dog has relieved himself, pick up the first dropping with the plastic wrap. Place that in the plastic bag and put it in your car. Drop this fresh specimen at the veterinarian's office on the way to your appointment and ask him to do a flotation. You can check back on the way home. If your dog has worms, you can pick up the medication for that specific worm and/or pay the bill for the flotation. Flotation of a stool sample is the best way of diagnosing worms. A second check may be needed to be certain that no worms have hatched after treatment. Ask your veterinarian if this is needed.

Never worm your dog with over-the-counter wormers. It is not a good idea. *Only worm your dog when it has been determined that he has worms,* and then only with the specific medication prescribed by your veterinarian for that particular worm. Some medications are to be sprinkled on food. Personally, I prefer a tablet, which I can thrust down the dog's throat. If he does not like the taste of the medicated food, he will not eat it and will not get the medication. If you are traveling with your dog, particularly if you are taking him to dog shows, have him checked frequently for worms. Those rest stops along the highways have signs pointing to the areas where you and thousands of other people must walk dogs. When you know how your dog gets worms, you realize how worm-infested those areas must be.

Tapeworms — These worms are different from the other three. They come in two types, but each needs an intermediary host. One type uses the flea for a host, the other uses mice or rabbits. The dog is more likely to get his tapeworm from fleas than from mice or rabbits unless he is out hunting and eating them. It is more likely that he will swallow a flea if he is nibbling at one. The flea larvae ingest the eggs of the tapeworm. The larvae grow into adult fleas, and the tapeworm eggs grow to be worms inside the fleas. The dog bites at and swallows the flea containing the tapeworm. The worm travels to the stomach, where it attaches itself and grows in segments. The dog passes the segments, and they can be seen around the anus and in the hair on each side of it, looking like tan grains of rice. This is the true evidence, since the segments will not always be found with flotation. See your veterinarian for medication. To keep tapeworms away, keep fleas away.

External Parasites

Fleas — Fleas have plagued man and beast since before recorded history. They are marvels of adaptability, adjusting to all climatic conditions. In the frozen Arctic they survive nine months of subzero weather and emerge from snow-buried bird nests, alive and sucking. That is what they do—suck blood, not bite. The flea has a sharp stylus on the end of his snout and cuts his victim to suck his blood. If your dog is so irritated that he bites and scratches himself until he bleeds, the flea does not even have to work for his meal. About 50 percent of all dogs are allergic to fleas to some degree and can develop skin rash from fleas feeding on them. About 20 percent of these dogs are hypersensitive, scratching and biting until they lose hair and even ulcerate the skin. The allergic agent is in the flea's saliva, which is injected into the dog while the flea is cutting him with his stylus. One flea will cut your dog once an hour, or twenty-four times a day; three fleas, seventy-two times a day. And if that is not enough, the flea is the carrier of tapeworm.

Flea collars were effective when they were first introduced several years ago. Now new mutations of fleas have survived to become immune to the poison in the collars. At best, the poison must be absorbed by the skin on the dog's neck, circulated through his bloodstream to his liver and kidneys, and excreted in his urine. This is very hard on some individuals. Also, some dogs develop skin irritation around the neck from the poison. The flea has to have moisture. If the flea cannot get it from the dog's mouth, he will travel to the dog's tail. To be entirely effective, the dog would also need a collar for his tail.

Powders and dips are available from your veterinarian and will relieve the dog temporarily. But as soon as the dog is back in the yard, he will get more fleas. Your veterinarian has pills that can be used in extreme cases. These will kill the adult fleas. They must be given to the dog on a very strict regimen and only with your veterinarian's prescription and approval. These will not keep flea eggs from becoming more fleas and infesting the dog. Nor will giving pills to the dog keep fleas off of any other pets in your household.

You *can* keep fleas out of your life and out of your dog's hair if you understand that the entire environment in which the dog lives must be treated—not just the dog. If you have other pets,

the dog will get more fleas unless the other pet is treated, too. If you see your dog scratching and biting, waste no time in checking him for fleas. You may not always see the fast-moving flea that is bedeviling your dog. You have an advantage with a white-coated dog like a Westie. If you cannot find the flea, you can find the flea "dirt." These are small black specks that are clearly visible in the dog's white coat. If you examine the speck under a magnifying glass, it becomes a small crescent, rather than a dot shape. If you place it on a piece of white tissue and moisten and smash it, the color will change to brownish red. This is the excrement from the flea, and it is a positive sign that the dog has fleas.

The best cure is prevention. Go to the garden shop and buy some *Sevin.*® This is an insecticide and comes in both liquid and powder. *Sevin* is compatible with both dogs and cats, even with puppies and kittens, if directions are followed. As with all such products, the directions and all information on the label should be read *in full* and *followed to the letter.* It should go without saying that the insecticide should be kept safely out of the hands of children.

Spray your yard and/or dog run as directed for fleas. Allow all sprayed areas to be completely dry before returning your dog to the yard or run. The powdered form of 5 percent *Sevin* can be sprinkled directly onto the dog, left for two hours, then brushed out.* This form of *Sevin* is also useful for dusting the carpet in the house, should your house become infested with fleas. It is especially good to dust into the corners and under heavy furniture, where fleas may lay eggs. If fleas are in the house, vacuum thoroughly every ten days to break the flea cycle. Throw away the dust bag from the vacuum so that any flea eggs in it will not become more fleas. Do check with your veterinarian regarding the use of *Sevin* as I have done, and follow directions.

I have had wonderful results with *Sevin.* I only hope that new mutations of fleas—clever rascals!—will not become immune to it. Another

---

*Sevin® and other flea preparations have been known to discolor some individuals of the white-coated breeds, like Maltese, Samoyeds, Papillons, and Westies.

benefit of *Sevin,* for me, is that it is highly toxic to bees. One of my bitches is a bee chaser, and I used to worry that she might catch one. A bee sting in the mouth could be fatal to a susceptible dog. Once the *Sevin* has been "painted" on my dog runs with an old broom, the bees disappear. Six or eight weeks later, when I see the bees have returned, I know it is time to apply more *Sevin* to the runs. If you have fruit trees that need bees for pollination, you may not want to spray your yard with *Sevin.*

One final word about fleas. Do not relax your vigilance in the fall of the year just because there has been some chill in the air. Fleas seem to know that winter is approaching and seem to be more determined than ever to get on a warm dog before the cold really sets in. I think that fall is the worst flea season of all.

I also feed my dogs brewer's yeast daily. A full discussion of its many benefits, including its help in keeping fleas away, will be found in the chapter on nutrition.

Ticks — Ticks are parasites that prey on dogs and people. They are seeking their only food—blood. There are several varieties, but the three most common are the Rocky Mountain spotted fever tick, the brown dog tick, and the American dog tick. Here in the South, we have a tiny variety known as the seed tick, so small that it is very hard to find on a dog. The Rocky Mountain spotted fever tick is responsible for carrying four diseases: Rocky Mountain spotted fever, tularemia, Colorado tick fever, and tick paralysis. Ticks can also cause skin problems and malignant jaundice in dogs. These highly undesirable tenants are not a bit choosy where they live. Their home could be on your dog, on you, in your dog's quarters, or in yours.

This repulsive arachnid is easier to deal with than most of the other parasites because he is easier to see on the dog or the person. Daily inspection of a dog being kept outside is a must during tick season. If a tick is found, it needs to be coated with some kind of oil, since oil tends to paralyze the tick. Petroleum jelly is usually found in most households, but linseed oil or any other fatty oil can be used. Coat the tick with the oil and wait a few minutes. Then use the tweezers to grasp the tick's body and pull straight upward, slowly and steadily. Go clear to the dog's skin

when grasping the tick to make certain that the embedded head comes free. Examine the tick when it is out to make certain that the head is attached. If it is not, use the tweezers to remove the head. The spot should be treated with an antiseptic like peroxide or even a dab of iodine. I make certain that the tick is really dead and gone by placing him in a piece of tissue and flushing him away.

Remember that ticks are nasty customers, even though they are easy to see. The tick may get off after he has engorged himself, then go and lay eggs in the house. If you live in a heavily infested area, you must make every effort to find and remove every tick from your dog. The dog must be checked thoroughly every day.

Mites — Mites are microscopic arachnids that invade ears. They also cause two types of mange. If your dog has ear mites, he may shake his head and/or do some scratching at his ears. The first sign of ear mites in my pricked-eared Westies is that the victim is not carrying the affected ear fully erect. The wax in a dog's ear is reddish brown in color and may sometimes be seen when you are cleaning the ears. Check the ear with a cotton swab, never inserting the swab more than about one inch. If the discharge is black, you can be nearly certain that ear mites are present. The dog should be seen immediately by your veterinarian, who will clean the ear and give you medication to rid the ear of mites. Sometimes a secondary infection will accompany the mites. If this gets into the inner ear, it can be a serious problem that is difficult to clear up. Other pets in the family should be checked and treated, too. If one has ear mites, chances are good that everybody has them.

Sarcoptic mange is caused by a mite that burrows into the dog's skin, where it causes intense itching. Naturally, the dog scratches a lot. Hair loss on the ear edges, hocks, and elbows is common. In severe cases, the entire body is involved. This mange is very contagious from dog to dog. The veterinarian can take scrapings and examine them for mites, and he will recommend treatment. At home, sanitary conditions are a must, which means daily changes of bedding to prevent reinfection.

Demodectic mange, or red mange, has two distinct forms. It is sometimes call "puppy

69

mange" because it begins in puppies; it is thought to be transmitted by an infected bitch to her young. Possibly the disease is caused by the puppies being allergic to the mange mites. These cigar-shaped mites, which live in the hair follicles, cause hair loss in small circular areas, usually on the puppy's face or forelegs. Infected areas are reddened and feel warm to the touch. This mange is thought to be spread by contact. Generalized demodectic mange is the second type. It is seen in older dogs that did not recover from the localized form as puppies. Treatment is variable in the form of drugs and dips. Correct diagnosis is essential, and only your veterinarian can determine the best treatment.

GENERAL COMMENTS

For the pet owner, it should now be clear that cleanliness is more than next to godliness. Recently I heard a little "fable." I do not know its source, since it was quoted to me by a friend. The story goes that two goldfish were swimming in a bowl. One fish commented to the other that he had heard a lot about God and wondered if there really was such a thing as a God. The second fish replied, "Well, of course there is a God! Who do you think changes our water every morning?" I love the story and find it profound. I pass it along as a reminder that your dog or other pets depend on you for their well-being.

You should be aware of the importance of keeping your Westie on his home territory and of keeping that territory as clean as possible. This type of care for dogs is what separates the amateur from the professional. Owners of more than one dog know the great importance of cleanliness. When you understand that many diseases and signs of parasites usually result in diarrhea, you know the importance of cleaning up stools. How else will you be aware that your dog has diarrhea? The dog certainly cannot tell you about it.

Simple diarrhea can be treated at home with a little *Kaopectate*® or *Pepto Bismol,*® following the directions for children. The dog should be put on a bland diet. Cook one cup of long-grain white rice in two and one-half cups of water. I add two

beef bouillon cubes for flavor. In a separate pan, cook one-half pound of ground beef in water to cover it. When the beef is cooked, drain the water to remove the fat. Then mix the rice and beef together. My dogs love this mixture. Everybody gets a taste, while the dog with diarrhea is served a complete meal of rice and beef. If this "treatment" does not clear up the diarrhea in twenty-four hours, the dog should be taken to the veterinarian.

If your dog is your best friend, remember that your veterinarian is your second best friend. He is there to help you take care of your dog. Nothing grieves a veterinarian more than a dog brought into his office too late for treatment. A dog shows you all his love, spirit, and gameness but seldom shows you that he is not well until he is refusing food or staying behind the sofa. You must watch for any changes in his habits, his stools, or his urine. Correct diagnosis is essential. Do not allow a friend or neighbor to make it for you. Always let your veterinarian decide what your dog needs in the way of treatment.

Like a healthy child, your dog will maintain a certain amount of natural resistance to various dog diseases. This does not mean that you can forego his booster shots for distemper, hepatitis, and leptospirosis. This shot is known as D-H-L and should be renewed annually. A new dog disease, called parvovirus, is considered quite serious, but vaccine is available. Ask your veterinarian to immunize your dog against this disease.

While diseases are most often seen in puppies, adults of any age can contract them. If you travel or have other reason to board your dog in a kennel, ask your veterinarian about the vaccine for parainfluenza (kennel cough). The cleanest kennel in the world has no defense against this airborne virus. The vaccine will not prevent canine cough, but it will protect the victim from the other respiratory infections that could complicate the illness. Do not forget his rabies shot. Most communities require the shot as a condition to buying a license.

The discussion of external parasites should have pointed out the importance of brushing your Westie daily. This takes only a few minutes and pays great dividends in his overall condition; it also keeps him clean. Directions for brushing the dog are found in the grooming chapter. As you brush the dog, you will be able to spot problems, such as irritated skin, tender ears, fleas, ticks, tapeworm segments, or anything else unusual. As you brush, make it a sensory experience for the dog, going all the way to the skin for stimulation. Make it a loving experience, too, by telling your dog that he is a good boy and that you love him. Your Westie will soon come running when he sees you get the brush. Cleaning his teeth, as described in the grooming chapter, should be done daily.

The late Lou Faherty introduces Fairtee Upsy Daisy O'Donnrich to his grandson, Seth.

Am. Can. Mex. Ch. Dreamland's Councillor

A top producing son of a top producing sire, Councillor was bred in Canada by Mr. and Mrs. Albert Kaye. His sire, Ch. Dreamland's Cyclone, produced fifteen champions. Councillor was shown to his American and Mexican titles by Neoma Eberhardt. Along with an outstanding show career, he produced twelve champion sons and daughters. Born in 1966, at this writing he is still alive and living with the Palmers in Ontario, Canada.

Ludwig photo

10 Feeding for Health and Beauty

The highlight of your dog's day (next to your homecoming if you have been gone a few hours) is mealtime. He does not care about the research, time, and effort that have gone into the making of the contents of his bowl. Nor does the average dog owner think much about it. The truth is that most dog foods are purchased by the dog owner on the basis of the clever promotion by Madison Avenue ad men. We have all been educated to believe that the dogs of America are more nutritionally fed than the children.

It must be remembered that your dog eats to satisfy his needs for calories, or food energy, not to fulfill his need for a particular nutrient. Yet the value of good nutrition throughout his life would be hard to overemphasize. Like you, your dog is what he eats. The properly fed puppy grows the properly sized organs to support him in good health. The properly fed adult dog shows bloom of coat, sound bones and teeth, and resistance and/or immunity to disease. Undernourishment of a bitch during her pregnancy causes the death of many puppies from "fading puppy syndrome." Feeding only a maintenance diet during pregnancy is one of the most common causes of reproductive failure.

There is no question among experts in dog nutrition that the commercially packaged dog foods are the easiest and most inexpensive choices for a balanced diet. The average dog owner cannot be expected to have the know-how to formulate a home-cooked meal which contains all the nutrients that a dog is known to need, in properly balanced proportions. This is particularly true of the correct balance of vitamins and minerals.

The National Academy of Sciences, National Research Council (NRC), Subcommittee on Dogs has studied what dogs require for a well-balanced diet. Its findings have been accepted by dog food manufacturers who meet the standards set by the NRC.

73

In 1969 the Federal Trade Commission (FTC) accepted the findings of the NRC. The FTC's position is that all dog foods which meet the *minimum* recommendations of the NRC are equal. With all due respect to the FTC, the following paragraphs on the formulation of dog foods will explain the fallacy of this position.

The requirements set by the NRC are for the maintenance of a mature dog kept in comfortable surroundings and at rest. The minimum recommendations of the NRC are too low for most dogs other than very sedentary types living indoors. Even the maximum recommendations fall short of the needs of some dogs at various times of their lives or under stressful conditions. Requirements for growing puppies, bitches in whelp and lactation, and dogs doing hard work—like the sled dog, the guard dog, and the show dog—are far different from the maintenance of a mature dog at rest in a warm house.

Another factor is the size of the dog. The Chihuahua and the Great Dane require different energy—or caloric—levels. Energy requirements are based upon a ratio of the weight of the dog to the dog's exposed skin area. The small dog has more square inches of skin per pound of body weight than the large dog and a greater exposed surface for loss of body heat through the skin. Therefore, the small dog needs a higher caloric intake per pound of body weight than the large dog.

Both buyers and manufacturers of dog food have recognized that requirements of the dog can vary according to what the dog is being required to do. For maintenance, the easiest method of providing a balanced ration is to include an optimum amount of calories along with the essential vitamins and minerals in minimal amounts. In this way, the maximum limit will not be exceeded, which is the conservative view. More important for the dog that needs levels above maintenance is a balanced diet in which the nutrients are utilized with the greatest efficiency. Cattle, hogs, sheep, and other animals also need levels of nutrients for growth, maintenance, and breeding. The NRC has made recommendations for the special needs of these commercially important animals, but not for dogs. Their recommendations for dogs cover only the dog's needs for calories to burn, plus minimum

requirements of vitamins and minerals. The calories are provided as carbohydrates, protein, and fat.

Carbohydrates — Carbohydrates are recommended by the NRC at a maximum of 60 percent of the calories, which allows room in the formula for other nutrients. A dog can utilize a high percentage of carbohydrates, with those in excess of his needs being stored as fat. In the temporary absence of carbohydrates in the diet, the dog will use protein and fat for energy. Therefore, carbohydrates stored as fat serve to prevent the loss of protein. In commercial dog foods, carbohydrates are provided in the form of cereal starches and various sugars. Carbohydrates in the form of fiber also provide for bulk, which aids in proper bowel function. In reducing diets, fiber is increased to give the dog a comfortably full feeling and make him less hungry. A high-fiber diet will also yield larger stools. Carbohydrate in the form of cereals is the least expensive source of energy for the dog, which is why most dog foods contain cereals in large amounts.

Protein — Protein in dog foods comes from two sources—plant protein and animal protein. The NRC recommendations are for a minimum of 15% and a maximum of 29 percent, or a mean figure of 22 percent of the "dry matter," which means the amount when all water is removed. The protein content is recommended to be 20 percent of the total calories of the ration. The amount of protein in dog food is usually determined by an analysis of the nitrogen content. Protein is the dog's only source of nitrogen and must be included in the diet. Protein also provides the dog with the essential amino acids that he is known to need. Plant proteins are lacking in four of the amino acids, and the least expensive way for a dog food manufacturer to add them is to include some animal protein.

Quality of the protein in the diet depends upon how digestible the protein is and how well it is absorbed and used by the dog. Digestibility relates to how soluble the protein is, while utilization depends upon the balance of the essential amino acids, in relation to each other. If one is relatively deficient, it will limit the rate at which the protein is synthesized. Therefore, it lowers the efficiency with which all the amino acids are used. Quality of protein is also dependent on the protein source. Proteins from plants are less well utilized by the dog than those from animals.

Proteins are the most expensive item in dog foods. Therefore, most dog foods tend to keep it at a minimum. It has been suggested that feeding dogs more protein than is absolutely necessary is wasteful. However, while the dog uses carbohydrates about as well as humans, the dog functions better on larger amounts of protein than do people. An automobile engine that is designed to run on high-test gasoline simply does not run at its best if the tank is filled with regular. High-test gasoline costs more, but the car owner does not consider that a waste of money. He knows that it insures the car's performance when taking the hills in high gear and protects the engine.

Fats and Oils — These make up the highest concentration of calories in the dog's ration. By weight, they have more than twice the calories of carbohydrates and proteins. The NRC recommends that a minimum of 5 percent of the total of the dry matter be fats. Fats aid in the absorption of the fat-soluble vitamins—A, D, and E. During periods of high caloric need, amounts of fat up to 40 percent have been helpful. A possible side effect of too much fat in the diet is diarrhea, and a definite side effect is weight gain and obesity.

The addition of vegetable oils provides the essential fatty acids. The chief one is linoleic acid; the other two are linolenic and arachiodonic acid. The vegetable oils are better sources of the fatty acids than animal fats, although lard and chicken fat are high in linoleic acid. These polyunsaturated fatty acids are recommended by the NRC at 1 percent of the total ration. Dogs getting too little fatty acid are seen with dry skin, harsh coat, loss of coat, body swelling, and moist dermatitis in the ear canals and between the toes. Too much fatty acid increases the dog's need for vitamin E. Lack of this vitamin can cause muscle weakness and dystrophy and reproductive failure. Also, because the caloric content of the diet is increased, the need for all other nutrients is automatically increased.

Vitamins — Vitamins in commercial foods are included in *minimum* amounts of all those which the dog is known to need. Vitamin K is not required except during therapy with antibiotics. Vitamin C is presumed to be naturally synthesized by the dog's own body and not required as an added nutrient. Biotin is not needed as an additive if the dog is on a good diet and is not being fed raw egg whites. All of the other vitamins—A, D, E, thiamine (B1), riboflavin (B2), niacin, pyridoxine (B6), pantothenic acid, folic acid, cobalamin (B12), and choline—are added to the ration by the manufacturer as additives or are provided naturally in the products used in the manufacture of the food.

Minerals — Minerals (also referred to as ash) are provided in commercial foods as a carefully balanced group. Some of them are included in amounts so small that it would be impossible for the dog owner to measure these micronutrients. Minerals interact with each other as well as with other ingredients in the ration. This interrelationship is in such a delicate balance that the change in the quantity of one can cause a change in them all. In commercial dog foods, the minerals are provided in minimum amounts so as not to exceed any maximum, which might cause toxicity.

Each dog will absorb the quantity of this balanced group of eleven minerals that his body needs and will absorb them as a group, not individually. If his requirement is only one-half of the amount provided, he will absorb only that amount. If the amount of the balanced group were doubled in the ration, the dog would absorb one-fourth of the amount provided, to meet his needs. If the amount were to be doubled, by the addition of one single mineral to the balanced group, the dog would absorb one-fourth of the total minerals. This would create a deficiency of all the other minerals.

For example, let us pretend that the balanced group is provided at the rate of one-half teaspoon per cup of food. If the dog requires only half that amount, he will absorb only one-quarter teaspoon. If we increase the balanced group to one teaspoon, the dog still will only absorb one-quarter teaspoon. If we add one-half teaspoon of the balanced group plus one-half teaspoon of calcium, the dog will only absorb one-quarter teaspoon of the total. Thus, we are really creating a deficiency of the balanced group, because the dog will absorb one-eighth teaspoon of calcium and only one-eighth teaspoon of all the other minerals in the balanced group.

A DISSERTATION ON DOG FOODS

Dry Foods — Dry foods are available in many forms, from meal to chunks. They are made from various cereal grains and/or soybean products. They are the least expensive form of commercial food, since cereals cost less than meat. Also, since they contain only about 10 percent moisture, the dog owner is not paying for a lot of water. Animal protein is provided in the form of meat and/or meat by-products to balance the essential amino acids. Average protein content of the dry matter is 25 percent. Fats are usually provided at 10 percent or less so that the fat will not soak into the bags in which the food is packaged. These foods are marvels of ingenuity. The animal protein is usually applied to the surface of the dry food to provide palatability. Some of these foods are expanded with air.

An eight- to nine-week-old puppy owned by Coreley Plasek of Darien, Illinois.

Dry foods are easy to store and to feed. Canine dental studies indicate that hard food is good for teeth and gums. Cereal foods contain starch, which is cooked during the drying process. Cooked starch can be assimilated by the dog, but the digestibility of energy is lowered. The efficient utilization of protein and some of the minerals is also reduced. Due to the drying process itself, the manufacturers have fewer ingredients from which to choose, since many components do not lend themselves to being dried. Some of the nutrients may be destroyed during the drying, and the process also lowers palatability. Minerals, especially calcium and iron, are poorly absorbed from cereal foods. Calcium is now supplied in large amounts in these dry foods, which is why supplementation for a dog being fed dry food is not necessary and could even be dangerous by creating a deficiency of other minerals.

Soft Moist Foods — These dog foods provide a manufacturer with a wider choice of ingredients because they require no harsh drying process. These foods are usually about 30 percent water, which must be considered in their analysis. The average carbohydrate level is about 45 percent. The carbohydrate portion is largely sugar, listed as sucrose (refined table sugar) or syrup. Sugars have a higher rate of digestibility than starch. Calcium levels in these foods are lower due to the more readily digestible energy source. One of the biggest advantages of these foods is that harsh drying is not needed, which means that fresh animal tissues can be used. Average protein level is about 29 percent, with fat averaging about 14 percent. Soft food is not as good for teeth and gums; therefore, some hard food, like *Milk Bone,*® should be supplied.

These foods cost about the same as canned dog foods. They are easy to feed and to store without refrigeration. They are marketed in patty form, in individual-serving plastic bags, and in large bags, which lowers the cost. It should be noted that once the package is opened the food loses its moisture very rapidly.

Canned Foods — These come in many types, from "stew" and "dinner" types to loaf types. All-meat, which means 100 percent meat, products are seldom seen. A meat content of 95 percent leaves room to add 5 percent essential nutrients, which allows the food to be termed "complete." The FTC requires that "meat" in food must be muscle meat. "Meat by-products" are organ meats (heart, lungs, spleen, etc.) and bone. If the food is 95 percent beef, the label is allowed to read "Beef for Dogs." If the food contains as little as 25 percent beef, the label will say "Beef Stew" or "Beef Dinner." If the label says "Beef Flavored," the food need not contain any beef at all so long as the flavor is present.

To compare these canned foods with dry and soft moist foods, the water content must be taken into account. Most canned dog foods are very high in water—an average of 75 percent or more. With the water removed, the food can be judged on a dry matter basis. The stews, dinners, and loaf types all contain some cereal and show an average carbohydrate level of about 30 percent. Protein levels in these foods average about 36 percent, with fats being about 16 percent. Due to the cereal, high levels of calcium are provided in these "complete" products, as in the dry foods.

These foods are very tasty and digestible. Their high fat content makes them high in calories, which makes them ideal foods for the small dog and the lactating bitch. These are also more expensive to feed than dry foods. The "all-meat" and/or "meat by-product" canned food is the most expensive. This food has a very high protein content—in excess of 50 percent of the dry matter. The fat content is also very high—about 28 percent. Other than racing sled dogs, which have been shown to perform well on a zero-carbohydrate diet when doing this demanding work, this type of food, as a regular diet, has no advantage to the dog. It is the most highly palatable, of course, and can easily produce obesity. Its greatest disadvantage is the high amount of nitrogenous waste excreted in the dog's urine. It has no particular offsetting advantage other than its high acceptability by the dog. This makes it a fine additive to a dry food diet.

Choosing A Food

Heaven knows that the dog owner does not lack a selection of types and flavors of dog foods. At the supermarket, much valuable shelf space is allotted to the stocking of prepared diets for our furry friends, each type labeled "complete" and "balanced." In addition, the manufacturers are required by law to include a "Guaranteed Analysis" and a list of ingredients on every container. Reading these can leave the dog owner with more questions than answers.

The "Guaranteed Analysis" lists by percentages the amount of protein, fat, fiber, and moisture in the food, and the manufacturer guarantees their presence in the food. The label will read "Not more than" or "Maximum" with a percentage figure. Literally translated, this means that the amount could be much less or even none. The line may read "Not less than" or "Minimum" with a percentage. This means that the manufacturer guarantees to include that amount but that the percentage could be considerably higher. In either case, the manufacturer would be within the law. The truth is that once a dog food has been processed, it is virtually impossible to identify the contents. In effect, the law is unenforceable.

The list of ingredients on the package is in the same order as it is on "people food." The ingredient in the largest quantity, by weight, is listed first, followed by the one in the next largest quantity, with the one in the smallest amount being last. The list does not include amounts or percentages of the ingredients, which does not give the buyer much information except in a most general way. And, as in the list of the Guaranteed Analysis, there is no assurance that the listed ingredients are, indeed, present. Dog food manufacturers are allowed to change their "recipes" to take advantage of the market by substituting one ingredient for another of lower price or higher availability.

For these reasons, the dog food buyer interested in the best nutrition for his dog is well advised never to buy the cheapest food on the shelf. The company that makes cheap dog food is using the cheapest ingredients available. The buyer will get exactly what he pays for. On the other hand, those expensive "all-meat" gourmet foods are no bargain in nutrition, either. The good reputation of the manufacturer is the best approach to selecting a food. Buy the food made by a company that does feeding research and does tests on its own products to maintain high quality.

The American Association of Feed Control Officials (AAFCO) has established "protocol studies" for evaluating its foods. These studies involve feeding one product to a group of dogs of all ages, from puppies to lactating bitches. Each group is studied for growth rate in puppies and condition of skin and coat in all ages, during illness and with medication, and with blood tests. The research is conducted by veterinarians and dog nutritionists at the manufacturers, and participation is voluntary. Interested consumers may write to the company at the address on the dog food package and request research results as well as a complete nutritional profile. If such a request is not answered by the manufacturer after about thirty days, write to other companies for their test results. Then choose your dog's food from a company that cares enough to do such research and shares the results with consumers. If you are interested in further information regarding the nutritional needs of dogs, you can write to the National Research Council and request their bulletin "Nutritional Requirements for Dogs."

I do not for one second believe that my live-wire Westies could stay in top condition on a dog food that meets the maintenance needs of a sedentary breed. Neither do I expect any dog food company to tailor a special diet for my breed. Knowing the contents and the shortcomings of all three types of commercial foods has helped me to create a diet for my dogs that appears to suit them very well. My own solution to the dog food dilemma is to feed a high-quality dry food in kibble-size nuggets. This comes from a manufacturer that does protocol studies and has sent me a complete nutritional profile of this product. This is the mainstay of my dogs' diet and is fed daily. I do not buy a high-protein dry food. I realize that the dry food is lower in protein than canned food and is slower to digest than the soft moist foods. Still, for economy and easy storage, coupled with the crunchy texture so good for teeth and gums, I prefer dry food. I improve the protein content by adding small amounts of various supplements. I vary the supplement daily, which makes for eager and nonfinicky eaters.

One simple way to do this is to add small amounts of canned food to the dry food. Each type is nutritionally complete, and the canned food contains additional animal protein. I prefer the loaf-style canned foods, since the contents of the can is uniform from can to can. Some of the "dinner" and "stew" types have too often been more gravy than anything else. My dogs have a generous tablespoon of canned food mixed with their half cup of dry food for their evening meal.

Supplements

Dried Brewer's Yeast — This is a daily breakfast supplement for my dogs. This is not to be confused with baker's yeast, which is totally different. Brewer's yeast is used in making beer and ale. When it is dried, it no longer ferments. For consumption by humans and dogs, it is also debittered. It is a fine source of high-quality protein with all the essential amino acids. It is also rich in the water-soluble B-vitamins, especially thiamine. This yeast is available from the health food store. I use the seven-and-one-half grain tablets and feed each dog three tablets every day. Many people give the tablets as treats, since most dogs accept them readily. It is also available in powder. One-fourth teaspoon is equal to one tablet. The thiamine contains organic sulphur, and sulphur is good for the skin. Sulphur is oxidized in the tissues and acidified in the urine, which wards off bacterial infection; it is also inexpensive to feed.

There has been much discussion of using brewer's yeast as a flea repellant. The theory is that after consuming brewer's yeast daily for about three weeks, the dog begins to smell like sulphur to the fleas, which then stay off the dog. My own Westies have been fed brewer's yeast daily for about two and one-half years. They are kept on cement runs but are allowed to run in the grass every day, weather permitting. The first summer that they were fed the yeast, they had one or two fleas. Since then, I have never seen another flea, and I no longer spray the yard with *Sevin*.

My "experiment" has not been at all scientific. I do not have a control group being fed the yeast while others are given a placebo. I do have pet owners on all sides who fight fleas all summer, and I have the only flea-free dogs in the neighborhood. I find it hard to believe that all the fleas in my yard simply packed up and moved next door. I can only credit the brewer's yeast. However, I believe that the effects are cumulative and that the longer the dog is fed the yeast, the more flea-resistant he becomes. I have read that it will also repel mosquitoes. I am unable to verify that and give daily heart worm medication to be safe. If the brewer's yeast does nothing but add protein and B-vitamins and ward off bacterial infections, it is still worth its weight in gold. If you want to try it, start your dog with one tablet the first week, two the second week, and then continue with three tablets every day.

Egg Yolk — This is the most complete food for meat-eating animals. Egg white should not be fed raw, since it interferes with the absorption of biotin, an essential B-vitamin. The whole egg, if cooked, is very good for your dog. Eggs are a poor source of niacin and a variable source of iodine and vitamin C. Otherwise, eggs are a complete food and are utilized 100 percent by the dog. No eggs unfit for human consumption are fit to feed your dog. Eggs with dirty or cracked shells can be a source of salmonella, to which dogs are just as susceptible as people. I feed my dogs hard-cooked eggs, which have been cooked about five minutes—just long enough to cook the whites. Sometimes I give them scrambled eggs, also not overcooked. Raw egg yolks are also very good for the dog.

Chicken — Chicken, like eggs, makes excellent food for dogs. Chicken is used as the main source of meat protein in many canned foods. The meat in chicken is higher in calcium than beef, making it a very good food for the lactating bitch. Chicken fat is high in linoleic acid. Whole chickens are the least expensive to buy. I cut one up and simmer it until tender. I add one chicken bouillon cube per cup of cooking water plus onion and celery salt. I use the breast and thigh meat for chicken salad or casseroles. Then I serve the meat from the legs, wings, back, and neck, plus all the skin, in small amounts on my dogs' dry food. I often measure the broth and cook two and one-half cups of it with one cup of long-grain white rice. My dogs love a spoonful of this, too.

Liver — This is another excellent supplement. Pork liver is the least expensive, and its nutritional profile is excellent. Liver is low in calcium and lacks iodine and the essential fatty acids. It is a fine source of vitamin A, but the amount is variable with the age of the animal from which it comes. The older the animal, the higher the vitamin A content. Liver should be

cooked, as should all other meat that is fed to your dog. This is especially true of pork, which could be a source of trichinosis.

Cottage Cheese — This is an excellent source of high-quality protein and the amino acids. It also makes an excellent supplement for the bland diet when mixed with cooked rice. Cheddar cheese is high in fat and should be fed sparingly, shredded over the top of food. It is high in vitamin A and riboflavin.

Unsaturated Fatty Acid — This is best found in corn oil because of the high linoleic acid content. My dogs are never dry and scaly, nor do they have any of the other symptoms of too little fatty acid. If signs of deficiency were observed, I would never add more than one-half to one teaspoon of corn oil. Too much fatty acid can cause your dog to be overweight, and you will need to increase all the other nutrients, especially vitamin E. Cooking fats, which are often stored on the stove top, can become rancid very quickly. These should not be fed to your dog. Fats that have been used and reused are also a no-no.

Vitamin E — This vitamin is needed by every cell. It is especially important in breeding stock, aiding fertility in males, and helping to prevent abortion of fetuses. The maintenance level recommended by the NRC is very low—forty-five IUs per kilogram (2.2 pounds) of the dry matter of the diet. Like most other dog breeders, I add vitamin E to my dogs' daily ration. I give each dog one 100-IU capsule on the morning meal. No signs of problems in dogs fed too much vitamin E have ever been recorded.

Vitamin C — This vitamin is presumed to be synthesized by the dog and is not included in dog foods. However, animal studies have proven that vitamin C maintains the competency of the immune system and is very helpful during stress. I find it difficult to find vitamin C in small-size tablets. I presume this is because so many people are taking the vitamin in larger amounts. So I simply cut the size I can find into pieces that are roughly equivalent to a fifty-milligram tablet and feed it every day.

Kelp — Kelp is one of the seaweeds and is rich in iodine and iron. The dry food that I give my dogs has iodine in the form of iodized salt. I feed less of the food than the manufacturer recommends, so I supplement my dogs' diet with iodine and iron in the form of kelp tablets from the health food store. These are ten-grain kelp tablets, which contain 150 micrograms of iodine and two milligrams of iron. Both of these amounts are very small so as not to imbalance the other minerals in the diet.

Iodine is an important component of the dog's diet, since it maintains the thyroid gland in good working order and the hormones in healthy balance. Adding a small amount of iron has been noted by many Westie owners as an aid in maintaining black pigment. My own dogs are fed two ten-grain tablets daily.

I discovered kelp during my first summer in the South. One of my bitches had "hot spots," a form of moist dermatitis. Its cause was undetermined but described as "allergy" by my veterinarian. All summer I applied two different salves that he prescribed in addition to two shots of steroid drugs. This resulted in a greasy dog with continuing "hot spots." In D. Mary Dennis' book *The West Highland White Terrier*, I read that "seaweed powder" helped eczema. I decided to try feeding my bitch some kelp tablets that I had on hand. I gave her twenty grains a day.

In addition, I applied a solution of *Mycodex*® shampoo (from my veterinarian) to the spots. Because we were showing the bitch, I did not want to bathe her. So I mixed a spot of *Mycodex*® about the size of a dime with one-third cup water. With a cotton ball, I applied this solution to the spots and to the surrounding areas and allowed it to dry. I applied it again three days later.

I began to see immediate improvement, but the weather had cooled considerably, since it was now October. I did not know what to credit with the cure. The following spring, during the first warm days, the "hot spots" appeared again. I decided to start feeding the kelp as an experiment, and the "hot spots" began to heal themselves. In brushing the bitch, I would find areas in which I had not known any "hot spots" existed. These were scabbed over, with healthy pink skin underneath. Now on daily kelp, the bitch never has "hot spots." I have suggested this "treatment" to other Terrier owners, who have reported the same good results.

Cabbage and Carrots — These vegetables were also suggested in Mrs. Dennis' book as food additives that were good for skin problems. I feed packaged, prechopped cabbage and carrots from the produce department to my dogs about once a month. I simply add a couple of tablespoons of the mixture on top of their food until the package is used. My dogs cannot eat it fast enough. The greatest benefit is that it keeps the dogs from eating grass.

The most popular theory about dogs eating grass is that the dog has something in his stomach which is not digesting, and the dog wants to vomit to rid himself of it. The dog will certainly vomit if he eats grass. However, it is known that a dog can vomit at will. Sometimes a dog will regurgitate the food that he ate an hour before, examine it, and reingest it. A bitch weaning her young will sometimes regurgitate her meal and allow her puppies to have this predigested food. Therefore, my own theory about grass eating is that the dog wants something green once in a while, and that he vomits because the grass is indigestible. When I see my dogs trying to get to the grass surrounding the runs, I buy the cabbage, and they stop trying to eat grass.

I am not a veterinarian or dog nutritionist. I offer all of the above suggestions on feeding on the basis of my own experiences in feeding my Westies. I hope that the information will make you a more informed buyer of dog food, since each type of commercial food has its merits and drawbacks. Whatever you choose from the supermarket shelf, remember that your dog is what he eats, so nourish him well.

11   An Introduction to Grooming

The grooming instructions in the following pages are intended to educate the first-time Westie owner in the care of the dog. The instructions are lengthy due to their detail so that the pet owner or the novice to showing will fully understand the procedures of stripping and cleaning a Westie. They are written for the newcomer and with the presumption of no knowledge whatsoever on the part of the reader, in an effort to make everything clear.

In the show ring, grooming styles vary from one part of the country to another. Professional handlers start fads by doing something a little differently, and others rush to follow suit. Therefore, these pages are not intended to represent the one and only method of stripping, shaping, and cleaning the dog. Other ways are equally acceptable. And by the time you have mastered the technique you will have come up with innovations of your own.

You will not be an accomplished groomer after one session at the grooming table. In fact, the first session will be the hardest. Your most needed "tool" is *patience.* Some people learn faster than others. In show grooming, some people seem to have a better eye for the subtleties of one-eighth inch here and one-quarter inch there. The pet owner may wish to master only the stripping of the coat to make for a neater appearance and a healthier skin under a hard coat. He will certainly want to learn to trim the ears, the head and tail, and the pads and the feet; "open up" the eyes; and how to brush and clean the dog.

One thing is certain. The average grooming parlor in the average city will probably send your Westie home looking like a cross between a Schnauzer and a Scottie. If that was not what you had in mind, learn to trim and care for the dog yourself. He will look and feel better, while you will take pride in his appearance and a job well done. For the price of two or three professional groomings—which have been done incorrectly anyway—you can buy the essentials in grooming tools.

For the future exhibitor, dog grooming is the most important part of showing. A poorly groomed dog will never be able to compete with his pristine peers in the ring. Between two dogs of equal quality, the better grooming will make the difference between first and second place, or between Winners Dog and Reserve Winners Dog. It takes work and practice to become proficient at grooming. If you think about it, in any activity—from enjoying a meal to climbing the Alps—preparation is 90 percent of the doing. It is learning to enjoy the preparation and practice that makes you happy. To be good at what you want to do, you must spend considerable time getting ready and not be impatient with it.

GROOMING EQUIPMENT

With any job, tools are available to help you do your work. Different breeds of dogs require different kinds of equipment. The tools described here are personal choices, selected by trial and error. Tools for a Westie are not easy to find in the local pet shop, where you will usually find those items used on the very popular breeds. The store will only stock items that have a fast turnover. If you live near a grooming parlor, it is a possible source of supplies if the shop owner is willing to order items and sell them to you.

The best sources of supplies, in my opinion, are the "wholesale" pet supply houses, which is where the grooming shops obtain their equipment. The various magazines for the dog fancy print advertisements for many of these supply houses. Most ads say that the supplier will send you a free catalogue or will credit you with the price of a catalogue on your first order. If you do not subscribe or have other access to dog magazines, your veterinarian's office usually has copies on the tables in the waiting room. You can make a list of names and addresses while you are there. Another source of this information are dog exhibitors and/or local kennel club members. Most of these people have ordered supplies from the wholesalers. Pet supply houses usually ship United Parcel Service, and some even have toll-free, long distance numbers for speedy delivery of your orders.

Another source is the nearest AKC-sanctioned dog show, where booths are set up by vendors of dog supplies. You will be able to see a bewildering assortment of brushes, combs, leashes, and other paraphernalia and make your choices in person. The selections are not always complete, and the prices are higher than those in the catalogue. This is why I prefer the catalogue order method. Even so, it is hard to find one catalogue that lists each and every item you like. Like one supermarket, the wholesale house may not have everything, either.

Restraints and Grooming Tables

The most important piece of equipment, in the beginning, is a restraint for the dog while you work on him. While it is possible to suspend a leash and collar from a door frame and move a table underneath it, this does not allow for much adjustment, and the light may not be good. A better solution is a grooming post, which consists of an adjustable upright pole with a horizontal arm at the top. A noose, which is like a collar with a slip fastener to tighten around the dog's neck, is suspended from this arm. A clamp-on style, which slips onto a table edge and fastens underneath the tabletop is available. This requires a table with no horizontal support underneath the table edge, which would prevent the clamp from slipping onto the edge. If you

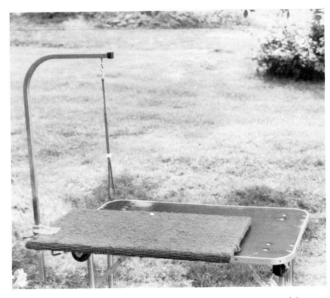

A clamp-on grooming arm can be attached to a table or to a piece of carpeted plywood.

82

have a sturdy table that meets this requirement, it is an excellent solution to the need for a restraint. A rubber tub or sink mat will provide a nonslip surface for the dog.

If you do not have such a table, a simple device to use on any table of comfortable height and sufficient sturdiness is a carpeted piece of plywood. You can have your lumber dealer cut a piece of plywood about eighteen inches wide, thirty-six inches long, and one-half- or five-eighths inch thick. This can be covered with a remnant of lightweight carpet or topped with rubber matting. The weight of the plywood will hold the device flat on the table, even when the arm is clamped to the projecting end. With the weight of the dog added, it makes a nice improvised grooming table. Clamp-on grooming arms are available from the wholesalers or from a national chain of retail catalogue stores. The post is inexpensive and should last as long as you have the dog.

Grooming tables are available in two styles. One takes the clamp-on grooming arm. The other has a hole in one corner of its top to allow a post to slip down into it and be adjusted to the dog's height. The tabletops, composed of metal-edged plywood about five-eighths inch thick, are covered with ridged rubber matting. If you are planning to show your dog, you will certainly want and need a table for working both at home and at shows. The sturdy metal legs fold up for storage or for hauling in the car. Tables are not inexpensive, but like the post, this is a one-time purchase.

Tables are usually thirty-one inches high, and the tops come in two sizes—twenty-four by thirty-six inches and eighteen by thirty inches. My personal preference is the larger table because it allows plenty of room for both the dog and the tools. I think that the convenience is worth the slightly higher cost. The smaller table takes up less space in the house and in the car and is large enough to hold the dog, so it may be a better choice for you. Some tables come with removable extenders for the legs, which make the tabletop higher. If you are very tall, one of these might be a good choice to consider. Some tables come with sturdy wheels attached underneath. With the legs folded flat, the table becomes a dolly for moving all the gear from the car to the grooming area at the show.

GROOMING TOOLS

Scissors

The next most needed item is a pair of thinning scissors. Like the post and a table on which

Grooming tables have legs that fold for storage. Some are equipped with wheels so that the table can be used as a dolly for moving all of the gear to the grooming area. Table pictured is twenty-four by thirty-six inches.

to work, these are a must. These should be 46S thinners. The number indicates that the scissors have forty-six slots in a single thinning blade and one unslotted blade. A good pair of thinners is an excellent investment. They should be carbon steel, which stays sharp almost indefinitely. However, they may rust and therefore should be kept in a piece of waxed paper with a drop of fine oil when stored. Stainless scissors will not stay sharp very long when used on a dog's coat. It would be safe to say that you would never need to sharpen the carbon steel scissors or buy a new pair if used on one or two dogs.

A second pair of scissors for straight trimming will be needed. I like a snub-nosed pair for trimming pads and ear edges. The rounded points cannot puncture a wiggly dog or puppy. These scissors are sold in the dog supply catalogues or at the cosmetic counter of most department stores, where they are called nose trimmers.

Brushes

My favorite brush is a wooden-backed pin brush. I like the *Safari #442.*® It is about nine inches long and has thirteen rows of ball-point pins set in a rubber base. This brush is excellent for daily brushing because it goes through the coat without removing undercoat. Since you will always use the brush in the same direction, the rubber base may eventually slip out of the wooden back. It can easily be reglued with *Elmer's Glue-All.*®

A "slicker" is a small rectangular brush with bent metal bristles and an angled handle. This is used for brushing up the hair from the toes and feet and for the leg and head furnishings. It will remove undercoat and should be used with caution elsewhere, unless, of course, it is your intention to remove undercoat.

A Terrier palm pad is an oval-shaped brush. It is composed of rubber with about twenty rows of ball-point pins. It has a strap on the back that fastens to fit your hand. The flexible rubber back makes the brush conform to the curves of the dog's body as well as to your palm. This is used for smoothing down the dog as a final touch-up.

A small, narrow-backed brush with "natural" bristles is very useful for applying chalk. This type of brush can usually be found at your variety or department store in the nail care section, where it is sold for scrubbing fingernails.

Combs

You will need two combs for two different purposes. One is the combination comb with coarse and medium teeth made of metal, like the *Greyhound.*® I like this particular comb because

84

Left side: 3/16-inch show lead and martingale lead. Upper row, left to right: wooden-backed pin brush, slicker brush, stripping knife, magnet stripper, chalk brush, spray bottle for dampening coat, French white® powder and block, Kote Glo® waterless-rinseless shampoo. Lower row, left to right: claw clippers, tooth scaler, 4-in-1 file for claws, Greyhound® comb with wide and medium teeth, Lambert-Kay® fine comb, snub-nosed scissors, 46S thinners. Lower front: pair of Terrier palm pads.

the points are very sharp and go through the furnishings without tearing them. This comb should always be used parallel to the dog to avoid sticking him. The other comb has fine teeth and a handle. It has about fourteen teeth to the inch. An example is the *Lambert-Kay,®* which has a heavier tooth at each end to protect the fine teeth. This comb has dull points and can go down through the coat to separate every hair without sticking the dog.

Stripping Knives

I like a coarse stripping knife, like the *Warner®*. It has about twelve teeth to the inch. The teeth are about three-sixteenths of an inch long, which is enough depth for the long coat of the Westie. I also have a fine stripper, called a *Magnet®* stripper. If you are not a finger stripper, you will like this knife for the parts of the dog that are kept very short. After the dog is cleaned and groomed, the *Magnet* stripper can be run over the coat parallel to the surface to smooth off any fly hairs on the back and tail.

Grooming Chalk

Several grooming powders are available, and the choice must be left to the individual. Some groomers love one kind and hate another—and vice versa. I have heard complaints that bad chemical reactions, causing discoloration of the coat, have occurred from time to time on some dogs being shown. I personally think that the discoloration is more likely to be caused by a chemical reaction between the chalk and the water being used to spray the dog. Water supplies everywhere are chemically treated for human consumption. Even rainwater, which used to be considered soft and pure, is now so full of pollutants that in some areas the acid will eat holes in the leaves of plants and crops. I use distilled water, which I know contains no chemicals. I also use *French White®* powder and block chalk, because they do the best job on my own dogs. I have never had bad results from them. I also like them because they are easy to get out of the coat.

Some Westie owners mix their own chalk using their private "recipes." Calcium carbonate is one ingredient used. This is a powder used in

making capsules and antacids. The drugstore can order it, but you will be required to buy a large amount. Since it must be 99 percent pure (being used for human consumption) it is quite expensive.

Another form of calcium carbonate is whiting from the paint store. My pharmacist says that the two products are the same but that the calcium carbonate has been purified and the whiting has not. Whiting is used in mixing paints and is very inexpensive. This can be mixed with boric acid, which is said to be very soothing to the skin. However, it is hard on the eyes unless made into a very dilute solution, as the directions on the bottle will tell you. Powdered magnesia is another ingredient mentioned, as is baby powder, which has a slight amount of oil to help keep furnishings soft.

Since French White® does a good job for me, I have never experimented with mixing my own chalk. French chalk is a form of soapstone (steatite) used for making tailor's chalk and for dry cleaning. That is exactly what I am doing—drycleaning the dog. Cornstarch from the pantry shelf is a good cleaner and is all that I ever use on puppies. It is also good for cleaning the extra-hard-coated dog. It has a slight softening effect that helps to prevent breakage and discoloration of the hard coat.

Shampoos

Waterless-rinseless shampoos are available for cleaning legs, feet, beards, and bellies, when and if needed. One of these is *Kote-glo®* and another is *Pro-Line Self-rinse Plus Brightener®*. These come in plastic bottles with squirt tops for easy application. Any good dog shampoo can be used by mixing a small amount with water in a pan. Work it into a good lather with a sponge, and apply the lather to the parts of the dog that need shampooing. Rinse this well with fresh water in the pan.

Odds and Ends

You will also want to use other grooming aids, such as a nail clipper and/or file, tweezers, and a tooth scaler. A spray bottle for water to dampen the coat is available from supply catalogues, or you can recycle one from a hair preparation or window cleaner (be sure that the bottle is thoroughly washed). A small amount of mineral oil on a cotton ball is useful for removing any chalk residue from the dog's black nose. Swab sticks for cleaning ears and a product like *Ear Rite®* are good to have on hand. A flat container with a tight-fitting lid is a helpful aid in chalking the dog. This could be a cookie tin or a plastic box used for refrigerator storage. I found a nice one that is five by eight by two inches at a *Tupperware®* party, or an eight-inch-round by two-inch-deep size would be good. That is large enough to work in and small enough to fit into the average grooming case, should you decide to buy one. A tube of cream hair conditioner, like *Wella Kolestral,®* found in the hair care section of the drugstore, is an often used preparation.

12 The Importance of Stripping and Grooming

Dogs come with two types of coat—the kind that sheds all over the house and the kind that does not shed. This latter type needs help in removing the old coat. Dogs also come in oily coats and "dry" coats. The dry coat, having far less oil, does not develop "doggy odor," which is due to the rancidity of the oil and the soil that it naturally collects. Westies do not shed, and they have dry coats. Next to their delightful personalities, this shedless, dry coat is the best reason why they are such wonderful little companion dogs. They are easy to keep clean with a brush and are best "dry-cleaned" with grooming chalk rather than with bathing. The breed is a joy to own if the owner knows how to keep the dog cleaned and groomed. You simply must go about it differently than with other breeds.

A Westie falls in the category of long-coated Terrier. He has a crisp, or "hard," outer coat with a profuse soft undercoat. He needed these two layers for doing his work in the Highlands. While running free over rough terrain and through the briars and brambles, he had no need to have his excess coat removed for him. Now, kept largely as a pet, he has no way to wear off his coat. It needs to be removed to stimulate new live coat to come in. Otherwise, too many hairs will grow in the same follicle, choking out the new growth. The dog that is not stripped becomes very itchy and can develop skin problems if he scratches himself a great deal. He needs more brushing to keep his skin healthy than the dog that has his dead coat removed. Also, the shorter coat is easier to care for and looks smarter.

Using the clippers on a Westie will shorten the coat but will not remove the dead hair. It leaves cut ends, causes the coat to curl, and makes the coat softer. Stripping the coat by pulling out the hairs in the direction in which you want the new growth to lie will train the new growth, and the dog's coat will fit him like a lovely jacket. While various publications state that the breed needs a little "trimming," the word is used in the sense of "tidying up" or "making neat" rather than actually trimming with the scissors or clippers.

The most common question is, "Doesn't stripping hurt the dog?" I have read that the nerve ends on these hard-coated Terriers do not lie close to the skin, which is why stripping does not hurt the dogs. I do not know whether this is true, but I do know that the dogs do not mind the stripping. The dead hair pulls easily with a fast tug. Some dogs have touchy areas, but they will let you know if the stripping bothers them. In those places, pull fewer hairs at a time, pull as quickly as possible, and pull a bit now and a bit later, returning to that area until you get it done.

A soft-coated puppy is stripped to bring in his hard coat, and the continued stripping keeps the coat hard. This hard outer jacket, which has very little oil, does not absorb dirt and is easily cleaned with a brush. This is one reason why a Westie should not be bathed. Water does not hurt the coat, but shampoo softens it. The soft coat will absorb dirt, and the dog will need another bath, and so on, ad infinitum. In fact, the more baths a Westie has, the dirtier he will become. Most breeds are bathed to remove the oil in the coat, which becomes smelly. The Westie has so little oil in his coat that frequent bathing will dry his skin and create skin problems. This is another reason why he should not be bathed. There are exceptions—like a chance encounter with a skunk, or some other unusual situation— but a Westie should have as few baths as possible. I sold a puppy to a very nice lady who later confessed that she had not really believed me when I told her that my dogs were never bathed. After she had owned her dog for about a year, she knew that I had spoken the truth when I had said that Westies could be bathless all their lives. If your dog looks dirty when you put him on the table, you will be surprised how clean and white he looks after brushing and the removal of the dead hairs.

An important part of stripping is that you can visually change the outline of your dog by the strategic removal of coat. This is why, at first glance, all the Westies in the show ring look very much alike. While you may have read that the dogs require very little trimming to show them in the ring, those words were written before the days of the professional handler. Like a master tailor, the professional groomer creates an individual jacket that enhances his exhibit. It is to

their credit that these groomers have contrived to make each dog appear to conform to the breed standard and have cleverly hidden the faults and shortcomings. There is no such thing as a perfect dog. Without their coats, the show dogs would not resemble each other so closely. So for the novice interested in showing his dog, there is more to stripping than merely removing dead hair and making the dog neat and tidy, if he hopes to be any real competition in the ring. The pet owner, too, can learn to improve the appearance of his dog by following the same procedures to whatever degree he wishes.

To shape your dog, it is vital that you know the breed standard and how your dog deviates from perfection. You must take an objective and dispassionate view. To you he is the most beautiful dog in the world, but remember, nobody is perfect. You must learn to fault your own dog. Once you recognize his shortcomings, you will learn to groom to diminish them. This is not to say that I advocate the showing of inferior Westies. Far from it! I do realize, however, that absolute perfection in dogs is unattainable, and I do believe in grooming to enhance each individual dog.

BRUSHING THE ADULT

The best place to start is with the lower furnishings. The "furnishings" are the long hair that a Westie grows on his head, legs, sides, chest, and belly. If you have taught your dog to lie on his back while his belly is being brushed, the procedure will be easier. If not, stand him on his hind feet and brace his body and forelegs on your left arm while you brush with a handled pin brush. If he has mats, work a dab of cream hair conditioner into them, rubbing it in well. Your fine comb will then remove them easily. If nowhere else, you will probably find mats where the forelegs join the body. If your dog is a male, trim the hair from his belly, just in front of the penis, with your snub-nosed scissors to keep that area clean. Also trim the hair from the penis, so that as little hair as possible will remain in this area to collect urine and dirt.

With the dog on all four feet again, start brushing the lower sides (the skirt). Do the

Stand the dog on his hind feet for brushing the belly.

Brush "apron" and legs.

Brush sides of the skirt, doing underlayers first.

Brush back from neck to tail.

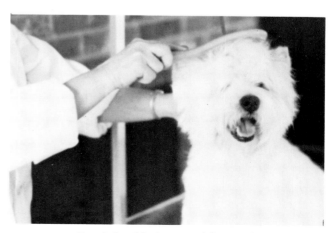

Brush head hair up and forward.

underlayer first by lifting the upper layers up and out of your way and brushing the ends of the hair first. Proceed by brushing a second layer and then a third, until your brush meets no resistance. This same method should be used on the lower chest (the apron) and the legs. Then the upper parts of the dog, which have shorter hair, can be brushed. Follow the lie of the hair, from neck to tail, down the center of the back. Brush the sides, chest, and rear downward. Brush the tail from base to tip.

Lastly, brush the head. Most people have a hard time deciding what is head hair and what is neck hair. The head "ruff," or "frame," starts at the base of the skull, goes across the base of the ears, then follows the jawbone down and underneath the chin, where it becomes the beard. All of the head hair should be worked upward and forward, both in stripping and in brushing.

THE BASICS OF STRIPPING

An adult Westie has three lengths of coat—new coat coming in, the coat of correct length, and the longest coat, which needs to come out. In addition, he has the soft and cottony undercoat, which you want to preserve, and the long furnishings on the sides, belly, chest, legs, and head. The soft-coated puppy, which needs to be stripped, has no outer coat, so he is really wearing only the cottony undercoat. The technique of

stripping either the puppy or the adult is the same.

Finger Stripping

This procedure is easier for doing puppies. The stripping knife can be used only in one direction. A puppy has not learned to stand in one position, and just as you are ready to pull the hair, he may do an about-face. With your fingers, you can pull from any direction, which makes it less frustrating. I have become so adept at finger stripping that I put the knife down unconsciously and work away with my fingers. I find this method easier on the areas of the dog that are stripped very short, and I urge everyone to learn.

In addition to your fingers, you will need a pair of finger stalls, like those used by file clerks—one for your thumb and one for your forefinger. Or, if you have a spare latex household glove, you can cut the thumb and finger from it. The rough surface helps you to grip the hairs better, especially when you are learning. A bit of grooming chalk on the hairs to be pulled will also give a better grip.

If you are right-handed, lift a small section of coat with your left hand. This allows you to see the various lengths of the hairs and where the hair is growing, for selective plucking. *Work in a good light.* When you lift a section, the hairs below it also rise. Pluck the hairs from *just below* those that are held in your left hand. Most first-time

90

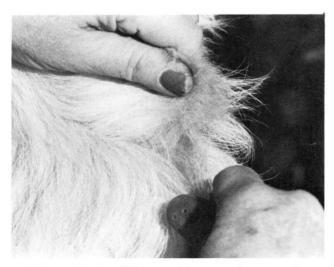

Finger stripping, lifting coat to see and remove the longest hairs.

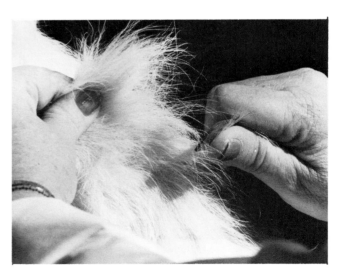

Using the stripping knife to remove the longest hairs.

groomers try to pull the hairs that are tightly bunched and firmly held in the left hand and find that they are not getting any hair. It is the hair falling free just below those in your grasp that you will pluck. In the beginning you will only get a few, but as you practice, you will be rewarded. Keep your right hand palm down, and grip the hairs between your thumb and the side of your bent forefinger. This is like a pinching action, or a combination of pinching and plucking. *Keep a stiff wrist*, and with a sharp tug, pull out the hairs.

The Stripping Knife

Using the stripping knife is very similar. Instead of gripping the hairs between your thumb and bent forefinger, grip them between your thumb and the knife, catching the longest hairs falling free in the teeth of the knife. *Keep a stiff wrist*, and pull the hairs out. If you flex your wrist, you will cut rather than pull the hairs with the knife. If this happens, you will have short hairs on one side of your knife rather than the long hairs that you had planned to pull out, caught through the teeth of the knife. An inspection of the knife contents will quickly show you whether or not you did it correctly.

The breed standard calls for an outer coat "of straight hard hair, about two inches long, with shorter coat on neck and shoulders, properly blended." This does not mean two inches of coat everywhere except the neck and shoulders. Basically, it means two inches of length on the top of the back and elsewhere as needed for blending. While you may see dogs in the ring with far less coat than two inches, do not be persuaded to follow suit. A dog in one-half inch of coat shows every flaw and bump and is not being shown according to the standard. The standard two-inch coat, lying perfectly, appears much shorter than it is. The standard also says that the coat is very important and is "seldom seen to perfection." How is "perfection" to be defined? I believe it is the standard two inches of outer coat, with the equally important softly supportive undercoat, so that when your palm is placed on the dog's back, your hand sinks into the coat.

STRIPPING TO TRAIN THE COAT

Before you begin to strip the coat, get firmly in your mind how the coat should lie. This applies to puppies as well as to adults. The hair must be pulled out in the direction in which you want the new coat to lie. From the base of the skull, at the center of the back of the neck, the coat lies straight back to the tail. At the skull base, the strip will be about one and one-half inches wide and will gradually widen until it is about the width of your palm at the base of the shoulder blades. The center strip will not be that wide on a puppy, of course, but will be in similar proportions.

The next section of neck, at the base of the ears on each side of the center strip, lies toward the lower end of the shoulder blade. The sides of the neck lie toward the front foot. The hair at the front of the neck has a natural sort of part and should lie to the sides, toward the shoulder point. Just under the ear, on the side of the neck, is a cowlick. The sideswept hair on the underneck meets the hair on the side neck in a kind of ridge. The front of the chest can lie straight down or from center to side. I prefer the latter so that the chest hair blends into the hair on the upper foreleg, which I also like lying sideways. The apron lies downward. The hair on the lower shoulder blade lies back and down. The sides, below the center back, lie downward. The rear area—the back end of the dog—lies downward. The foreleg furnishings pluck at right angles to the leg bones all around the circumference of the leg.

These are the various directions in which you will strip the coat. Most new owners ask how often this is necessary. This question is difficult to answer, since each dog grows coat at his own rate. The season of the year also affects how fast the coat grows. In the fall, the dog grows coat for the coming winter, and in the spring he grows coat more slowly. In warm climates he may grow no undercoat at all in the hot summer months. The show dog will need more frequent stripping on the areas that are kept very short, especially in the neck areas. A dog being shown needs stripping of the longest hairs once a week, which is called keeping him in a "rolling coat." Coat that is removed during the resting stage of growth (telogen) will begin to grow new hairs at once. New hair growth is stimulated by the removal of the "dead" hairs.

As a minimum, the pet Westie would certainly need stripping in the spring and fall and would need shaping up to look his best for the holiday season. The owner-handler who hopes to do well in the ring should remember that his competition may be the professional handler, who is grooming his client's dog at least twice a week—every Saturday and Sunday at the shows, and in between times. Do not be put off by that statement. Rather, let it be a guide to the amount of work you must do to prepare your own dog for competition.

In addition, the show dog will need work well in advance of entering the ring. Three to six months may be required to bring the dog into coat—coat trained to lie perfectly and with the correct depth and texture. If you are starting with a "show prospect" puppy, regular work will pay off in having him in shape sooner. It will also train the dog to be accustomed to the grooming table and to being worked on. The greatest benefit will be to you, the groomer, since you will develop more confidence with every session. You will give yourself time to learn from your own mistakes.

SHAPING THE DOG

Keep the breed standard in mind. The object of shaping the dog is to make him look level in the back (his top line), short in the back (tight-coupled), with laid-back, sloping shoulders, good reach of neck, and chest overhang with straight front legs set well underneath it. The dog should have flat elbows, a high tail set, and well-angulated rear legs for close-in rear movement. His head should wear a full ruff in proportion and balance to his size, with the smallest possible ears, deep-set eyes, and a well-defined stop. The dog must also be flat sided and not present a barrel-ribbed, short-legged appearance. His side coat should always maintain this flat-sided look, even when he moves out. There should be no flyaway hair to spoil the clean outline of the dog when he is moving.

Any adult Westie that has never been stripped will undoubtedly be wearing a great deal of neck hair. If left in his natural state, a Westie will grow so much hair on his neck that it will be hard to tell where his head starts, where his neck ends, and where his shoulders begin. This full neck ruff can be seen on Westies in early photographs of the breed. For doing his work, it gave

him protection from the slashing teeth of his cornered adversary, but now it is removed to show off his beautiful "chrysanthemum" head. And, puppy or adult, this is a good place to begin.

Sides of the Neck

These are the sections just below the base of the ears. Separate the neck hair from the hairs that were brushed upward to form the head ruff, and tighten the noose of the grooming arm to form a line of demarcation. Apply a small amount of chalk to the hairs that will be stripped.

Separate head hair from neck hair, and tighten the noose of the grooming arm to form a line of demarcation.

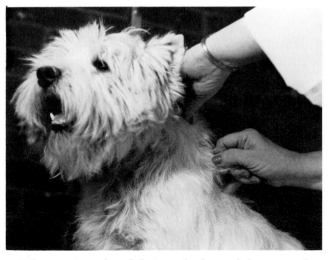

Lift a section of neck hair at the base of the ear, and strip toward the lower end of the shoulder blade.

Lift a small section of neck hair at the base of the ear and grip the longest hairs, those falling free, between your thumb and bent forefinger or knife blade. *Keep a stiff wrist,* and give a sharp pull. These sections are pulled toward the lower end of the shoulder blade. Pluck all hairs that are longer than three-quarters of an inch in length. If the dog has not been stripped before, you may be getting down to the skin, and some may show through. The new hairs will come back lying the way in which you are training them to grow. This area will fill in quickly and will always be kept very short, so some skin showing for a while is all right. If you chalk the dog after stripping, there will appear to be more coat anyway.

Front of the Neck, Underneath the Chin

This section is very tender on most dogs. It is hidden by the ruff and beard. While all areas of the dog are improved by stripping, this area can be an exception. Hold the dog's chin up and use your thinners to smoothly feather this part. "Feathering" is done by shifting your scissors blades between each cut so that each time you cut to a slightly different length. This area should be very short—about one-half inch long. Hold the points of your thinners upward so that you cut with the lie of the hair, not across it. On the show dog, only the part that is hidden by the

Use the thinners to feather off the coat under the chin.

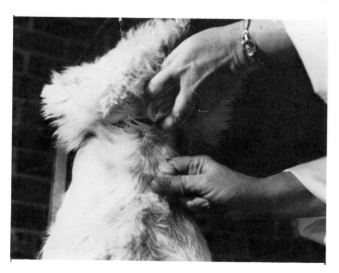

The show dog should have the balance of the neck stripped.

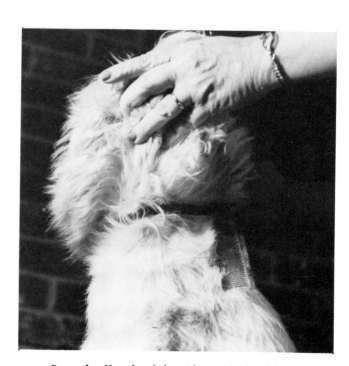

Smooth off ends of the ridge with the thinners.

93

beard should be trimmed. The lower area of the front of the neck should be plucked smooth and flat, pulled from center to side. The pet can have all of the neck feathered short with the thinners. Here, too, you may very well see some skin when the hairs are trimmed one-half inch in length. The hair in the neck areas grows fairly fast, and the new coat will soon fill in the area. A sort of ridge is found where the sections under the ear and the chin meet. This should be smoothed off with the thinners, including the ends of the cowlick, so that it lies flat.

Front of the Chest

If the front of the chest is plucked very short and flat all the way down to the breastbone, the dog will be visually shortened when viewed in profile. Here it is important to know if your dog has a correctly laid back shoulder blade or is upright in the shoulder. The dog with the upright shoulder blade has a wider angled joint between the shoulder blade and the upper foreleg. This structure also makes for a shallow chest overhang. This dog should not have his chest hair removed all the way down to the breastbone. Allowing the apron to begin *above* the breastbone will improve the dog's appearance by making him seem to have a better front overhang of chest than his body structure has provided. The dog with the well laid back shoulder should have his apron begin just below the breastbone to show off his overhang. In either case, the chest hair should be very short, about one-half inch in length. This hair can be plucked straight downward or from center to side. I find that it lies better if trained to the sides, where it will smoothly join the hair on the upper foreleg. The pet can have this area trimmed very short and flat with the thinners.

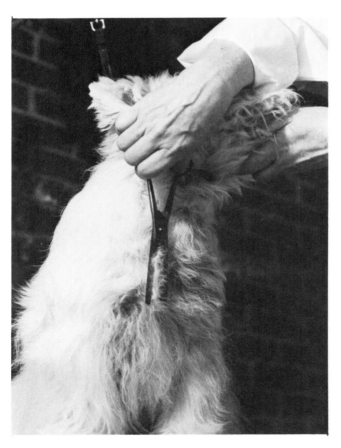

The pet can have all of the neck feathered short with the thinners.

Chest hair stripped to be very short, to below the breastbone, and trained to lie to the side.

94

Upper Foreleg and Point of the Shoulder

The upper foreleg, or humerus, joins the lower end of the shoulder blade to form the "point of the shoulder." It also joins the lower foreleg at the elbow. You have already stripped the adjoining chest and made that hair very short and flat. Lifting the hair on the humerus and lower shoulder blade will help you to see where the hair is growing. The hair on the lower shoulder blade should be plucked backward and downward, or at an angle toward the elbow. It should be very short. If your dog is upright in the shoulder, do not strip this area short for more than two and one-half inches above the point of the shoulder. This is so that enough hair will be left above that for better blending of neck into shoulder, which will be done later. If your dog is very narrow in the front, strip enough to make the coat lie flat, but leave enough to visually lend width to the front, when viewed head on. If your dog is well laid back, pluck this area short and flat higher on the shoulder blade to an imaginary line drawn down diagonally from the inside ear edge.

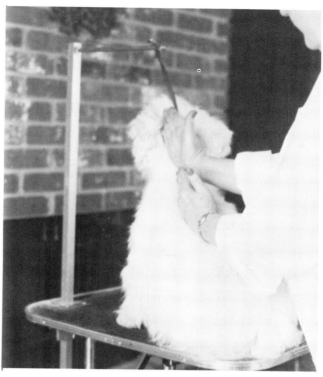

If the dog has a well laid back shoulder, pluck hair short to an imaginary line drawn diagonally down from the inside ear edge.

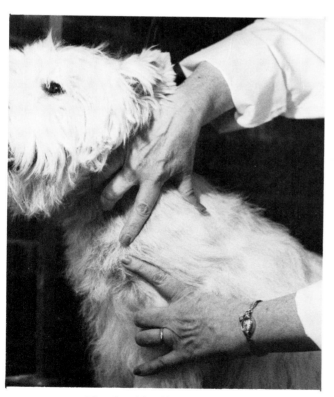

The shoulder blade and the upper foreleg bone form the point of the shoulder.

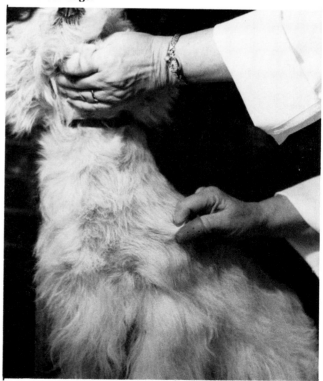

Pluck hair on the lower shoulder blade backward and downward.

95

The hair on the humerus should also be very short and flat and plucked toward the rear, or sideways, to train the hair to lie smoothly flat. For the narrow-fronted dog, leave enough to match the hair on the shoulder point in length.

The hair on the humerus should lie smoothly flat all the way to the elbow joint. At the lower end of the humerus, where it joins the lower foreleg, is a horizontal indentation in which you can place your finger. Make the hair above the indentation very short and flat. This is so that your dog will not look "out at the elbow" when he moves. If your dog happens to be out at the elbow, strip a little lower than the indentation. This lends the appearance of flatter elbows. On pets, I have shortened these areas with the thinners, but if you plan to show your dog, have the patience to strip them so that they will be trained to lie beautifully.

Lower Forelegs and Feet

Leg furnishings should be encouraged to thicken and improve in quality by constant stripping of the longest hairs. All furnishings grow very slowly, and if you plan to show your dog, plenty of time must be allowed for their growth. Even six months will not be enough for regrowth if you remove furnishings heavily. They seem to grow at the glacial speed of about one-eighth inch per month. On my own dogs, continual stripping of the long fine top hairs is the better course. This also should be done on a puppy. Encourage furnishings to grow by massaging

96

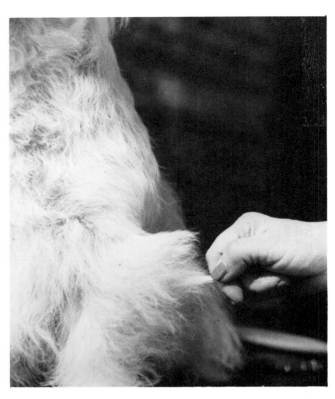

Strip longest fine hairs from leg furnishings at right angles all around the circumference of the leg.

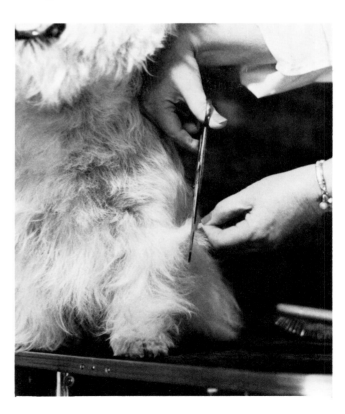

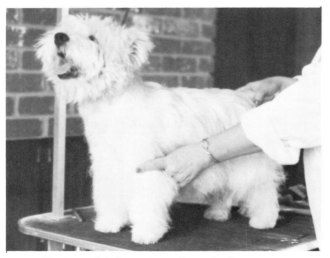

Horizontal indentation where the humerus and lower foreleg join.

Even up the hair tips with the thinners, as necessary.

some greaseless conditioner like *Wella Kolestral®* (available at the drugstore in the hair preparations section) into them often. A small amount applied frequently will keep the furnishings soft enough to prevent breakage. In stripping, pluck the hairs at right angles to the leg all around the circumference of the leg. After you have plucked the longest hairs, some evening up with the thinners will probably be necessary. Parting the hair vertically with your comb or fingers from elbow to ankle into sections about one inch wide makes it easy to even the hair all around the leg.

The feet should be trimmed to nice rounds with the snub-nosed scissors. First lift the foot and trim the excess hair from around and between the pads. The pads of any dog need to be kept trimmed so that the dog does not get wet feet and develop fungal infection. A Westie, to be properly gaited, literally walks on his toes. When his pads are trimmed and his claws are short, you will see the largest pad, since all of the dog's weight should be on his toes when he is standing. The edges of the feet may be trimmed in one of two ways, or a combination of both. While you have the foot up for trimming the pads, you can trim the outer edge from underneath. Or you can trim the edge while the dog stands on the foot. Hold the points of the scissors toward the tabletop as you snip the excess hair from around the foot. Do not trim any hair from the top of the foot, only from the edge. If the dog does not want to keep his foot on the table for you, simply lift the other foot so that he will have to stand on the one on which you are working.

Use your slicker brush to lift the hair of the foot from the toes to the ankles. The object of grooming the front legs and feet is to create the illusion that the dog has a nice straight front, with columnar legs which culminate in toes. Leave enough hair on the ankles to achieve this effect, so that when the hair of the feet is brushed upward, all blends together as one. If the foot appears to have been set on afterward, a Westie will not look up on his toes. In fact, the dog can appear to be down in the pasterns and flat-footed. Quite properly, a Westie should be allowed to toe out, since as a working dog he would need to toe out. In the show ring today, a straight front with straight feet is much admired by some judges, and, to be sure, the degree of

Trim hair from the outside edges of the feet, lifting the opposite foot, if necessary.

97

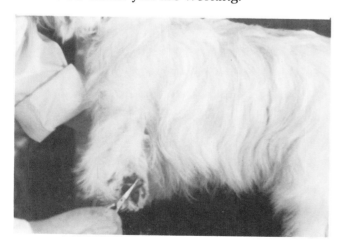

Trim excess hair from around and between the pads.

Use slicker brush to lift the hair on the foot.

toe-out is a factor. If your dog toes out, you can visually straighten his feet by trimming the outer edges very short and leaving more length on the inside edges. The difference between the two lengths will be only a subtle fraction of an inch but will make for an improved appearance. The dog that is out at the elbow should have a little extra length of coat on the outside of the leg, especially at the ankle, to make the legs appear more straight.

Center Back Strip, Neck, and Shoulders

This is the center area of the back, from the base of the skull, between the ears, all the way to the tail set. For the puppy, or for the adult that has never been stripped, pluck all of the longest hairs from the skull base to the tail set. You also can start at the tail set and work to the base of the skull. This is to improve the quality of the back hair and train it to lie flat. In about four weeks of weekly stripping of the longest hairs, new coat will be coming in and lying correctly. As the puppy grows, this section should be stripped as often as needed to keep the coat length at about two inches or less. The same holds true for the pet.

For the future show dog, this section is very important in his future shaping. It will become his "top line," which is the top of the dog's silhouette when he is viewed in profile. The width of the skull base on an adult Westie is about three inches. The exact center of this section should start at the skull base at about one and one-half inches. The remaining one and one-half inches of this section will be about three-quarters of an inch in width on each side. As it descends the neck, the strip will widen, as does the neck, so that at the base of the neck the center is about two inches, while the two side sections widen to cover the upper shoulder blades. Continuing to the tail set, the center section will widen to about the width of a palm.

Every Westie needs some hair on the top of his neck, or his head resembles a blossom on a stem. The length of the hair should be about one inch just behind the head ruff and should gradually become longer as it approaches the shoulder blades. How much longer the coat on the shoulders should be depends on the structure of the dog.

The Steep Shoulder

The dog with the upright shoulder should have hair about one inch long at the base of the skull to as much as three inches in length at the base of the shoulder blades. To lengthen the dog's neck, the head ruff should start slightly higher than the base of the skull. The hair on the top of the neck should have as much depth as possible, especially at the base, where it joins the shoulder blades. Just above and over the upright shoulder blades, the dog needs as much coat as he can "carry," which means as much coat in length and depth that will lie well and not separate or part in the middle. The top line should slope from the skull to behind the shoulder blades, with the back leveling out behind that. This is to make the dog appear to have a longer neck, more sloping shoulders, and a shorter back than what Mother Nature gave him. A bitch may have a longer back than a dog. She, too, will benefit from similar treatment of her top line.

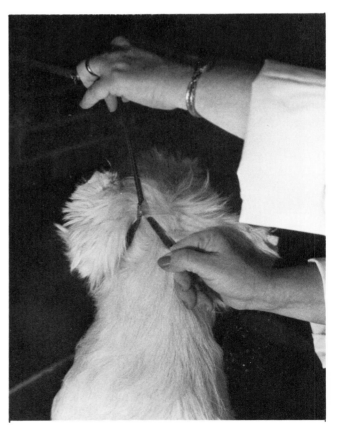

Begin to strip the topline at the base of the skull.

98

When the coat on the point of the shoulder was stripped short, it was not stripped very high up on the steep-shouldered dog. This was to allow room to blend the long hair on top of the shoulder blades into the short hair on the point of the shoulder. When the dog is off the table and has had a good shake, the longer hair on top of the lower neck and shoulder will fall slightly toward the shoulder point and will lie to the right and left of center. Put the dog back on the table and finger strip a few hairs at a time until you have removed enough coat from these areas to achieve a nice blend of coat that will give a sloping appearance where the coat of the upper shoulder and the coat of the shoulder point meet.

The Laid Back Shoulder

The dog with the well laid back shoulders also needs his neck blended so that it joins his body, merging into nicely sloping shoulders. The hair on top of the neck should be about one inch long at the base of the skull and should gradually lengthen to about two inches at the base of the

shoulder, where it joins the coat on the back. The longer hair of the sides of the center section should be selectively plucked to a nice blend. You stripped the shoulder point higher and will have a narrower area in which to blend from longer neck hair to the short hair on the point of the shoulder. If the dog has a bumpy withers muscle or a dip behind the shoulder blade, leave enough coat to cover it and level out the back behind that.

Leave enough coat on the shoulders so that you will get a better merge of shoulders into back.

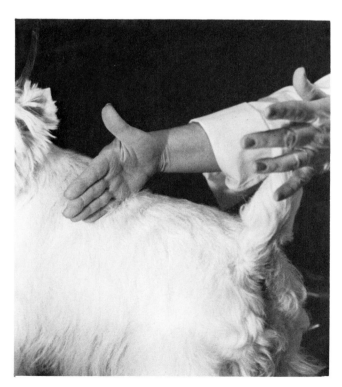

If stripping the "top line" from the tail to the neck, strip only about halfway up the back.

"Neck: should be sufficiently long to allow the proper set of head required, muscular and gradually thickening toward the base, allowing the neck to merge into nicely sloping shoulders."

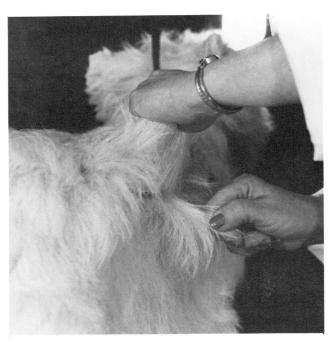

Lift the coat on the rib cage, and pull some hair from the underlayers for flatter sides.

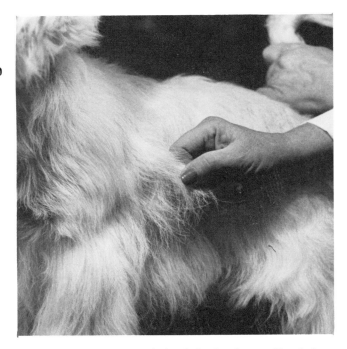

Selectively pluck, just behind the foreleg, to blend the short coat of the shoulder into the longer skirt.

The Top of the Back

If you wish to strip from the tail set up to the shoulder, strip the back only about halfway up to the neck. If you strip the back all the way to the shoulder blades, you may not leave enough coat for a nicely sloping top line. After stripping about halfway up the back, start at the skull base and work toward the shoulder so that you will get a better merge of shoulders into back. You can always remove more coat from the back to level it out higher. If the back hair is removed too high, it cannot be put back onto the dog.

In working from tail to neck, or from neck to tail, make certain that you are stripping for a level back. If the dog decides to sit while you work, get him on all four feet. If his tail set is a little low, leave hair on his back in front of the tail to improve the top line. If his rump has a little rise, take the hair down a little more, or use your stripping knife as a rake to remove a small amount of undercoat, just enough to level the rise.

I believe that the British standard perfectly describes how this top line should appear: "Neck: Should be sufficiently long to allow the proper set on of head required, muscular and gradually thickening towards the base, allowing the neck to merge into nicely sloping shoulders." And: "Body: Compact. Back level, loins broad and strong." Remember that this top line is very important, since it forms the outline of the dog. This profile is what the judge sees first when you enter the ring and he says, "Take the class around." I always think that a good judge picks his winner on the first circling of the ring. His later inspection of the dogs on the table further substantiates that first impression and helps him with the other placements.

Upper and Lower Sides

The coat will be about the same length where the upper sides join the center back. It will be gradually longer as it descends the dog and becomes the longer skirt. Where the back and sides join, strip the longest hairs, plucking downward toward the tabletop, on the area over the upper ribs. As you approach the flank and the point of the rump, angle your plucking slightly toward the rear. On a fully furnished Westie, the long side furnishings begin about halfway up the rib cage. These may be quite long and full, giving the dog a rounded appearance in the ribs even though he has the correct flat-sided, heart-shaped ribs. You want him to look flat sided, as the standard states. You cannot pull the sides only from the top layers. Once again, the key word is "blend." This can best be done by lifting the coat about midway down the rib cage, pulling some hair from underneath, and alternately pulling from the top layers. If you try pulling only from the top, the shorter hairs on top will lie in a sort of ruffle which will be impossible to blend with the lower skirt. Taking some of the hairs from underneath will allow the upper layers to blend smoothly in graduated lengths.

The trickiest area is on the side front, where the hair is very short on the point of the shoulder and the humerus, and where it meets the longer hair of the upper rib. On the lower rib, just behind the foreleg, the coat must become the long skirt. This narrow vertical strip needs careful and selective plucking so that its upper end blends with the two inches of coat on the back, while the lower end, by the lower foreleg, is left long as part of the skirt. This requires lifting the hairs to see where they are growing and removing a few hairs at a time until the coat is

well blended. If you get the dog off the table and watch him move, both head on and from the side, it will help you to remove enough hair for a smooth outline.

You will want to get him off the table anyway before considering that you have finished the sides. Your dog will look very different after he has given a good shake, and he may be a far cry from the carefully brushed dog on the table. You are not going to show him on the table, and he is going to shake himself as he gaits in the ring. Now you will be able to see where you need to remove more coat. It is the best possible way to learn—remove some hair, watch the dog move, then remove some more hair until he looks perfectly flat and smooth even after a good shake and run. A useful adjunct to your grooming area is a mirror in which you can see the dog from a distance as you work. You will get a better perspective. Also, you can see the side that you have done, which makes it easier to get the two sides alike.

The best Terrier handler I know comes to the ring with the Westie underneath one arm. The dog is set down in the ring, and his side coat is set in place with a quick comb or a smoothing palm, if that is all time permits. The professional handler may have a very tight schedule of ring assignments, and may not have the time for

Shorten skirt enough to give "some light under him."

extra grooming in the ring. Nor does his entry need it. It is this same kind of "unflappable" coat that you are trying to obtain. Remember, too, that if you are finding it necessary to do a lot of combing or brushing in the ring, the judge is going to think that you are not ready for your class. This is not the impression you want to give.

The longest fine hairs at the bottom of the skirt should also be finger stripped. You may need to do some evening up with the thinners, taking care to give a natural appearance. These hairs may also be "tipped," which is shortening the hairs with your stripping knife and flexing your wrist to cut them, a few at a time. The breed standard says that a Westie should not be too low to the ground, so make the skirt short enough to give "some light under him."

If you are stripping a puppy, I recommend that you let these side furnishings grow, since it takes the average Westie a year or more to become fully furnished. These areas grow very slowly, and puppies romp and roll, frequently breaking off the hairs. Keep the furnishings soft with hair conditioner or with baby powder when he is cleaned. It has a small amount of oil in it. Then begin removing the long fine hairs as the furnishings begin to come on.

Thighs, Rear Legs, and Feet

Check the rear structure of your dog to see how well it conforms to the breed standard. Like the shoulder structure, you need to know the dog's angulation or lack of it. The upper thigh-bone should angle forward from the ball joint in the pelvis to the knee (stifle). The lower legbones should angle backward to the point of the heel (hock). The hocks should not turn inward. These are termed "cow hocks." A dog that lacks angulation at the knee is said to be "straight in the stifle."

The side, or point, of the rump should be stripped to match and blend with the upper flank by plucking the hairs at an angle toward the hind foot. The hindquarters should be broad across the top, according to the standard. I like Barbara Hand's description in her book, *The West Highland White Terrier*, in which she says that the hindquarters should have enough width across the

top so that, when viewed from the rear, it is impossible to see anything forward of them. The upper thighs should be nicely flat, as are the sides of the dog, and should be blended in graduated lengths. Just above the knee, longer hair must be left to appear as a continuance of the skirt. It should also lie flat like the skirt. If your dog is straight in the stifle, grow more hair on the thigh and on the back of the hock. Even up the long hairs at the bottom of the thigh to a naturally curved line upward to join the skirt on the flank. The long fine top hairs on the lower rear leg should be plucked to remove flyaway hairs. Some shortening with the thinners or stripping knife may be necessary for a smooth appearance.

The back feet must have the hair trimmed from the pads. Like the front feet, these are trimmed to neat rounds, either from underneath when the foot is lifted or while the dog stands. The largest pad on the back foot should be completely exposed and be seen in its entirety (when viewed from the rear) when the dog moves out. Like the front feet, these feet should be an extension of the leg. Use your slicker brush, and lift

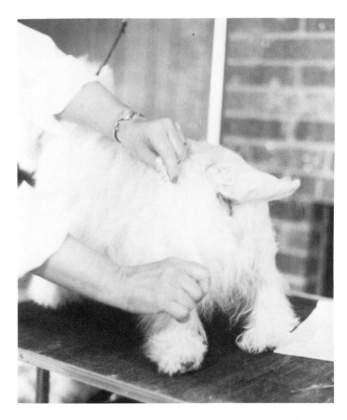

Blend coat on the upper thigh to match the sides.

the hair upward from the toes to the ankles. A Westie should have well-bent hocks, which give him the correct close-in rear movement. If your dog lacks angulation here, leave more hair on the inside of the hocks. The back of the hocks should be trained to stand away from the leg. Pluck, and, if necessary, trim the hocks to present a neat and straight appearance.

Tail and Rear

Tails come in individual sizes, different in length and in circumference as well as in the amount of hair and its texture. As with every other area, stripping will improve the texture and quantity of the hair. The tail is an important part of the dog, lending balance and smartness to the overall appearance. It should resemble a flat-sided carrot, the flat side being the back side, and should look as short as possible. Find the end of the tail with your fingers, and trim off any excess hair with a blunt cut. This allows you to see what you have, lengthwise. Chalk the underside

of the tail hair, and pluck the hairs from base to tip. This is the flat side of the carrot and may also need a bit of trimming with the thinners. The pet can have the back side of the tail trimmed without the stripping.

Regard the tail as a four-sided object— bottom, which you have just made flat, right and left sides, and top. Using a comb to part off the sections may give you a better perspective. If the

"When viewed from the rear, it is impossible to see anything forward."

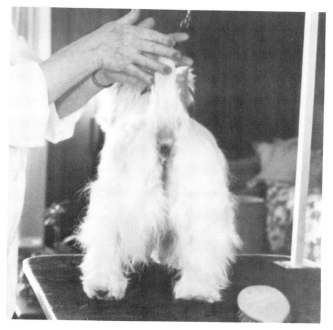

Pluck flyaway hairs from hock for smooth appearance.

Lift rear foot up and back, to trim pads.

103

dog has soft and/or sparse hair on his tail, pluck the longest hairs to help thicken the tail and improve the quality. If the dog naturally grows a lot of hair, shaping his tail can be done with the thinners. The pet can have his entire tail shaped with the thinners. The front, or top section, should be a little longer than the two sides, because the extra length of the hair on the front improves the appearance of the tail set.

On one of the side sections, start at the base of the tail and trim or strip to the point of the tip. Then trim the opposite side to match in length. Lastly, trim the top section, leaving this hair slightly longer than the hair on the side. The object is to trim the tail broadly at the base and end in a point. The shaping must depend on the girth of the tail itself. Some dogs have tails with little taper due to the thickness of the tail muscles and the underlying bone, while others have slimmer tails that are easy to taper. If you imagine a bunch of carrots, some very pointed and some the same thickness for almost the entire length, you will understand the different tails found on Westies.

If the dog has an overlong tail, it will appear shorter if the tip is trimmed further down, making a more elongated and very skinny point while leaving the base relatively fat. If the dog's tail has a slight curve in it, leave longer and fuller hair on the inside of the curve. Trim the base of the back of the tail very close, but leave some hair on the back of the tip. Trim the front of the tip very closely. This will make the tail appear to be more straight. You should also try to train the dog to carry his tail straight. The muscle that holds the tail erect is on the top side of the tail. This muscle needs to "learn" to pull the tail up straight.

At the spot, or semicircle, where the tail and the back join, you may need to remove a few hairs from the back as well as from the tail, so that when the tail is carried up, it fits nicely into the hair of the back. This area of the back seems to grow the hardest hair. A dog that seems reluctant to carry his tail well up will improve his tail carriage if some of this very hard hair, right at the tail set, is removed. Tail muscles respond to reflex, and those hard hairs seem to tell the dog to hold his tail away from them. Just remove a

Pluck hairs from base to tip of tail.

104

Trim tip of the tail with a blunt (straight-across) cut.

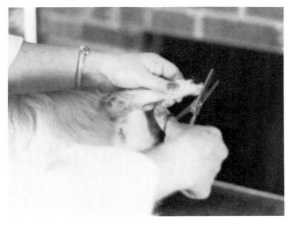

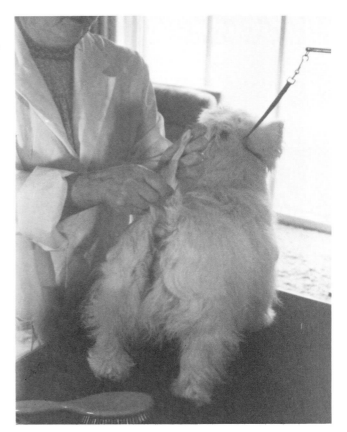

few hairs at a time, only enough for a nice "fit" of tail into body when the tail is erect. Do not get carried away and leave a bare spot.

Like the chest, a good flat rear visually shortens the dog and improves his profile. However, care must be taken not to remove too much or the appearance of an otherwise good tail set will be spoiled. Trim the hair right around the anus with the thinners all the way to the skin. This makes for a cleaner dog, since fecal matter will not cling to the skin as it will to hair. On each side of the anal opening, for about three-quarters of an inch, shorten and feather the coat to be smooth and flat. Below the anal opening, the hair has a natural part and lies to either side. You will see dogs in the ring which show a strip of skin in this part, sometimes almost black if the dog is well pigmented. You will also see dogs on which none of the skin shows, where the hairs have been brushed together. A great deal depends on the amount of coat the dog has. I find this a tender area on my dogs, and I always use

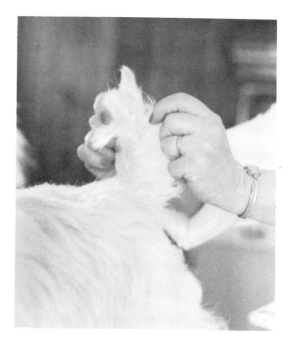

Part off the tail into sections to give a better perspective.

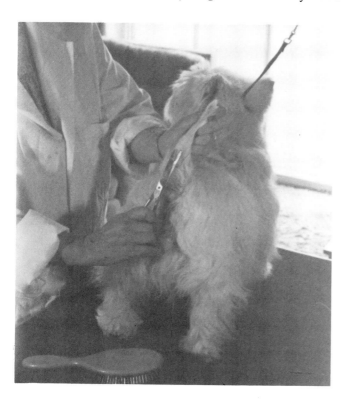

Trim back side for flatness, if needed.

105

Trim tail to be broad at the base and taper to a point.

the thinners rather than strip the hair. I know that stripping would improve the amount of coat, but it hurts. I brush the hair together and feather for flatness, while leaving enough hair for a gentle slope in the outline of the dog, when viewed from the side.

From this one-and-one-half inch center section to the outer sides, the coat must become longer to blend with the length of coat on the sides of the thighs and rear legs. This can be stripped, or the pet can be trimmed with the thinners, points up. Pluck the hairs downward. If the dog has a low tail set, improve his appearance by leaving the hair below the tail a trifle longer.

Every dog needs a little hair on the lower rear, between the legs, to cover the testicles or vulva. Let the hair blend with the long hairs on the inside of the back legs, and even up the ends, as needed, to make an inverted "U."

The Head

The head is usually done last because it is the part that the dog likes to have shaped the least. Also, once the excess hair is removed from the body, it is easier to judge how much trimming and shortening is needed to make the head fit the body for size and proportion. The head hair is softer than the body hair, but it will improve in texture with constant plucking of the longest hairs. This should be started when the dog is a puppy so as to provide him with the best possible adult head furnishings. When all the hair on top of the head is brushed upward and forward, from behind and between the ears, any hairs that are longer than his ear tips should be pulled out with your fingers, gently, as few at a time as possible. Constant plucking will result in

If necessary, remove a few hairs from the back to get a nice "fit" of tail into body.

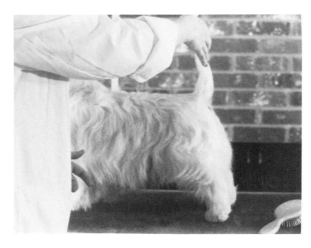

Leave enough hair for a gentle slope in the outline, when viewed from the side.

Blend sides of the rear to match thighs and rear legs.

Feather the coat of the lower rear for flatness.

106

better texture, but this hair will never be as hard as the hair on the back.

The ear edges should be trimmed with the scissors on both sides of the tip to the edges of the ear leather and down each side about one-half to five-eighths of an inch—about a thumb's width. You can feel the ear leather through the hair with your fingers, which makes it easy to trim the ear tip to its shortest length. The back side of the ear tip should be smooth and velvety. You can finger strip here or use the thinners to smooth and feather off the hair until the tip is left with only very short hair. Make your first cut with the thinners across the base of the triangular ear tip—in other words, about a thumb's width from the end of the tip. Working up the tip, lift a very narrow layer of hair with the straight edge of the thinners, and make a second cut across the lie of the hair. Continue to the tip of the ear in this manner.

To trim the side edges of the ears, work from the front side of the ear. Regard the front side of the ear tip as if it were the corner of a square (ninety-degree angle). Using the thinners, trim the hairs on the outside edge of the ear to continue one side of this imaginary square. Trim the inside edge (the edge closest to the center of the dog's head) the same way. Most publications tell you to remove the hair from the back of the ear about halfway down, making this longer tip a narrower triangle. If you do this, the dog's ears look larger and on a large-eared dog, it is a disaster. A wider-angled, square-trimmed ear seems to fit right down into the furnishings of the head and looks much smaller, better becoming any dog, especially the one with large ears.

The inside, or front side, of the ears should be finger stripped to be free of hair, both on the lining and in the ear opening. Put some chalk on your fingers, and pluck any hairs that are on the lining. Remove all of those in the center of the ear flap so that you have hair only in a nice clean

107

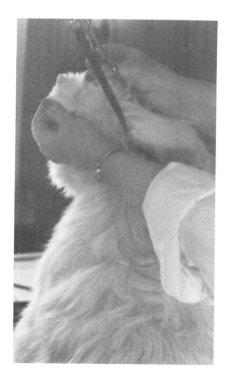

Smooth small triangle of the tip of the ear to be short and velvety.

From the front side, trim the outside ear edges to a ninety-degree angle (one corner of a square).

Finger strip the ear lining to leave a nice clean line on the two edges, and clear the ear opening of hairs.

line on the two edges. The ear opening should be hair-free for good circulation of air into the ear. Pluck all you can with your fingers, or if the hairs are growing down too far to grasp (or if you have large fingers), use tweezers. After the hairs have been pulled, it is a good idea to treat the ears with a little *Ear Rite®*, or similar product, on a cotton swab. Apply it only to the outer folds and where you have pulled the hairs to forestall infection. Antiseptic powders are also available for this purpose.

The hair behind the ears, the back of the skull, the top of the head, and down across the forehead should be finger stripped of the longest hairs by plucking upward and forward. If the dog has large ears, leave the hair a little longer and more full. Some trimming may be necessary to even up the hair and preserve more fullness. Use the thinners for this trimming, or tip off the ends of the hair with the stripping knife. The breed standard says, "Considerable hair should be left around the head to act as a frame for the face to yield a typical Westie expression." I take the word "considerable" to mean exactly that. I like the dog to have a head that resembles a lovely "football"

type chrysanthemum. I see dogs in the ring with far less furnishings, trimmed down to resemble the furnishings of a puppy. I do not think that this excessive trimming is correct, but I leave this decision to the groomer.

Some of the forehead hair will fall to the sides, in front of the ears. This should be left long enough to lie across the ear opening to diminish the size of the ears when viewed from the front. Some trimming may be necessary at the brows. The standard calls for deep-set eyes under overhanging brows. But the Westie's whole expression comes from his bright, hazel eyes, and some shortening of the brows is needed to allow the eyes to be seen—and to see as well. Comb the hairs growing *between the eyes* upward, and catch them between the forefinger and index finger of your left hand. While they are held thus, trim the ends where they curve forward over your forefinger. Use the same method to trim the hairs growing above each eye.

Where the rounded skull joins the flat plane of the muzzle, there should be a well-defined "stop." Hold the dog's chin in your left palm, and

108

Trim, if necessary, to even up the hair between the ears.

Hold hair growing between the eyes between your forefinger and index finger, and trim ends where they curve forward over your forefinger.

pluck a few hairs from this juncture of skull and muzzle—or tip the hairs with your stripping knife. Do a few hairs at a time, enough to "open up" the eyes, in a narrow line from the inside corner of one eye across to the inside corner of the other eye. This will make the stop more defined and will seem to shorten the muzzle. This will improve the dog with the shallow stop. Combined with the upward curving hair between the eyes, you create the illusion of a better stop. The dog with an overlong muzzle will also need more hair on the back of his skull so that his muzzle will seem to be shorter than the distance from the stop to the back of the head. If the dog has overlarge eyes, leave some hairs jutting upward from the muzzle to partially hide the eyes.

The sides of the cheeks of a fully furnished Westie will need some thinning, since the hair grows very thick. You can thin these areas by finger stripping. You may also need to use your stripping knife like a rake to avoid a muttonchop effect in the jowl area. Go clear in to the skin, and rake outward with the stripping knife to remove the excess. This thinning of the cheek hair makes it easier to brush and comb. The beard should be stripped to be about one and one-half inches in length. This area may need some raking underneath the jaw. On the lower lip, just to the rear of the lower canine teeth, is a fold in the lip. Here there is a tuft of hair that is usually discolored, and the hairs are reddish brown. These tufts should be trimmed to the lip line with the snub-nosed scissors. Spread the fold in the lip with your fingers, and trim away the dark hairs.

Some trimming will be needed to shorten the head ruff until it is fairly round. Remember

Location of "stop."

Pluck a few hairs from inside eye corner to inside eye corner

Rake excess coat from jowls with the stripping knife.

Rake excess coat from beard underneath chin.

Trim dark hairs from lower lip.

that you have both width and depth and that you are not trimming for a "dinner plate" appearance, but rather a round head with depth. The outside edge of the ears have already been trimmed. The widest part of the head should be at the level of the eyes. In trimming the cheek hair, the edge above the eyes will round in to meet the trimmed edge of the ear. The edge below the eyes will round in to meet the trimmed beard. It is best to trim a fraction of an inch at a time until you have the head to a proper size for the dog. A large head will look in better balance on a large dog, for example, so make the size of the head fit the dog. If you have a mirror, you will get a better perspective. If the dog's head is narrow, shorten the top hair and the beard slightly, while leaving the sides a little longer to lend the appearance of more width.

Trimming the bottom layer, or the edge nearest the neck, and the back layer of the head

nearest the neck a fraction shorter than the rest of the ruff helps to lend support for the upper layers of the frame. I like to leave the ruff a fraction longer than it needs to be so that I can go back around the tips, at right angles to the edge, to avoid a too-scissored look and to give the head a shaggier appearance.

SHORTENING THE CLAWS

The claws should be very short so that the dog can properly gait on his toes. Long claws are bad for the feet, causing the toes to splay. Most breeders have the dewclaws—those on the inside forelegs—removed when the puppies are about three days old. However, this is not required for showing the dog, as it is in some breeds. Check to see if your dog has them, and if he does, include them in your care of claws. Otherwise,

110

Widest part of head hair should be at the level of the eyes.

Edge above the eyes will be round in to meet the trimmed edge of the ear.

Edge below the eyes will round in to meet the trimmed beard.

Trim underneath the edge a fraction shorter to lend support to the frame.

Go back around the outer edges of the frame, at right angles to the edge, for a shaggier look.

they will grow in a circle and will grow back into the leg.

I have never found a Westie, or any other dog, that likes to have his claws trimmed. Puppies do not seem to mind when they are very young, and the claws are easily trimmed with the scissors. The claws on an adult Westie are very big and tough. I do not wish to discourage any brave soul from trimming claws, and, indeed, I recommend a "guillotine" type trimmer. This tool has a blade that slips down when the handles are gripped and that clips off the end of the claw. Care must be taken not to cut into the quick, which is very painful for the dog and will make the claw bleed. You should have a preparation like *Quik Stop®* on hand. This is a styptic powder that you can insert into the open end of the bleeding claw.

Claws can also be filed, which is the method I prefer. Files sold for pets are fine for smoothing, but they will never file the heavy claws of a Westie. You can make a giant emery board from a flat, narrow piece of wood, like a wooden paint stick, or even an object as small as a tongue depressor. Your hardware store has emery cloth in sheets. Ask for extra coarse. Cut a piece twice the width of the wood strip plus one thickness. Fold it over the wood slat, and staple the open edge through the wood so that the emery cloth will stay in place. This makes filing claws easy. Recently, a very thoughtful friend gave me a

wonderful present. It is a *Black Diamond®* eight-inch, 4-in-hand file. This dandy tool has four different file surfaces, one of which files claws in a hurry, and another which is finer and smooths them off. I am very pleased with it and hope that you can find one at the hardware store. If not, the improvised emery board, plus a pet nail file for smoothing, will do the job.

Your dog will not absolutely love having his nails filed, but he will quickly come to realize that it does not hurt. Do remember that all friction tends to build up heat and becomes painful if continued for a long period. Just hold the claw between your fingers and file across it while it is firmly held. You can do this while the dog is on the grooming table, or you can sit on the floor together. The front claws will need the most frequent shortening, since the dog wears down the back claws by scratching the dirt or cement with the back feet after relieving himself. File the claws a couple of times a week, and your dog will soon have nice short claws with the quicks receding into the base. Get them at least short enough so that they do not touch the tabletop when the dog is standing on his toes.

THE EYES

Your Westie's eyes should look bright and clear, with no dampness or mucous in the corners. Westies come "naturally equipped" with a small granule of black matter in the inside corners of the eyes that will probably be there daily. I use the word "granule" because it is rather like a grain of sand, and, like sand, it is dry. I have never met a Westie that did not have it, or one that it ever troubled. Wetness from the eyes is another matter and should be examined by your veterinarian. It could be a pollen allergy or something equally simple, but it should be checked, along with any redness in the white of the eye, which is also unnatural. Generally speaking, Westies do not have eye problems as do most of the other breeds that are white. This is because of the dominant gene for the white coat color. In other breeds, except the Samoyed, the white coat color is from a recessive gene.

111

Filing claws with 4-in-1 file.

CARE OF THE TEETH

Your dog's teeth should be cleaned daily. Starting this early in his life will avoid many future problems. It is true that a dog does not have any digestive enzymes in his mouth and that all of his food is digested in his stomach. This is why dental caries in dogs is rare. But the teeth will collect tartar, just as your own teeth do. Teeth cannot live with tartar at the base, and the gum will recede, causing the teeth to loosen. Cleaning the dog's teeth with baking soda will correct the pH balance in his mouth and retard formation of tartar. Start by cleaning one or two teeth with a washcloth dipped in plain water. Gradually, clean more teeth. Then add some baking soda to the damp cloth. Soon your dog will learn that having his teeth cleaned is a regular part of his day. You can get a small brush and eventually change over to that. You can also switch to *Peak*® toothpaste, if you like, since it has a soda base and no detergent to make the dog sick should he swallow some. It has a nice minty scent, pleasant for the owner.

If your dog already has tartar that you want to remove, tooth scalers are available from the pet supply catalogues. Brace your thumb at the end of the tooth and use it as a fulcrum. Scrape from the center of the tooth upward to the gum line and from the center of the tooth down to the end. With a little practice, you will soon master it. Heavy deposits of tartar should be removed by your veterinarian. This requires tranquilizing the dog, which makes it cost a little more than having your own teeth cleaned. However, due to the large supply of blood vessels in the dog's mouth, any infection that develops here quickly spreads throughout his body. If your dog has bad breath and his teeth and gums appear to be clean and healthy, have him checked by your veterinarian. The problem could be the result of a metabolic disorder, indigestion, or an infection that is being transmitted through the blood to the lungs, where it causes bad breath.

13 Dry Cleaning the Westie

In the grooming chapter, it was explained why your Westie should not have any more baths than are absolutely necessary. Instead, a Westie should be cleaned with grooming powder. A little shampoo is also needed, preferably the waterless, rinseless kind. Having had other breeds, I can say that cleaning a Westie is far easier than giving a dog a bath. It also takes less time. I find that I can clean and chalk the dog at the show site, with every hair in place for the judge, in about one hour. I do not believe that I could wash, dry, and brush the dog, making him look so neat, in twice that time. I also find that cleaning up some chalk dust is far less work than cleaning the hair from the drain, the splattered suds from the tub walls, drying the bathroom floor, and doing up all the wet towels.

Chalking makes the dog look bandbox clean and has the extra benefit of keeping him clean longer. It adds body to the coat and improves the texture. The silicones in the chalk make the dog even more soil-resistant than he is in his natural state. Owners often ask if the chalk causes skin problems. I have never heard of or owned a Westie that had skin problems due to using chalk. Bathing this dry-coated dog and thus removing the small amount of oil in his skin is far more likely to cause problems if done frequently. Dry skin is itchy skin. Also, the dog that is not stripped can become itchy and an itchy dog can do an unbelievable amount of damage to himself in a few hours if left unattended. The chalk merely removes the soil from the coat, while the stripping keeps the new growth coming in. Both are beneficial.

To clean your dog, cover the table with several layers of newspaper. A terry towel can be laid over these, but it is not necessary. You will need two small towels, one to dry the parts that you are going to shampoo and one for later use on the dog's back. You will need the chalk, your brush, your metal combs, and the shampoo. The waterless shampoo comes with a squirt cap, so you can apply it directly to the dog. You can also use any good shampoo. Mix a small amount with some water in a flat pan and work it into a good lather with a clean sponge. You will apply only the lather to the dog.

Start with a foreleg. Apply the shampoo to the leg and massage into a good lather, or apply some lather from the pan and work it into the coat. Now do the same to the rear leg. If the skirt and belly area are dirty, suds them. Move to the other side of the dog and repeat the same sudsing of legs and belly. Then suds the beard and the outer edges of the ears if they need it.

Take your terry towel and begin drying the first leg that you washed. The waterless shampoo is also rinseless, but the regular shampoo should be rinsed out of the coat with a pan of water before drying. Towel dry all of the damp areas, rubbing briskly. This helps to stimulate growth. Leave all of the parts *slightly* damp.

Now you are ready to apply the chalk to these parts. Some people try applying the chalk directly from the container because it has a shaker top. It is much easier to apply if poured from the can into a flat container and applied with a small bristle brush or your hands. Remove the top layers of damp newspaper from under the dog. If your container is large enough, you

Apply the shampoo to the foreleg, and work into a good lather.

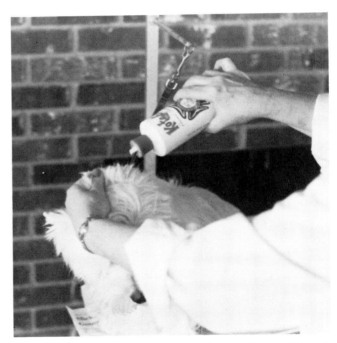

Suds ear edges and beard.

114

Suds belly and skirt.

can stand the dog's foot right down into it and work the chalk into the damp hair of the feet and legs. Shake the foot over the container to remove all the excess chalk. After you have chalked the feet and legs, chalk the skirt and belly furnishings. You can hold the container right up under these areas and apply the chalk easily. Then brush the chalk into the head furnishings that you have shampooed.

If you are using regular shampoo, squeeze out the sponge until it is barely damp, and rub the back from the neck to the tail to dampen the back. *Never* rub from tail to neck because you will loosen up the tight back coat. Or, you can simply dampen the back, chest, rear, and tail, and any other parts not shampooed with a light spray of water. I recommend that you use distilled water, especially on a show dog. A gallon of it is very inexpensive and will stay fresh indefinitely if kept

capped. I have heard of some strange chemical reactions that have been blamed on chalk and that have resulted in discoloration of the coat. The distilled water has no chemicals in it and cannot react in any way with chalk.

Now you are ready to chalk the sprayed areas. You can use block chalk on the flat areas of the back, chest, and rear or apply the powder with the small brush. Apply the chalk carefully to the muzzle so as not to get it in the dog's eyes. The object of applying the chalk to the slightly damp coat is to finish the drying, since the chalk will absorb the moisture as well as the soil. It takes a bit of practice to learn how much towel drying and chalk are needed. Do not leave the dog wet, only slightly damp, and use as little chalk as possible. Train your dog not to shake while the chalk is on him. He will love the rubbing and will shake because it makes him feel so

Hold foreleg over chalk container, and apply the chalk.

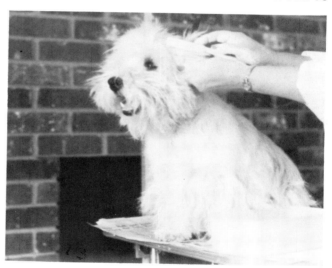

Applying chalk to ears with the brush.

115

Place container of chalk underneath the dog for chalking skirt.

Applying chalk to muzzle and beard.

Spraying the dog's back to dampen the coat.

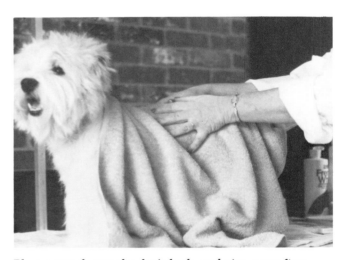

Use the pin brush to brush out the chalk.

Place a towel over the dog's back, and give some firm slaps to loosen chalk.

116

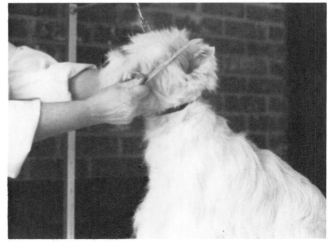

Comb all of the lower furnishings with the wide-spaced teeth of the combination comb.

Work the comb through the head furnishings, upward and forward.

good. If he starts to shake himself while you are chalking him, put your hand on the back of his neck and give a firm "No!"

Return to the first leg you chalked. Take the pin brush and begin to brush out the chalk. Brush directly toward the tabletop. Then hold the chalk container underneath the table edge, and brush the chalk from the table back into the container. This is not only less messy, but it saves chalk. Pin brush the other three legs and the side and belly hair, again brushing the excess chalk back into the container. At this point, you may want to remove another layer of newspaper from under the dog to provide a chalk-free surface.

Place a clean towel on the dog's back, and give some firm slaps on the back to work the chalk loose. Then brush all the other areas, including the head. With all areas well brushed, take the combination comb and, with the wide-spaced teeth, comb all of the lower furnishings— feet, legs, sides, belly, chest apron, rear, and tail. If this comb has very sharp points, be sure to use it parallel to the dog. Work the comb through the hair of the head, combing all the hair from the base of the ears and the base of the skull upward and forward. Work the brush through the coat from neck to tail. Place the towel on the back again and give some firm slaps. You may want to remove another layer of newspaper for a chalk-free surface.

Pat the back to see if any chalk still remains. If so, brush well again with the pin brush. *All* of the chalk *must* be removed from the dog before he can be shown to the judge. Using the fine end of the combination comb, work through all of the furnishings, including the head. Pat the back again to bring out any remaining chalk.

Use your slicker brush, and brush up the hair on the front feet, from the toes to the ankle, so that the hairs are lifted and the feet and legs blend together. Brush all of the hair on the front legs upward. A gentle shake will settle it in place and give a nice, full look. Use the slicker or a Terrier palm pad to go over the head, brushing upward and forward.

By now it is presumed that the dog is clean and dry. You should be able to use the fine comb to go through the furnishings, meeting no resistance. If the dog is still damp, continue to pin brush until he is dry. The dog *must be dry* so that all of the chalk will come out. The slightest bit of dampness will retain chalk. If the dog's back is now chalk-free, put a dab of *Wella Kolestral*® between your palms, and rub it lightly down the dog's back and upper sides. Use the Terrier palm pad to smooth it into the coat and to lay the coat nicely flat. You should now have a sparkling clean Westie, chalk-free, with every hair separated.

You need to learn to get the coat to the proper dampness before applying the chalk. You must continue to work on the dog until he is completely dry and free of chalk. Use the chalk sparingly, since all that you put on the dog has to come out. Do not pin a towel around him and return him to his crate. All he needs to do is scratch himself once or shake himself, and neither the towel nor the coat will be in place. Do not leave him with a wet coat, which he can shake into standing on end. You will never get the coat to lie flat. Keep the dog on the table until you are satisfied that he is dry and that all of the chalk has been removed. It is better to chalk the dog that has been shampooed and is completely dry than to have too wet a coat. Some handlers always prefer to dry the dog thoroughly and apply chalk to the dry coat.

If you are fooled into thinking that the dog is dry and that all of the chalk is out, you will be in trouble in the ring. Between the time that you think you are ready for the judge and the time that your class is called, the coat will dry. If the dog shakes, out will rise a cloud of chalk, and you will be excused from the ring for that show. Some judges try hard to find traces of chalk on Westies. I recall one who even checked soles of feet. Chalking is the accepted method of cleaning, and everyone knows that it is used, but not one trace of it can be found on your exhibit.

Westie exhibitors have been heard to complain that since chalking is the accepted method of cleaning, what is the objection to a trace of it on the dog? If any at all were allowed, the judge would have to decide how much was "a little" and how much was "too much." The AKC dog show rules prohibit the use of any substance that will alter the color of a dog being shown. Chalk in the dog's coat would certainly make him appear whiter. Being excused from the ring is a blow to the exhibitor. It is also a blow to every other exhibitor. By getting excused from the ring, you reduce the entry by one dog or bitch. If your dog made enough entries for a major, being excused reduces the points from three to two. Whatever the points were, this is a disappointment for everyone, not only you.

If you have a place to groom where you will not mind the blowing chalk, you can use a blow dryer. If the dryer has a brush, always use it in the directions previously discussed. You will still need to learn how to dry the dog manually, since electrical outlets are not always available at the show sites, especially the outdoor shows. You should time yourself so that you know how long you will need to prepare your dog for the judge. If the weather is humid, it will take a little longer to get the dog dry. At an indoor show, I still prefer to dry the dog manually. Blowing chalk dust everywhere is not going to make you popular, especially if you are grooming near somebody's black Poodle. Have some consideration for your fellow exhibitors and for the club giving the show by making as little mess as possible.

To be competitive, you really do need to groom your Westie at the show site. He will never look the same if done at home the previous night. But it does not take five pounds of chalk to get the dog clean. If you can set up to groom by other Westies, so much the better. You will learn a lot by watching other Westies being groomed. You can talk dogs as you work, which makes the day even more interesting and rewarding. Some of my best "Westie friends" were made in the grooming area at the show site.

118

Sparkling clean Westie, chalk-free, with every hair separated.

14 Dealing With Special Problems

After the dog has been cleaned and chalked, he will appear to have more coat everywhere, including those places that looked a little bare due to their shortness. The chalk gives body and fullness to the coat. The head hair between the ears may not stand up as well as you would like, or the toes may look a little brown, or the beard may look stained. These and other problems and how to correct or improve them will be discussed here.

GETTING THE HEAD HAIR TO STAND

Head hair is never as hard as the hair on the neck and back, and some dogs have soft head hair in spite of much stripping. Several products can be used to help give the hair enough body. The one that works best depends on the degree of softness of the hair. Fabric finish, used to give a crisp finish to the laundry, can be lightly sprayed on the hair, followed by light chalking and brushing upward and forward. A *small* amount of petroleum jelly worked into the hair at the roots and some chalk applied will give body at the base and help the hair to stand. Use the petroleum jelly sparingly. If one application is not enough, repeat the process. This same method, substituting *Wella Kolestral*, can also be effective. Hair-setting gels, like *Dippity-do®*, or lotions, like *Breck Basic®*, lightly applied and brushed dry, can help. I suggest that you experiment with these on your own dog to see which one does the best job. If you are grooming for show, experiment both on damp and dry days to learn which to use if the weather happens to be hot and humid.

STAINED FEET AND BEARDS

I am convinced that brown and rusty beards are caused by water chemicals, mostly chlorine. Westies that swim regularly in chlorinated pools will turn pink all over. The best solution is prevention. The simplest method is to dry the dog's beard after he has had a drink. If possible, also chalk the beard. Not all dogs will drink it, but about three drops (use an eye dropper) of lemon juice in the drinking water will help to keep the beard whiter. I have attached an *Insta-pure®* water filter to my kitchen faucet. I can see a vast improvement in the color of beards after using it for about three months. It took some time for the old hairs to grow and new, whiter beards to appear.

Failing all else, the show dog can have his beard bleached. In a small bowl, mix about one tablespoon of grooming chalk with enough 3-percent hydrogen peroxide to make a solution about the consistency of paint. A new, clean, one-inch paintbrush makes an excellent applicator. Brush the stained areas of the chin and mouth with the solution. It is best to do this at the beginning of a grooming session, while the dog is on the table. The solution should dry in about an hour, while you are working on the dog. If it is not completely dry by that time, you can use a blow dryer. You could also brush in some more chalk to absorb the dampness, then brush it all out. Depending on the degree of stain, you may need more than one application.

Reddish-brown toes are caused by the dog licking his feet. Some dogs simply seem to be clean feet "freaks" and clean their feet daily. I have one of these. Since the water filter has been in use, his toes, like his beard, are white. Other dogs lick their feet because the feet itch. The dog often nibbles as well as licks. You need to discover which type your dog is, so that if his feet itch, you can make him more comfortable. Sprinkle his feet lightly with a little *Desenex®* foot powder. This will stop the itching. It will also stop the licking if the dog does not like the taste—and most dogs do not. If necessary, bleach the toes at the same time you do the beard.

TEMPORARY COAT COLOR

Temporary color in the coat is another problem and it is one of the reasons why, as the standard says, the coat is seldom seen to perfection. Usually the color can be seen in the dorsal streak, this center back area of the coat taking on a tan or yellow tinge. Removing too much live coat by stripping the dog down heavily has been cited as a cause of the color. Southern dogs will often turn tan in the strong sunshine. Friends of mine who own black Scotties and Cockers complain that their dogs become bleached to reddish brown by the sun. Some Westies "burn" only the tips of the hairs of the coat, each hair tip on the back turning brown. In all climates, the coat that is very hard is the most vulnerable to discoloration. Still, one of my bitches who loves to sun her chest and belly by lying flat on her back yellowed all of her chest, leg, and belly furnishings during our first summer in the South. These are examples of possible causes of *"temporary"* color in the coat. These dogs were white until some outside influence caused the coat to discolor. This condition corrected itself when new coat came in. Some Westies have yellow or tan dorsal streaks all the time. This is a matter of the dog's genetic background, the coat color harking back to a Cairn Terrier ancestor, long forgotten for generations.

120

Bleaching the beard, using a narrow paintbrush to apply the solution.

I have known one or two Westies that discolored a spot on the coat by constant licking and nibbling, just as the toes can become discolored. I discovered that the dogs had had fleas and had been nibbling at the spot, and the saliva had turned the area pink. It was hard for me to believe that the owner allowed the dog to lick and nibble long enough to discolor the coat!

Bleaching of Westie coats is done for the show ring, but it is never discussed. If it *is* discussed, it is always the other fellow who bleaches his dog, never the person discussing it. *I recommend it ONLY for the dog that is naturally white but has somehow managed to become discolored.* I am not even certain that it would help the dog whose genes have given him the color, and AKC rules specifically prohibit using any substance to alter or change the *natural color* of a dog. *Neither do I recommend bleaching for the extra-hard-coated dog*, since you might get breakage of coat if the bleaching further crisps it. Overuse of bleach, or any other grooming product, could eventually damage the coat and should be used with discretion.

The ingredients are the same as for the beard except that you will need more of both, and the consistency should be thicker. You will need about one-third cup of chalk, with enough 3-percent hydrogen peroxide to form a fairly thick mixture. The mixture should be heavy enough so that the dog cannot lift the coat on end if he shakes himself. The mixture can be applied with an old toothbrush by working from neck to tail and keeping the coat as flat as possible.

This is best done when the dog can be crated for the time the coat takes to dry. You will find

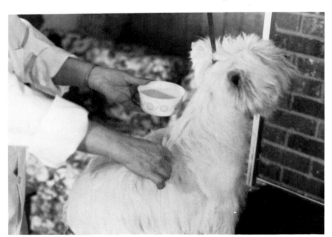

Bleaching the back, using an old toothbrush to apply the paste.

that one-third cup of chalk is quite a lot. Cover the floor around the crate with newspapers to make cleanup easier. Even so, you will have a lot of chalk to remove from the coat when the paste dries. If more than one application is needed, allow several days between them.

For my own dogs, I mix one-half part distilled water with one-half part *Roux Fanci-Full,®* a hair tint, in color #49, Ultra White Minx, to use as a spray-dampener for the back or other parts that need whitening and brightening. This hair tint shampoos out and therefore presents no danger of overdoing it and dying the dog blue. This half-and-half mixture is the standard content of the spray bottle in my grooming case, and it is always used instead of plain water for spraying the areas to be dampened.

THE EXTRA-HARD COATED DOG

It is true that most Westies never need a bath. Now we come to that well-known "exception that proves the rule." This is the Westie with the extra-hard coat. This dog has a coat more like a Wirehaired Terrier. The coat is very brittle and breaks so easily that you can see the broken hairs as you brush the dog. The dog will not grow coat, because the hair is too brittle to get any length. This dog needs a bath for the very reason that most Westies do not—the shampoo softens the coat. Choose a good nondetergent shampoo, one that does not sting the eyes, like baby shampoo, and give the dog a bath.

Most bathing instructions fail to stress the importance of keeping water out of the dog's ears. A dog's ear canal goes very deeply into his head and has a curve at the bottom. Water has no way to get out, since it cannot drain upward. Water in the bottom of the ear canal can cause fungal infection and a painful and smelly ear. Pricked-eared dogs like Westies have very few ear problems, but there is no need to invite problems. Most instructions say that you should put cotton balls in the ears, but I have found that the dog shakes them out before the bath is well underway. Use a sudsy washcloth for the dog's face and head. Then, as you rinse, use your index finger to gently plug the ear and act as a deflector for the water. Rinsing only from the back side of the ear will allow the water to run down both sides rather than into the ear.

121

Partially towel dry the dog, then blow dry the coat. If your dryer has a brush, use it gently to smooth the coat into lying flat, brushing only with the lie of the hair and never against it. When the dog is perfectly dry, chalk the coat lightly and brush out the chalk. This extra-hard-coated dog should always be chalked dry. Corn-starch, which has a slightly softening effect, also makes a good cleaner for this dog.

The rain-soaked Westie needs similar treatment, especially the soaking wet show dog. Westies usually do not care about the weather and enjoy the rain and snow. But your show dog cannot be allowed to dry with his coat in disarray and standing on end. If necessary, use the dryer or rub a towel down the back from neck to tail. Then chalk the dog to absorb the excess moisture, brushing the coat nicely into place until the dog is dry.

THE IMPORTANT UNDERCOAT

Throughout the grooming instructions, the importance of the undercoat has been stressed. This is another reason why the Westie's coat is seldom seen to perfection. It is sometimes hard to maintain the furry undercoat, especially in the summer months and/or in the warm climates. It is particularly important to try to maintain all that you can on the neck and the back. The grooming instructions have mentioned only brushing the dog's back because a comb will sometimes remove undercoat. The slicker brush does the same. You will find that, as you strip the dog, you loosen a little undercoat, which is only natural. But never use any brush or comb that gathers undercoat as you work.

When warm weather approaches, the dog may shed the undercoat. Even the pin brush (which will not remove the undercoat if it is tight) will gather soft undercoat as you brush. One of my dogs began to shed undercoat in January after we had had an especially warm December. "Ho hum. Who needs all this, when it is shirt-sleeve weather?" he seemed to say. This is very frustrating for the owner who has big plans for showing. It should be noted that if the undercoat is loose enough to be brushed out with the pin brush, it is better to get it out of the coat.

It will come back in sooner if this is done. Otherwise, the loosened undercoat will "hang up" in the outer coat, usually along the sides of the dog, where it will create feltlike mats. These must be worked out of the coat. Massage a dab of *Wella Kolestral®* into the mat, and use the wide teeth of the combination comb to ease the mats out of the coat.

This is why keeping the dog in a "rolling coat" by stripping the longest hairs weekly is so important, especially for the show dog. You will be removing a little of the undercoat as you pluck the long top hairs. These hairs are in "telogen," the resting phase of the dog's coat, and new hairs will begin to grow at once. Otherwise, new growth occurs much later if the hair is allowed to shed naturally.

Many exhibitors of Westies drop out of the shows for the summer, not only because the weather is hot, but because they like to strip their dogs of the winter coat. They feel that the new coat will come in sooner and that the dog will therefore be in better coat sooner for the fall shows. I live in the South and feel that my dogs need coat for protection from the heat, as much as a dog needs a coat for warmth in the winter. Therefore, while I remove excess coat in the spring, I never strip my dogs heavily. The "rolling coat" method works best for me.

A Westie was bred to be weatherproof, so a little foul weather will certainly not hurt him. But if you own a "show prospect," you will have to treat him accordingly. The breed thrives in all climates, from the tropics to Alaska, but not with the ideal show coat. The "show prospect" will have to be maintained as such, at least until he finishes his title. The dog cannot be out adventuring in the woods, chasing rabbits and tearing off furnishings. He cannot be out getting sunburned in the southern sun. Think about how the professional handler maintains his client's dog while he is showing him. The dog is traveling in the handler's van *in a crate*, with air-conditioning in the summer and heat in the winter. He is getting his exercise in a pen or with roadwork on a leash. This is not to say that you must crate up your dog every day. Just use your common sense to keep your dog in as good a coat as possible while he is being shown by keeping him out of problematic situations.

"WINTER" OR "SNOW" NOSE

This condition is a fading of the dark pigmentation which is evident in the change of color from black to liver brown, or a faded dark grey. This condition is also seen in the Samoyed, the other breed with a dominant white coat color. Sometimes other black "trimmings" are affected in addition to the nose. Various reasons for the condition have been advanced, from lack of trace minerals to the use of plastic feeding dishes and plastic toys. Lack of sun in the winter months is another theory. In many dogs, pigmentation will return during the summer months, while in others it will continue to worsen with each succeeding winter.

One of my bitches developed winter nose when we lived in Pennsylvania. While watching her, I discovered that she was a lover of shade. She never stayed in the sun for more than one or two mintues, while the other dogs basked in it. I decided to give her some liquid cod-liver oil—the naturally fishy smelling variety. I added one-half teaspoon to her food daily throughout the winter, and by spring the pigment was returning.

Lack of iron has been suggested as another cause of fading pigment. Dogs that are not helped by a small amount of cod-liver oil will be helped by kelp tablets. As discussed in the chapter on nutrition, kelp is a daily additive to the diet of my own dogs. Each ten-grain tablet contains two milligrams of iron. This tiny amount is not enough to imbalance the other minerals, but it does seem to help maintain the pigment and to restore it to faded noses.

Ch. Heritage Farm's Jenny Jump Up, top winning Westie bitch of all time. "Jenny" was bred by Nancy Johnson. "Jenny" was the dam of eighteen puppies before beginning her show career at about the age of five years! During the relatively short time that she was shown (only about one year), "Jenny" won four all-breed Best in Shows, three Specialty Best in Shows, twenty Terrier Group Is, fifteen Terrier Group IIs, eight Terrier Group IIIs, seven Terrier Group IVs, and Best of Breed seventy-seven times. This little girl was always a crowd-pleaser, one of those rare bitches that made everyone, even competitors, happy when she won. "Jenny" is owned by Marjadele Schiele, O'The Ridge Westies, Barrington, Illinois. *Photo courtesy Martin Booth Photography, Inc.*

15 Training for Showing

Training your dog for the show ring should be started as soon as you have decided that you own a "show prospect" and plan to show the dog. If a kennel club is located in your area, you can enter your puppy when he is three months old in a "fun match" or "puppy match," depending on when the match is held. Westie breed clubs also hold puppy matches. There could be several fun matches held by nearby kennel clubs. If you plan to show your dog, by all means become affiliated with a dog club so that you will know about all the activities.

In addition to the matches and shows, kennel clubs usually hold conformation training classes. Some clubs hold them year-round, while others hold them for six to eight weeks before their AKC licensed show. These classes are wonderful training for both you and your dog. Sometimes a nominal fee is charged; other times the classes are free. The trainers are usually kennel club members who donate their time to help people learn to show dogs. The classes, usually held once a week, give the dogs the opportunity to learn under conditions similar to those at dog shows.

At the classes, your dog will encounter people who are strange to him. This will help him to become accustomed to having someone who he does not know inspect him. He will learn to gait in a line of other dogs. People at the classes who understand dogs can help your dog to stand quietly while a stranger inspects the dog's teeth. These are all activities with which he should be familiar before being entered at a dog show.

If no training classes are available in your area, check out the local Obedience group. You can enroll your dog as a means of getting him with a group of other dogs. You can explain that you do not wish to qualify the dog for an Obedience title. Your dog can learn to "Heel" and "Stand" rather than "Heel" and "Sit." The instructor and other dog owners can go over your dog as if for inspection, and the dog can learn to have someone examine his teeth. These classes, too, are usually held once a week.

THE GAITING PATTERNS

On the other days, you should work with your dog at home. Put on his slip collar and leash and work on the pavement. Gait the dog on your left side, with his head even with your left foot. As you work with your dog, always say his name first, then give him the command. For example, say "Duffy, heel!" Swing your left foot forward and move the dog along at your left hip. Gait the dog about twenty feet, then turn and return to the starting point. In the show ring, you will always want to keep the dog on the side where the judge is standing. Imagine the judge standing at the starting point. When you turn, the dog will turn in a half circle and remain on your left. In this "Straight Up and Back" pattern, the judge will see your dog's rear movement going away and his front movement returning. Keep the dog moving in a straight line, and keep enough slack in the lead so that the dog is, not "strung up" too tightly.

Practice moving in a circle, which is what you will do when you first gait in the ring. You can also practice the figure eight, which is taught in Obedience training. This pattern will not be used in the conformation ring, but it is an excellent exercise for training the dog to follow the handler. Next, practice the triangle. Gait about twenty feet and turn a corner. Gait about fifteen

126

Ch. Carus Limelite, bred by Charles and Caroline Rarey and owned by Mrs. J. H. Baldwin of McKeesport, Pennsylvania, is a beautiful and "typey" Westie dog, always owner-handled to his title.

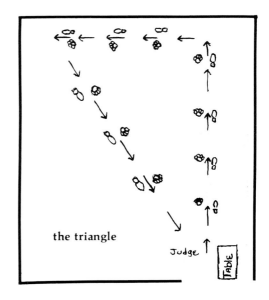

the triangle

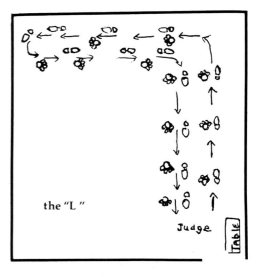

the "L"

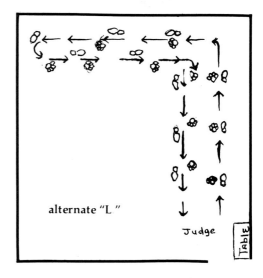

alternate "L"

feet and turn another corner, returning diagonally to your starting point.

Than you are ready for the "L." In this pattern, you will gait about twenty feet and turn the corner. Gait about ten feet. At the end of the "L," both you and the dog will turn so that the dog will be on your right side, which means that you will have to change hands on the lead. This is to keep the dog to the judge's side. It is best to change hands on the lead just before you reach the end of the "L" so that you will make a smoother turn. At the corner, turn and go back to the starting point. The dog will still be on your right side. There is an alternate method of completing the "L." As you approach the corner, change the lead back to your left hand. As you get to the corner, move the dog in front of your body and proceed back to the starting point with the dog on your left side. This looks very nice in the ring. It is only slightly more difficult to teach to the dog, who may resist moving in front of you when you reach the corner.

If you plan to take your dog to the outdoor shows, practice gaiting in the grass as well as on pavement. I need to move my Westie at a slightly faster pace when gaiting in the grass, because it seems to help him get his feet up out of the grass. Often, grass at outdoor shows is coarse and stiff, even if well mowed. Outdoor show grounds are not smooth and level like the rubber mats at indoor shows. You and your dog should learn to gait on both surfaces. If you are going to the outdoor shows, do not let rainy days keep you from working with the dog. Put on your raincoat and take the dog out to work. A dog that has never been shown with the rain pelting down may have a big disadvantage at a rainy day show. Training him to work in the rain could very well give you the winning edge someday.

As you practice the various patterns, imagine that you are bringing the dog up to the judge. Give the dog a command to stop so that you are about three feet from the imaginary judge. Keep the dog standing alert by training him to wait for a piece of bait. In the early training, have a piece of bait in your hand. Train the dog to stand about three feet from you until you give him the bait. If he approaches you, place your foot gently against his chest to keep him at a distance. Then give him the bait. Gradually lengthen the time it takes for you to get the bait out of your pocket so that your dog will learn to be patient until the bait is handed to him.

Practice moving in a straight line and in a circle at various speeds. Begin at a very slow speed, accelerate to a trot, then return to a slow pace. Give your dog commands to follow along with the different speeds. For example, say "Duffy, slo-o-o-w, slow, now faster, faster," as you move along. This is to teach the dog a smooth transition from one speed to another. In the show ring, you may need to slow your pace if the handler ahead of you is moving more slowly. If your dog must slow abruptly, he will break his gait and appear awkward. Your dog must learn to stay even with your hip and follow wherever you go at whatever pace you set.

While you are working, you must learn to fold the leash into your left palm. Pivot your left wrist back and forth as you grasp the leash into folds about four inches in length. This allows you to extend the leash by releasing one or two folds. It also allows you to shorten the leash by taking up slack in short folds. Learn to move without swinging your right arm. Most people swing both arms when walking as a matter of propulsion and balance. Your left arm will be holding the leash and guiding the dog, which gives every new handler a compulsion to swing the right arm. A widely swinging right arm can be a real distraction from the dog. Press your right elbow firmly to your side, and train yourself not to swing that arm.

127

Keep the dog alert by training him to wait for a piece of bait.

You should also train yourself to focus attention on your dog. Learn to walk with your upper torso turned slightly to the left so that your shoulders are at an angle. A Westie is a small dog, and this posture subtly attracts the judge's eyes to the dog. You will also get a better view of your dog if your shoulders are turned toward him.

At first you will teach the dog to follow your pace. Next, you must teach yourself to gait at the dog's best pace. A good place to practice this is at a shopping center, in an area where the storefronts are windowed. Gaiting in front of the windows provides a mirrored reflection of dog and handler. Keep your eyes on the mirrored dog. Pace him so that he exhibits the best front thrust and smooth drive behind, head up and tail up.

Practice this as often as possible. You need to memorize the pace at which you move the dog. When you have mastered that, practice watching the dog from above, which is what you will be doing in the show ring. Watch his front feet thrusting forward so that you get the feel of his best movement. These trips to the shopping center are also excellent training for the dog to ride in his crate. By going daily to this strange territory, he develops much self-assurance.

Choose the early morning hours in the beginning. Put your dog in his crate before he has been fed, and drive to the shopping center. He will not be fed in the morning before a show either, so this is good practice. In the morning,

128

traffic will be at a minimum at the shopping center. This will make the dog's first visits there less confusing. After several trips, go later in the day. By about one o'clock, many trucks, cars, and people will be around. In addition to gaiting in front of the windows, take the dog for a walk around the parking lot, where he will encounter strange feet and noises. If he shies, just tell him in a cheerful voice how silly he is and keep going. If you encounter dog lovers who want to talk to you, stop and chat. Put one hand under the dog's lower jaw, and invite the stranger to pet him. A dog has to drop his lower jaw in order to bite, so this should be perfectly safe.

When leaving for the shopping center with the crated dog, remember to take some treats for baiting. Also take a roll of paper towels and a plastic bag and/or the pooper-scooper. Your dog may decide to relieve himself, as do most dogs, after the excitement of going for a ride in the car. Be prepared to clean up any droppings so that your dog will not be guilty of "fouling the footway," as the British say. No shopper should be allowed to accidentally step into your dog's droppings. He is your dog, so clean up after him.

STACKING

In addition to learning to gait, your dog must learn to "stack." This means that he must stand in the show pose, both on the ground and on the table. The puppy becomes accustomed to standing in one spot when he is groomed with the noose of the grooming arm around his neck. This makes training the dog to stack easy. If you are starting with a puppy, place the three middle fingers of your right hand between his front legs. Lift his front so that his feet are just off the floor. As his toes drop downward, allow his body to come down to stand on them. With your left hand, press lightly on his shoulders, and he will firm them up under the pressure. Grasp him under the neck with your right hand to hold his head in position. Run your left hand down his back to the tail. Then place the middle fingers of your left hand between his back legs, lifting the hindquarters slightly off the ground. As you set the rear back in place, move his rear feet slightly backward. Again stroke the back from neck to tail, this time exerting gentle pressure to make

Train yourself to focus attention on your dog by turning your upper torso slightly to the left.

him firm his stance. Push his tail into the upright position.

Use any word of command that you prefer—Stack, Stand, or Show. Just be consistent. Also be consistent in the order in which you arrange the various parts in the stack. Do it the same way every time. If you have a mirror, you will be able to see if his feet are correct and the tail is really up. From the reflected image, glance at the dog. This way you can remember how he looks from above when he is correctly stacked to look his best.

When you are stacking the dog on the ground, you will need to get down with him. Squatting, and sitting on your heels, can get quite uncomfortable during a big class, while kneeling makes getting back up very awkward. Most professional handlers kneel on the left knee, keeping the sole of the right foot on the ground. It is easier to rise from this position. If you are not very tall, and if you have a well-trained dog, you can just bend from the waist to reach down and hold the tail in an upright position with your left hand. Then, by taking up the slack in the leash in your right hand, you can keep the dog's head upright.

As the puppy gets older, you will want to have him on a leash on the table. You can use the martingale or a narrow lead of nylon tape with a slip clasp. This is the lead that most handlers use on the adult dog. The most commonly used width is three-sixteenths of an inch. This is a very narrow width but is much like the noose on the grooming arm. The "collar" should be worn snugly under the neck and across the base of the ears and skull. In this position, the narrow lead makes only a fine line of demarcation between the hair on the head and the hair on the neck. For gaiting the dog, the clasp is tightened to fit snugly but not tight enough to choke the dog.

When stacking the dog, learn to fold the lead into your right hand. With your fingers, loosen the clasp and pull it upward so that the collar forms a triangle behind the dog's ears. This helps to get the ears up. Terrier handlers lift the front of the dog with the lead until his feet are just off the floor or tabletop. This places the legs in correct position when the dog is lowered and it does not hurt the dog. He will only be suspended for a moment. Then firm the shoulders and continue the stacking. Set the back feet of the groomed show dog by grasping the point of the hock, first the left, then the right. Use your palm or comb to settle the side furnishings quickly, first the left, then the right. Remember that the left side of the dog is the one that the judge usually sees.

Lift the front of the dog with the lead (note toes dropping down).

Firm the shoulders with a little pressure.

Nervous hands sometimes have damp palms (and who isn't nervous in the ring?). In using the lead to set the front and in grasping the hocks to set the rear feet, you have not smashed down the carefully brushed-up feet. Put the tail into position with the tips of the widely spread fingers of your left hand. When the judge views your dog in profile, your fingertips will be practically invisible along the tail.

To train your dog to carry his tail upright, tickle the tail up the back. Tail muscles work on reflex. The tail will pull forward and upright, away from your tickling fingers. The moment that the tail is held upright, stop the tickling. At the instant that the dog is holding the tail upright without stimulus, praise him. It will not take long for him to get the idea.

Training the dog to stand for the inspection of teeth requires the help of friends who know dogs. Each person should try to examine the dog's teeth while the dog is on the table. If the dog absolutely refuses to have his teeth examined, set him up with his back feet at the edge of the table. Place your left hand underneath the tail and your right hand underneath the dog's neck. As the dog backs away from the tooth inspector, assist the dog right off of the table! Make certain that you have a good grip on the dog. Obviously the dog should not be dropped, only made to think that he is falling. It should also be obvious that this is easiest to do before the dog becomes very large. It is a highly successful method. It should be done every time that the dog backs off from anyone trying to check his teeth. Put the dog in the same position and try again. Three "falls" off of the table are about average before you have a dog that is happy to stand for tooth inspection.

Some judges like the dog to be stacked at the front edge of the table. If your dog rears back,

Grasp the point of the hock to set back feet.

If the dog does not want to have his teeth inspected, support him firmly under the neck and under the tail, and "drop" him off the table.

Put the tail into position with the tips of the fingers.

130

like a rocking horse, tug backward on his tail, or give a small shove on his chest. The dog will quickly right himself. This is the same reverse psychology as used for the tooth inspection. If you try to pull the dog forward, he will resist all the more. Personally, I like my dog on the front edge of the table where the judge has easy access to the dog's head and teeth. Stack your dog in the center of the table, too, so that when you are in the ring, you can do what the judge prefers.

Some handlers prefer to toss the end of the lead up and around their necks when stacking the dog on the table. This leaves both hands free for stacking the dog. You may wish to try this method to see if it is easier for you than folding the lead into your right palm.

Your Westie will learn more and in less time with short training sessions, repeated often. Lavish on the praise for good work, and have a romp with the dog when the session is over. Work with the dog when he is "up." That is, work with a hungry dog. If he has just been fed and is wanting to take an after-dinner snooze, he will not have much enthusiasm. Work for varying periods of time. If all sessions are the same length of time, the dog will soon learn to let down after that time has elapsed. If your own schedule permits it, vary the time of day so that the dog becomes accustomed to working at different hours. Dog show judging schedules vary from show to show.

If you have difficulty teaching any one thing, work with the dog until he has done it correctly. Give instant praise for the good work, and proceed to another activity. In this way, your dog will learn what is expected of him. If you make him repeat the exercise, he may not do it correctly twice in a row, which would necessitate doing it again and again until he does it right again. If a Westie gets bored, you may as well give up for the day.

**American Canadian Bermuda Ch.
Laurie's Piper of the Rouge**

Like father, like son. Piper is a champion son of Am. Can. Ch. Shipmate's Hannibal, and like his sire, is also a top producer. Bred by Leonard H. Hunter, he was out of Ch. Annie's Memory of the Rouge and received by Mrs. Dorothea Daniell-Jenkins as a "return puppy" from his litter. Born in 1967, and still going strong, he is currently the sire of twelve champions and may outdistance his sire. His dam has a total of five champions to her credit.

Booth photo.

131

132

English and American Ch. Ardenrun 'Andsome of Purston was bred in England by Mrs. C. Oakley and imported by Dr. Alvaro Hunt, Bayou Glen, River Ridge, Louisiana. During his show career, "Andy" was the top winning Westie dog in the country, winning the Terrier Group 119 times, plus 39 Best in Show awards and six Specialty Best of Breed wins, which included two wins at the annual parent club Specialty at Montgomery County, Pennsylvania, where the entries are enormous. "Andy" is also a top producing stud dog, currently the sire of 16 champions with more to come, and including a finished litter of four (see page 34).

16 Show Biz

Dog exhibitors need to be a hardy lot. The old slogan above the New York City post office, which reads in part, "Neither snow nor rain nor heat nor gloom of night," would seem appropriate to describe the dedication of the devotees. Dog shows, like the NFL games, are held in spite of weather. On occasion, a show has had to be cancelled, in part or in whole, due to flood, tornado, or blizzard, but these are the rare exceptions. Entries have a three-week closing date, and no exhibitor worth his salt will let a little inclement weather keep him away from the show site with his exhibit, once the entry has been mailed. People who have trouble all week hearing the alarm clock that summons them to rise and shine for work seem to have no trouble at all in loading up the show gear and dogs to set out before dawn for a dog show.

In the old days, dogs and handlers traveled to shows by rail and Model T. Now, show dogs are transported by jet and in fancy motor homes, vans, and even subcompacts. Getting into the back of the station wagon to clean up the results of nervous diarrhea or car sickness may be all in the day's work. Donning your raincoat over your nightie to walk the dog on the motel parking lot, where you will encounter everyone you know, is an experience that many exhibitors have handled with aplomb.

The show site is a kind of organized pandemonium. It could be likened to being backstage before the curtain goes up on a big Broadway production, with the harried stagehands and the cacophony of the orchestra tuning up. In the grooming areas, the stars are being cleaned and brushed, sprayed and dried, clipped, combed, and scissored. Each one must be ready at the appointed hour to perform for the sole critic, the AKC-licensed judge. For each hopeful handler, every dog show is Opening Night. Never doubt that exhibiting dogs is a form of show business.

It is also a sport. Before the entries are mailed, hours are spent training the dog and training yourself to show your entry to his best advantage. This is equal to the time spent in perfecting any other sport. The golfer, the tennis player, the skier—all have spent many hours practicing their chosen sport. Showing dogs is more like a "team" sport, since you and your dog will be performing together. No serious dog exhibitor will simply put a leash on the family pet and lead the dog into the show ring.

For all this time and effort, the dog exhibitor receives nothing tangible except a strip of satin ribbon, purple for Winners, if he is lucky. Sometimes a trophy is donated by a local fancier of the breed as an extra bonus. To the uninitiated, showing dogs seems to be an activity for which insanity must be a prerequisite. Each exhibitor knows that only about 10 percent of the dogs present at the show will be winners that day. Still, more than 800 AKC-licensed, all-breed shows are held annually, in addition to the approximately 1,200 Specialties and all of the "fun matches." There certainly must be an awful lot of "nuts" out there.

Before I became interested in showing, I, too, thought that these people were demented. I thought that the dogs could not care less about being shown and that it was merely a big ego trip for the owners. That was before I discovered the pleasure in working with a really good dog. In the old days, I never realized the rapport that is established between dog and handler.

I also discovered that the dogs love the shows—at least mine do. The fun of sharing the day with your dog, the friendships made, the lessons learned, the anticipation of winning—all bring the fancier to the show site. Like golf, showing dogs can be a humbling experience. One day you are a hero, the next day, a bum. Every handler knows that you "can't win 'em all." However, the judge's placements at one show are only one person's opinion for one day. Wait till next week!

It is wonderful for dog exhibitors that all judges do not like the same virtues or loathe the same faults in dogs. If they did, each judge would select the same dog at every show. Eventually, other owners would decide not to make the effort to bring a dog to the show—and that would be the end of the dog shows.

Judges are all human, so every judge views the dogs brought into his ring with a different eye. Sometimes a breeder becomes a judge. During his experience as a breeder, he may have found one fault that he thought was intolerable in the breed. In the ring, during judging, he feels compelled to put down every dog with that fault.

134

The show site is a kind of organized pandemonium, with the "stars" being readied to perform.

Or, he may subconsciously look for some admired and elusive quality that his own breeding stock consistently failed to produce. When he finds it in a dog in the ring, he places that dog Winners. Some judges, regrettably, look only for the beauty of the dog, or the quality of coat and general condition, or the showmanship. Other judges look for the correct movement, which goes with correct structure and type. If I were a judge, movement would be my first consideration. But what one judge sees in a dog can be very different from what the previous judge saw, or from what the next judge will see.

If a judge loves your dog at one show but passes over the dog when you show under him again, you will wonder why. It may be that the second time your dog did not show well. Dogs have "off days," just like people. The dog also may have had different competition at the second show. In the company of these dogs in the ring, your dog has not looked as good as he did before. Anyone who reads show results published in the *American Kennel Gazette* will tell you that on three consecutive days, at three consecutive shows, under three different judges, with the exact same group of dogs in the ring, the placements may be totally different. The judge that did not like your dog the first time may put the dog up when he judges him again. This is why exhibitors know that tomorrow or next week their dogs may just as easily be Winners as those dogs that won.

The dedicated breed fancier knows the importance of the dog shows. The show ring is the Moment of Truth. Every dog looks great in his own backyard. It is at the show site, in the company of other dogs of his breed, that the dog can be evaluated. If you plan to become a breeder, there is no better place to learn what the word "quality" means. If you already are a breeder, the dog shows help you to evaluate your breeding program, since you and other breeders will be showing your best specimens.

No "short course" for showing dogs is possible. It is a hobby that takes time to master. In the days when the AKC licensed professional handlers, an apprentice needed to work for five years before applying for a license. This time was spent working with a professional, showing dogs every weekend of the year except for vacations. No owner-handler can be expected to know all of

the ropes in less time than that. During this time, you will thrill to your success and learn from your failures. A good friend once told me that you must have a good dog in which you believe, and you must show him until you finish him. I know that she was right. If you have a dog that you have shown ten times to ten different judges, and the dog has not taken Reserve Winners in competition, it is time to reevaluate your concept of the breed standard and the dog.

GETTING INTO SHOW BUSINESS

Everyone interested in registered dogs should have a copy of the AKC booklet "Rules Applying to Registration and Dog Shows." A booklet on "Obedience Regulations" is also available. These are obtained by writing the American Kennel Club. This information will tell you what you need to know about entering and showing your dog in either Conformation or Obedience. Any copy of the *American Kennel Gazette*, published monthly, will have a list of the annually licensed show superintendents, who accept entries.

Most clubs that host shows hire a superintendent whose staff prints a Premium List from information furnished by the club. This is an announcement of the show, its date and location, the breeds that will be judged, and the judges who will be present. The Premium List also mentions any trophies being donated, routes to the show site, local motels that take dogs, and all other pertinent information of interest to the exhibitor. Also included are official entry forms that give entry fees and the closing date for entries. Blank spaces are provided for the owner or handler to fill in the information about his dog—such as the dog show class in which he will be entered, his registered name and number, birthplace and birthdate, his sire and dam, plus the name of his breeder and his owner. This information will be used in the printing of the show catalogue, which will be available at the show site.

One of the official entry forms must be filled out and mailed to the office of the show superintendent in time to be received before the closing date. You must include a check or money order to cover the entry fee. Acknowledgement of your entry will be returned, along with a Judging Program, about seven to ten days before the show. The program tells you what time your dog will be judged and the number of the ring in which the judge will see him. If the judge were running late, your dog could be judged a little later than the stated time, but he can never be judged earlier.

When your entry is returned, the excitement begins. The Judging Program shows the number of Westies that will be shown. It lists the breed, followed by three numbers. For example, it may read: "West Highland White Terriers 10-6-2." This means that ten dogs, six bitches, and two "specials" will be entered at the show. The "specials" are the finished champions that have been entered for Best of Breed competition. If enough Westies are entered for a "major" (three, four, or five points), this adds to the anticipation.

Each year, the AKC reviews the entries of all the breeds of dogs that were in competition at shows the preceding year. Based on the number of dogs and bitches being shown, a decision is made concerning how many of each sex must be in competition for winning one to five points in the coming year. This annual review is done to assure the AKC and the exhibitors that the points are awarded on the basis of real competition and that no "cheap" champions are being made in the ring. The new point schedule for each of the districts is published in the April issue of the *American Kennel Gazette*. The new points go into effect annually on May 15. The points are also included in the front of every show catalogue.

If there are enough entries for two majors, one in each sex, it is really exciting. On the other hand, the program may read: "West Highland White Terriers 1-0-0," which means that only one dog has been entered. This is very disappointing to you, with the only entry. If you have a good dog, do not decide to just stay at home. Your dog will have to take Best of Breed, which entitles you to take him into the Terrier Group ring. This ring is considered the professional handlers' world. Do not be intimidated by that. If you have mastered the grooming skills and have a good dog, you will have the opportunity to place the dog in the Group. Just remember the

owner-handled Siberian Husky that went Best in Show at Westminster in 1980. Remember, too, that a dog taking Group I from the classes will be awarded the points figured at the highest rating of any breed in the ring. If another Terrier breed in the Group ring has taken five points that day, and you take Group I, your dog will be awarded five points, too.

Dog exhibitors in your area will be glad to tell you when nearby shows are to be held. Clubs that give shows have established weekends on which their shows are held. For example, a club may hold its show on the Saturday or Sunday of the fourteenth week of the year, every year. Some clubs hold two shows each year, one in the spring and one in the fall. If you do not know any exhibitors, the April issue of the *American Kennel Gazette* has a Master Show Dates list. Since a corresponding date table is also published, even an old April issue probably will contain information about the shows in your area.

Regular exhibitors are on the mailing lists of the show superintendents and regularly receive Premium Lists for the coming shows in their area. To get your name on the mailing lists, write to the superintendents, stating that you are a new exhibitor and wish to have the Premium Lists mailed to you. This takes time—rather like getting your first copy of a new magazine. In the meantime, if you want to enter a show, all you actually need is *any* official entry form. This can be a form from any Premium List for any show. Simply strike out the name and date on the official form, and print in the name and date of the show you wish to enter. You may even change the name of the show superintendent. You do need to get your entry to the correct show superintendent's office before the closing date, along with the correct entry fee. Any dog exhibitor will have a form that you can use, perhaps even an extra one for the show that you wish to enter.

GETTING THE SHOW ON THE ROAD

If you plan to exhibit your dog, you will need to line up your gear. In the beginning, you may want a checklist to be sure that all items are present. Once you become an old hand, you will seem to know when even one item is missing from the accumulated gear that is ready to go into the car. You will need your grooming table and arm; your box of grooming supplies and tools; some terry towels and newspapers; a smock or jacket to cover your clothing while you groom; and, if you are female, an extra pair of panty hose—just in case. For the dog, you should take a jug of water, a feeding dish or pan, and food and treats. Folding chairs in which to rest at the show site are usually always needed. Lunch from home and a thermos of coffee or your favorite beverage will be welcome. Food stands at dog shows are usually very crowded, and one must often wait a long time to buy a hot dog or hamburger, the usual fare sold. And, of course, you will want your dog and his crate, his collar with his license and rabies tag, and his leash. His show lead should be in the grooming box. Do not forget the rain gear, especially if this is an outdoor show. Also, do not forget the pooper-scooper, a roll of paper towels, and some trash bags.

These are the items needed for a nearby show. If your dog is to be shown at 8:00 A.M., you may need to drive to the city where the show is being held the night before in order to be at the show site in time to groom your dog and have him at ringside at the appointed time. In that case, you will need items for staying overnight. Show superintendents set the times for the judging of the various breeds. This means that *some* breed must open the show, in every ring. One of them could be Westies.

If you are staying at a motel or hotel with your dog, learn good habits from the beginning. Do not allow your dog to soil the room, the carpet, the bedspreads, or any other object. Dog clubs find a steadily decreasing number of motels and hotels that are willing to take dogs due to thoughtless and uncaring dog owners. It is incredible that so much damage is inflicted on innkeepers' property. Some states have gone so far as to ban all dogs from hotel and motel premises. Barking dogs that disturb other occupants are another problem.

Staying overnight with a dog is not that difficult. When you arrive, crate your dog. Take him out to relieve himself—on his leash, of course—and take along paper towels or the pooper-scooper. He is your dog. Clean up after him. Do not leave the dog unattended while you go to

dinner. There are plenty of fast-food restaurants with carry-out food. Take the dog along to get food, then return to your motel to eat it. Crate your dog for the night, and keep him quiet.

At the show, you will be on your feet for much of the day. Comfortable shoes are an absolute necessity. Clothing varies with the season but should be of the correct weight for comfort. Sometimes a suit of long johns would feel good at an outdoor show on a raw day. Male handlers should be neatly dressed in casual attire, with a tie and jacket in most cases. The basic rule of etiquette in dress for male handlers is that if the judge is a man and is wearing a jacket and tie, the handlers follow suit. A blazer jacket, with its handy pockets for carrying bait and a comb or brush, is a good choice. Female handlers should be casually dressed in a skirt and jacket, or pants and jacket. The woman handler needs pockets, too. Remember, ladies, you are there to show your dog to the judge. I have seen amateur women handlers in the ring whose lack of proper undergarments has made me wonder exactly what they had come to show. Long hair should be tied back or otherwise confined in some becoming way. Jangling charm bracelets and similar items of jewelry have no place in the show ring. Shoes for both men and women should have nonslip soles. Women's shoes should have low heels or wedge soles. Color of clothing should be selected to set off the dog. For example, white clothing does not enhance your white Westie. Because you will be chalking the dog, dark clothing will need to be covered with a grooming coat or smock while you are preparing the dog.

OPENING NIGHT

Plan to arrive at the show site with plenty of time for parking the car, unloading the gear and the dog, and getting it all to the grooming area, with about two hours to spare before judging. Westies must be groomed at the show site if they are to look their best for the judge. On one occasion, I decided to try grooming dogs at home the night before, with only "touch-up" grooming at the show. This was a local fun match where no points would be awarded and where I knew that my dogs would be the only Westies entered. Believe me, they would have represented no real competition had any other freshly groomed Westies been present. My dog did win the Terrier Group, but that was because he showed well, not because he looked his best.

If the show is outdoors, try to set up to groom under a tent or some other place in the shade. Otherwise, your dog will get very hot in the full sun, and so will you. At an indoor show, I prefer to groom as near as possible to the ring in which my dogs will be judged and/or near other Westie people. Get to work cleaning, drying, and chalking your dog, and be certain that he is *dry* and that *all of the chalk is out.* Then return the dog to his crate to rest and await his turn in the ring. If he has not been given the chance to relieve himself, allow him to go before he enters the ring.

This schedule should give you time to freshen up and go to the ring to watch your judge doing other breeds (be sure that someone keeps an eye on your crated dog). It is a good idea to watch the judge while he is doing other breeds so that you can observe his ring procedure. Most judges have preferred patterns of movement of dogs in their rings, and, once adopted, the same procedure will be used all day. The exception might be for a breed with only one or two entries. Your dog will have been assigned a number, which is in front of his name in the show catalogue and on the returned entry form. Before leaving the ring, ask the ring steward (when he has a free moment) for the arm band with your Westie's number on it. This is what you will wear as identification in the ring.

About fifteen minutes before you are due at ringside, put your dog back on the table. Pound his back, brush his head, and check him *thoroughly* for any traces of chalk. If you find any, work until you remove it. Then give the dog a final combing or brushing. Put on your jacket and arm band, and pick up the bait and any comb or brush that you want to take to the ring with you. If someone is with you, let him carry the show catalogue and a pen to mark the placements of the judging, for future reference. You probably will not remember who placed where, once the show is over. Pick up your dog and head for the ring. Break a leg—as they say in show business.

ON STAGE, EVERYONE!

At ringside, keep your dog in control at all times. Keep him next to you and away from other dogs. When your class is called, enter the ring and set up your dog quickly so that the judge will see him at his best. In the ring, a handler seems to need three sets of eyes: one on his own dog *at all times,* one on the judge, and one on the dog ahead. Your most important focus of attention must be on your dog, with an occasional glance at the judge and the other dogs. You will learn to take in a good bit with your peripheral vision. No judge likes handlers to stare at him. If the judge speaks to you, give him your attention and a courteous answer. Otherwise, volunteer nothing to him. Remember that the judge is here, often without pay, to spend the day appraising dogs for exhibitors. His schedule is very tight. He is expected to judge twenty-five dogs per hour. If you have watched his judging of other breeds, you will know the preferred procedure in the ring.

The first movement of dogs in the ring is in a circle. The judge will indicate his readiness for the class to begin. If you are not the first in line, allow plenty of room between your dog and the one ahead so that you can gait your dog at his

138

Keep your dog next to you and under control at ringside.

best pace. If your dog is one of those that wants to lunge after the dog behind him, try to be the last one into the ring and take last place in line. After the class is taken around, the handlers and dogs return to one side of the ring and await the examination of dogs on the table and the individual gaiting. While the judge has his attention on the dogs on the table, let your dog relax a little, especially if the class is large. Stand facing him in the line, and offer him a treat. Or you can drop to one knee facing him, keeping him in the show stack. You need to watch the judge frequently. While he is looking at one dog, he could glance over his shoulder at your dog. Be sure that your dog is in control and is looking his best.

As the judge finishes with each dog on the table, he will ask the handler to gait the dog in the preferred pattern. If your dog is to be next on the table, place him there as soon as the dog before him begins the individual gaiting. This gives you time to set your dog up on the table for the judge. The judge will usually first examine the dog's head, including the teeth. Stand far enough away to allow the judge a good view. Then the dog's body and coat will be examined. If the judge ruffles up the coat, brush it back into

place as soon as he has finished examining it. Then the judge will examine the dog's rear structure and check the dog for testicles. At all times, control your dog, but stay out of the judge's way. You will next be signaled to gait your dog in the pattern that the other handlers have used.

Go to the starting point and await the judge's signal to start. At the corners or turns, glance up at the judge and make eye contact. As you return to the judge, stop your dog about three feet away, and get your dog alert with a piece of bait. Some judges throw keys or other objects to alert the dog. If you have done a good job of training your dog to stand alert to await a small treat, this is all that is needed. The judge will want to see the dog's expression, so do not block the judge's view. Then you and your dog will return to the end of the line. Set your dog up while you wait for the other dogs to be gaited.

What happens next will depend upon the size of the class and the judge's preference. He may rearrange dogs in the line or motion some dogs out of line, directing them to circle again. He may select two dogs to gait side by side across the ring for another look. He may have the dogs come to the center of the ring and "spar," nose to

While one handler is doing the individual gaiting, another handler sets up his dog for inspection on the table.

139

The first movement of dogs in the ring is in a circle. Allow plenty of room between your dog and the dog in front of you.

nose. I deplore this practice. It is done to arouse the Terrier "spirit." I feel that it gives all the Terrier breeds a bad public image to present them as fighting dogs in the ring. Terriers were developed to fight game, not other dogs. If they had been scrapping among themselves, they never would have caught the fox. Still, I have shown under judges that even sparred the bitches. If the class is small, the judge may simply have the group circle the ring again. During the final circling, the judge will point to his placements, "one, two, three, four," and in a wink, the judging is over. These dogs which have "come in in the ribbons" then line up with their handlers before the numbered placards in the ring, where they will be handed their ribbons by the judge. If you have placed in the ribbons, thank the judge for your award as he hands it to you, and leave the ring.

If your dog has taken second place in his class, do not leave ringside. After Winners Dog (or Winners Bitch) has been selected, Reserve Winners must be chosen. The Reserve Winners class consists of all the first-place class winners plus the second-place winner from the class in which the Winners Dog was entered. For example, if the first-place Open Dog is awarded Winners Dog, the second-place Open Dog must compete for Reserve Winners Dog. Or, if

Winners Dog was awarded to the first-place Puppy Dog, the second place Puppy Dog must compete for Reserve Winners Dog. If your dog took second place, he may be needed for further judging.

It is up to you to watch the judge's placements of the dogs and know the number that was awarded your dog. As the handlers stand in front of the numbers on the placards, the judge will mark his book from the arm band numbers of the handlers. On more than one occasion, a ring-wise handler has forced a novice handler into a lower position in the line. It has happened that newcomers have been jostled from first to second, or from second to third, by some unscrupulous person who was counting on the novice's confusion and naivete. Do not allow it to happen to you. If you have paid attention and know that you are right, refuse to budge. Just say politely, "I am sorry, but the judge placed me here," and stand your ground.

Always remember to congratulate the winner before leaving the area. If you did not win, be a graceful loser. Your turn to win will come. Winning is a lonely business. After the judging, all the losers will have each other for company and can gather together to discuss dogs and the judging. Wait till next week!

When you and your dog return to the grooming area, offer the dog a drink from the jug of water that you have brought from home. Water often varies from place to place, which is why you should bring water from home. Your dog may not like the taste or smell of the different chemicals used to treat the water, and some dogs get diarrhea from drinking strange water. Remember to give him a small amount of food or some *Milk Bone®*. Now that he has done his work for the day, he should be rewarded, both with food and the praise of his master.

Outdoor shows can get very hot for your dog. He will suffer from the heat more than you will. Always keep him in the shade, even if it can only be the shade of your own body. On hot days, see that he has plenty of water, even if you have to dry and chalk his beard again before the judging. An automobile parked with closed windows is like an oven. When you return to load up, get the car cool for your dog as soon as possible. Load the dog last so that he is in a hot car for the shortest possible time.

140

The judge inspects this dog's coat quality and depth.

17 The Professional Handler

A handler is anyone who shows a dog in the ring. It could be the dog's owner, a member of the family, or an interested friend. A professional handler is one who accepts a fee for handling another person's dog. In most cases, the dog lives with the professional handler and travels to the shows until he gets his title. Then the owner may wish to have the dog campaigned as a "special," being shown in Best of Breed competition and, it is hoped, on to a Group I and even Best in Show.

The professional handler was an American innovation in dog showing. In the days when travel was slow and there was considerable distance to cover between shows, dog owners often needed someone who was free to take a dog on the show "circuit." Over the years, the ranks of handlers have vastly increased. Now, between 2,000 and 3,000 handlers show dogs for owners nationwide. Many of these people make handling their sole occupation and livelihood. The services of handlers are gradually becoming more in demand in Great Britain and other countries.

Due to the high cost of gasoline, the use of professional handlers undoubtedly will grow. The handler often travels with twenty or more dogs in one vehicle, whereas the owner-handler usually travels with one or two. The handler charges a fee for the dog's room and board, plus a fee for handling the dog in the ring. Grooming and conditioning of the dog are included in the services. In addition, the handler mails in the entries for the shows and bills these costs to the owner. If the dog is shown in the Group ring and takes a placement, the handler usually charges another fee, depending on the placement. If the dog is shown in the Best in Show competition and wins that plum, the handler again charges an extra fee. If trophies are won, these go to the owner; if any prize money is won, it goes to the handler.

Owners often consider a "pro" handler a luxury that they cannot afford. In reality, the fees paid to a handler may be less than the cost of finishing the dog yourself. While the board bill may seem higher than feeding the dog at home, it covers the cost of conditioning and grooming the dog, and while the fee for handling the dog in the ring may seem high, it covers the cost of transportation to the show site. This fee may not be more than the owner's transportation and motel bill, plus meals. The entry fees would be the same, no matter who showed the dog. Handlers who really know their "onions" and their dogs will get the dog finished faster than most owner-handlers. The handler will set the dog down in the ring looking his absolute best. He knows what the judge is looking for in a dog, and he knows how to get the best out of the dog.

Handlers often travel to Great Britain and bring Westies back to the United States. The dogs are usually sold to a client, with the handler often conditioning the dog for its new owner and showing the dog to its title. Many handlers of top-winning dogs "special" the dogs for the owner, charging the owner an annual fee with bonuses for Group placements and/or Best in Show. It adds greatly to the prestige of any handler to have a top-winning dog in his entourage.

Many owners of show dogs would never set foot in the show ring. Still, they want to own a dog with a "Ch." in front of his name and a certificate from the AKC to frame as proof. After that, they are content to keep the dog at home and enjoy owning a champion. To other owners who really enjoy working with dogs, the only way to finish a champion is to do it yourself. These people get much pleasure and pride from knowing that their dogs are always owner handled. However, many of them may need the

142

Above:

They have done it again. George Ward and "The Pedlar" have just been awarded Best of Breed at the parent club's floating specialty held in Louisville, Kentucky, in March 1973. The Pedlar's proud owner looks on as Judge, the late Dr. Frank Booth, presents the award. Ch. Purston Pinmoney Pedlar's forty-eight Best in Show wins have never been equalled. "The Pedlar" was bred in England by Mrs. J. M. Fulford.

Below:

A legend in his own time is George Ward, considered by many to be the top Terrier handler living. Mr. Ward has been handling Terriers all of his life, having shown many of the top winning dogs to hundreds of Best in Show awards. Here Mr. Ward waits at ringside with Ch. Purston Pinmoney Pedlar and his owner, the late Mrs. B. G. Frame. Mrs. Frame was a Westie fancier for thirty-plus years, owning and breeding many fine dogs under her Wigtown prefix and under the Wigmac prefix with Mrs. E. P. McCarty.

services of a professional handler if unforeseen circumstances arise which prevent them from finishing their own dogs. It may be that the dog needs to be taken to a district where the entries are large enough for "majors," since every dog needs two major wins under two different judges in order to complete his title. Sometimes owner-handlers will seek out a professional handler at the show site and hire his services to take a dog into the ring as a "walk in," feeling that the competition at the show that day is keen and that the handler will show the dog to better advantage.

Thus, the role of the professional handler in the "dog game" continues to grow, and the numbers of persons engaged in handling dogs for their owners grow along with the need. Until 1978, the AKC licensed all professional handlers. It was the AKC's decision concerning which breeds a handler was qualified to show before a license to handle those breeds was granted. When licensing was discontinued, the ranks of handlers swelled. Now, on the entry forms and in the show catalogues, anyone showing a dog for his owner is listed as the "Agent." There are two organized groups of handlers, the Professional Handlers Association and the Dog Handlers Guild. The PHA has been in existence for several years, while the DHG is a newer organization. These two groups represent only a small percentage of working handlers, but they have established codes of ethics for their members to follow and screen applicants carefully before admitting them to membership.

Owners who feel that they cannot finish a dog themselves often wonder when they should hire the services of a handler. I always advise owners to train the dog for showing themselves—in the backyard, on the pavement, in classes, and at fun matches. Groom the dog yourself to accustom him to being on the grooming table. Condition the dog yourself with exercise and proper nutrition. Then hire the services of the best Terrier specialist that you can find. Your dog will be home in no time, finished.

If you send your dog to a handler out of coat, out of condition, underweight or overweight, and untrained, the best handler in the business may need to keep your dog for several months before the dog will be in shape to be shown. It takes time to get a dog trained and in

good coat and weight. If you decide to do it this way, understand that the dog could be gone for months on end.

Carefully check out the handler before you ship or drive your dog to him. Talk to other owners who have used the handler's services. They will be able to vouch for his ethics. If the handler has been showing a top-winning dog for several months, you can rest assured that his relationship with the owner is impeccable. Instead, talk to owners for whom the handler has showed a dog only a short time, perhaps until the dog finished his title. Ask if they were satisfied and consider the handler to be ethical.

For example, it is not considered ethical for a handler to show two dogs (or bitches) of the same breed in the classes, but some handlers have been known to do this. The two dogs could be entered in two different classes and have to compete against each other in Winners class for the points. Some owners have complained that their dog was taken into the ring "looking like a bum," making points for the other dog. In some instances, the other dog belonged to the handler.

Handlers decide their own itineraries—such as South for the winter months. If your dog is going to a handler to get his majors, be sure that he will be entered at shows in a district where the entries are consistently high. The handler may be going to an area where the entries of Westies, as well as other breeds, may be small. If the handler has a dog that is being "specialed," he may wish to enter the small shows in the hope of placing the special high up in the Group judging, and your dog will be entered at those shows. If the entries are too small for majors, the handler will not show your dog, and you will not be charged a handling fee, but your entry fee will be forfeited and the weekend wasted while the board bill mounts. Have it fully understood that your dog will stay with the handler until the dog gets his majors. It could be that the handler knew all along that he had a previous commitment to show another dog in two months but did not bother to tell you. Then you will be told that your unfinished dog is being sent home.

Some dogs are so unhappy with a handler that they have to be force-fed. It is natural for a dog to feel strange away from home and to skip a few meals at first. But some dogs must be force-fed to keep up weight and even to stay alive. The handler may never advise the owner of this. If I knew that my dog was that unhappy, I would have him sent home at once, as I believe most owners would. Of course, a greedy handler is not going to tell you. Reports of inhumane treatment of dogs circulate in the show world, from claws being cut so short that the dog had to lift his feet very quickly (which was why it was done) to dogs being kicked into submission. I remember one incident that really upset me. The handler of a male Maltese had wound a rubber band tightly around the dog's penis so that the dog could not urinate on his freshly cleaned, long side furnishings, which would have made extra work for the handler.

These samplings of some of the pitfalls in hiring a handler are offered to alert the dog owner to problems that may arise unless the handler is ethical and humane. There are *many* expert and ethical handlers in the business of showing dogs for owners. Get two or three opinions on anyone whom you plan to hire. Just be sure that you are sending your dog with someone who you can "trust out of town."

144

Fairtee Chortle Checkmate, C.D., and his owner Mary Robinson wait their turn to try the high jump during open obedience class practice.

Barber photo

18 Fun
Further Afield

Beyond the confines of the Conformation ring lies a whole world of fun with a Westie. Most people do not start off with a show specimen. Being "pet quality" does not make the dog some kind of second-class citizen. This dog can have other training and other titles after his name. Whether Champion of Record or pet, a Westie has other dimensions to be enjoyed by his owner. These are Obedience, Tracking, and Working Terrier trials. For these sports, the Terriers are an underdeveloped resource for fun, awaiting discovery by the owner and by the public.

In a Westie we have a small and compact dog of high intelligence, full of bounce and energy. To him, "sport" is the name of the game. His independent spirit and dominant characteristics make him something of a challenge. These are the qualities which all true Terrier lovers appreciate the most. Perhaps that is because these people have the same qualities as the dogs: spirit, spunk, determination, and drive.

OBEDIENCE TRAINING

Classes in Obedience are to be found almost everywhere. This training is for every dog, regardless of breed. Basic Obedience training results in a dog that heels on a slack lead, sits and stays on command, and comes when called. This makes every dog a better companion. Most Obedience classes today place the emphasis of the training on the dog whose owner plans to enter the dog in Obedience Trial competition. For this reason, puppies under six months of age usually are not accepted for classes, even though only about five percent of "students" are eventually entered at the trials.

This is unfortunate, because the best time for training a puppy has already passed. Between three weeks and four months of age, the puppy is the most receptive to learning what the owner wants him to do. If he is not taught, he will learn on his own, but not what the owner wants. I have heard Obedience training for Westies criticized "because it breaks the spirit." Nonsense! Teaching a dog to please his master establishes trust and confidence in the handler, not fear of him.

A puppy should be taught to heel on a slack lead, sit, fetch, and come when called before he is four months old. This does not need to be intensive training. Fifteen minutes a day spent with the puppy, in simple exercises and with firm but gentle correction, is all that is required. Remember to have a romp before and after the serious training, with lavish praise for good work. If you have done this early training, you will be ahead of the game in Obedience classes. However, no dog is ever too old to learn.

Many Obedience trainers have been seen to look skyward when a Westie shows up for class. These trainers do not understand the breed's ability to learn and willingness to please. Neither do they understand the nature of the dog. The classes are really organized to teach the owner how to control his dog and to teach the dog by repetition. The Westie, being brainier than most,

learns very quickly. He will be bored to death with doing the same exercise again and again. In Obedience training, the dog is being taught to please the owner. The Westie loves to please, but he wants it to be fun.

The minute that you sense a lagging interest, stop. Leave the class and take the dog for a short exploratory walk. Then return and work with the class some more. Your Westie will still learn all that the other class members have learned. Reinforce the lessons with daily work at home. Short sessions of fifteen to thirty minutes, working with the dog until he has done each exercise correctly once, exuberant praise for this good work, instant correction as needed—these are the keys to training a Westie. Long, boring sessions and ironhanded methods will get you nowhere with a Westie.

If you come to an impasse on some exercise—and this happens with all breeds—it is better to begin at the beginning and relearn the entire exercise. Break it into its simplest parts. Then put the parts together and praise the dog when he has done it right. There are tricks to all trades, dog training included. Individual dogs may need individual ploys, and problems in training may need individual solutions. Sometimes several different ideas must be tried to find the right one for an individual dog. Sometimes it becomes a matter of using enough imagination to outsmart the dog. This is what makes the inexact science of dog training such an interesting hobby. If there were no challenge, there would be no reward.

Whether you plan to enter the trials or not, you and your Westie will enjoy the training. A Westie enjoys the social outing as well as the learning. Remember the basics—instant correction, lavish praise, consistency, and patience. Add determination and imagination, and your Westie will soon have his Companion Dog degree.

TRACKING

For the outdoorsman, some Obedience clubs offer Tracking Tests as an adjunct to their Obedience Trials. A Westie, with his most excellent nose, is a "natural" for this work. It is surprising that so few Westies have been entered at Tracking Tests, considering the breed's natural

146

Windermere of Rosewood, C.D.X., T.D. ("Windy") is up, up, and away over the hurdle. "Windy's" owners are Vern and Mary Bell of Belvar Westies, Durham, North Carolina.

Left: Windermere of Rosewood, C.D.X., T.D., starts at the flag to follow the track. Below, top left: "Windy" follows the track with her owner-handler, Mary Bell. Below, top right: "Windy" is game for following the scent through the tall brush. Below, bottom left: She works one of the turns in the track. Below, bottom right: But, that does not keep her from finding the glove at the end of the track. "Windy" is the second Westie ever to get a Tracking Degree. There is an advanced degree in tracking, T.D.X., and she is working toward that, as well as her Utility Degree in Obedience, with her owners, Vern and Mary Bell, Durham, North Carolina.

Bell photos

instincts as a hunter of small game. A dog does not need a Companion Dog degree to compete in Tracking.

Training your dog and training yourself may take months of work. People who are "hooked" on tracking claim that it is the best of all possible sports with a dog. In Obedience, the dog is pleasing the master. In Tracking, the dog is pleasing himself. You will be out in the open walking a half-mile or more. A tracking lead is twenty to forty feet long. This is attached to the harnessed dog, who will be far out ahead of you, following the scented track. At tests, the track is laid with right-angle turns so that there will be two different wind directions. As the dog follows the invisible trail of scent, he must take into account the wind, weather, and the very air. The handler must learn to "read" his dog, as the dog leads the way to the leather glove or wallet at the end of the track. This very special communication between handler and dog, as they share a secret knowledge, is a rare experience granted to the tracking enthusiast.

Even if you are not the outdoors type, tracking could be just fascinating enough to get you out for some healthful outdoor exercise. Your Westie will be very glad that you decided to go! Training can be started in your own backyard. Seek information on the training from your local Obedience group. The Westie being shown in Conformation should not be taken tracking, because working in the brush is not conducive to growing coat, but the pet or the Champion are both excellent candidates for the fun of tracking.

WORKING TERRIER TRIALS

These trials are another outdoor sport held in many parts of the country by the American Working Terrier Association.* Many owners of Westies and other small Terrier breeds feel that just because their dogs are city dwellers is no reason to allow them to lose their innate ability as

---

*To contact this group, write to Mrs. Patricia Lent, Dogwood Cottage, R.D. 2 38A, Franklinton, North Carolina 27525. Mrs. Lent has written a book "Sport with Terriers" (Arner Publishers 1973), which is recommended reading.

hunters. If you are interested in seeing your Westie "in action," you will want to learn about the training and the trials.

Eligibility for the trials is limited to Terrier breeds which are small enough to get through a nine-inch drainpipe. (An exception is made for one of the Hounds—the Dachshund.) Novice A class is for puppies six to twelve months of age. Novice B class is for older dogs that have not competed before or that have not yet scored 100 points in Novice. Open class is for entries which have already scored 100 points in Novice.

Before the trial, wooden forms are buried in the ground to make a nine-by-nine inch tunnel, with about nine inches of soil piled on top. Scent is laid at the entrance to the tunnel to attract the dogs. At the end of the tunnel are steel bars and the "quarry"—some caged rats. Both the bars and the cage prevent injury to any of the animals. Above this, at ground level, is a flap which can be raised so that the judge can observe the dog. The Novice tunnel is ten feet long with one right-angle turn. The Open tunnel is thirty feet long with three right-angle turns. The Novice entry must enter the tunnel and find the "game" in one minute and "work" for thirty seconds (give voice, dig, bite the bars). The Open entry must find the "game" in thirty seconds, although he must travel three times as far and turn the extra corners. He must "work" the "game" for a full minute. The dogs are timed with a stopwatch.

Dogs are worked individually, with other dogs present being crated or leashed. The dog is released at a flag ten feet from the tunnel opening. Any handler who fears that his dog may take off for the hinterlands when released tells the spectators before he releases his dog so that all those present can help if this should happen. The handler of the Novice entry is allowed to walk to the tunnel entrance with his dog and give one command. The Open handler must release his dog at the flag, give one command, and remain at the flag. Dogs scoring 100 points in the Open class are awarded the Certificate of Gameness.

After the trials, Novice clinics are held. Entry fees for the trials are very low, and many owners enter dogs that have never been to a trial, often with rewarding results. If permission is granted by the landowner, some groups hold hunts after the trials. Any dog bringing a woodchuck (groundhog) to ground is granted the coveted Certificate of Gameness. Many landowners welcome this easy way to rid the property of vermin. Many of the dogs entered at the trials are Champions of Record or are on their way to their titles.

The American Working Terrier Association has done much groundwork in the recent years since this group started, standardizing the trials and spreading the word about this whole new way to enjoy a Terrier. The trials are attracting more and more enthusiasts and spectators, even though this is a "show" where all the action takes place underground. As for the dogs, they are in their element, doing what they were bred to do. Any game dog will be delighted with this sport. He will be hoping that he is going hunting again every time that he goes for a drive. Do not omit the bitches. Generally, a bitch is a better hunter than a dog.

There is much more to a Westie than that spruce "soap carving" gaiting jauntily around the show ring. Under that cute and cuddly facade lies the heart of a courageous hunter, useful as well as beautiful. This is an all-around dog that can be enjoyed in many ways.

Warren Ashbrook, Pittsburgh, Pennsylvania, watches his bitch, P. J.'s Good Witch of Oz, pick up the scent at the flag. Note the judges behind the brush. Then, "G. W." locates the entrance to the tunnel and is about to enter and find the "game."

149

150

Ch. Charlain's Holly-Go-Love-Leah

Holly is the dam of five champions of the six puppies that she produced by two different sires. She was bred twice to Ch. Sno-Bilt's Aquarius and once to Ch. Hilltop's See More-o-Me. Each breeding resulted in a litter of two puppies. Five of the six completed their titles. The sixth puppy went Winners Bitch at the huge Montgomery County specialty in her first show, a five-point major win. She accrued about nine points toward her championship before being sold to a new home where she was retired from showing. This is a fine example of "quality not quantity" breeding. Holly was bred and is owned by Frank and Carol Boatwright, Downers, Grove, Illinois.

19 The Joys and the Problems of Breeding

When owners of registered Westies consider breeding dogs, they should recall the line from the marriage ceremony admonishing that it "should not be entered into lightly, but soberly and advisedly." Breeding dogs can be rewarding, but it also can be a heartbreaking experience if things go awry. Before anyone decides to embark, he should know as much as possible about becoming a breeder. Too many people believe that breeding dogs results in large bank accounts. That is the first idea from which the newcomer to breeding must disabuse himself. Once he understands that breeding dogs will probably cost him money, not make him money, he is able to view breeding in a different light.

The responsibilities of the breeder are many. First comes the selection of the breeding partners. Once the breeding has been accomplished, there is the care of the bitch during her pregnancy, with a high-quality protein diet and daily exercise. When it is time for the puppies to be born, the breeder must be prepared to spend many anxious hours at the whelping box, assisting with the delivery. In some instances, help from the veterinarian may be needed.

The neonatal puppies must be kept in a warm environment. Some puppies may need supplemental feeding around the clock. If the dam has problems, the entire litter may need feeding, around the clock. In purebred dogs, the neonatal death rate is estimated to be as high as 40 percent. The experienced breeder knows this and is prepared to give as many hours as it takes to see the litter through the first three or four weeks.

Once the puppies are on "all fours," at three weeks of age, the dam takes less interest in cleaning up after them. When weaning begins, at five weeks, and the puppies are eating some meals of food other than breast milk, the dam will abandon her duties of cleaning the nest entirely. This work then becomes the duty of the breeder. Each puppy will relieve himself about five times a day, and the puppy pen must be kept clean.

Many trips must be made to the veterinarian, too. The dam should be seen shortly after whelping, especially if she has retained any of the placentas. Weather and circumstances permitting, the dewclaws should be removed before the puppies are one week old. At four weeks, the puppies should be taken to the veterinarian for worm checks, and at six to eight weeks, they should have their first shot of measles vaccine. The veterinarian will advise the owner when the second and third shots are needed. Male puppies must be carefully checked for the descent of testicles.

Then comes the responsibility of getting the puppies into good homes. Everyone who wants a puppy is not necessarily a person who should have a Westie, or even any dog. Careful screening of prospective puppy buyers is absolutely essential. You brought these helpless little darlings into the world. It is your responsibility to find them good homes. To that end, you must

When the puppies are eating some meals of food, the work of keeping the quarters clean becomes the duty of the breeder.

152

be willing to help the new owner of the puppy for the life of the dog, in every reasonable way. The buyer of a puppy may need education in the care of the breed, and you must be willing to assist in all areas in which you are qualified. For Westies, this means instruction in the care of the dog as well as in the technique of stripping the coat and cleaning the dog without bathing. If you sell a puppy to a buyer who is not happy with the dog or who for some reason cannot keep it, you must be prepared to take the puppy back and find it another good home. If you are not interested in the puppy's welfare, why did you bring it into the world?

There are only two good reasons for breeding dogs. The first is if *you personally* want all of the puppies. If proper buyers do not materialize when the puppies are young, you may have the puppies a long time. You cannot just give puppies away when you tire of cleaning up after them, or because their stay is running over into your planned vacation. No one really cares as much about a free dog as he does about a dog that costs money. Many recipients of free puppies take them out and sell them. It is a good idea for the new breeder of Westies to keep the entire litter for five or six months so that he can learn how the puppies develop.

The second reason for breeding dogs is to get the best possible specimens. The world is already too full of dogs, as officials of humane societies everywhere will testify. If you are not really trying to breed for the best dogs, why are you breeding? No bitch will "be a better pet" as a result of having a litter, nor does a bitch "need to have a litter or two." She will never miss the experience. Then there is the too-often-advanced reason that the children "need to witness the miracle of birth." *Hogwash!* There are far better ways of teaching children about the facts of life. Even if your only interest is the money that you plan to make, you should recognize that your expenses in raising the best litter will be no more than those for raising a mediocre litter. In fact, a litter from high quality and healthy stock may cost less to rear and will certainly command better prices when the puppies are sold.

Breeding for the best dogs must always mean using only sound and healthy stock, with excellence of temperament a prime consideration.

Excellence of conformation is important, but not at the expense of good disposition. "A sound mind in a sound body" is just as important in dogs as it is in people. Every breeder owes it to the puppies and to their buyers to turn out good pets. Show homes are not to be found in every neck of the woods, especially by the newcomer to breeding. Most buyers are seeking a pet, and it is up to the breeder to sell well-adjusted puppies.

This is particularly true of puppies of any of the Terrier breeds. All of these breeds were developed to be independent workers. This work required dogs with dominant characteristics. The puppies need much human socialization, beginning when they are very young. Like all breeds of dogs, they need an introduction to children before they are twelve weeks of age. Dr. Michael Fox, the noted authority on animal behavior, says that to dogs, children look totally different than adults. To be well-adjusted, any dog needs to learn what children are, even if you have to borrow some little folks from your neighbors. If you cannot devote the time to seeing that your puppies are well socialized, you are doing both the puppy and the buyer a serious disservice, not to mention the entire breed.

A "Golden Rule" of the breeder/seller of dogs is to "always be ethical." You may plan to breed only a litter or two and think that ethics can scarcely be important. The "dog world" is one in which most people involved with the same breed know many others. When one Westie owner encounters another, the first topic of conversation is usually the source of their dogs, their parentage, and their breeders. Make certain that anything said about you reflects your integrity. No matter how "small" you may start out in dogs, you may someday be "big" in dogs. If that day comes, as it has to so many others, anything unethical that you have done will come home to haunt you. Believe me, if you have ever misrepresented a dog, cheated anyone in any way at any time, the word will get around in dog circles.

If you have been honest and ethical, that word will spread, too.

The breeder of Westies must study the breed standard and always breed to it. The members of the West Highland White Terrier Club of America agree to accept the breed standard and to breed only to it when they agree to uphold the constitution of the club. Any serious breeder loves the breed enough to try to maintain correct type, not just pay lip service. Breeders must always be willing to help newcomers to Westies. Most people are not lucky enough to start out with a top-quality dog. New people need the help and education that a serious breeder is willing to give, remembering when he was starting out himself. This means giving much time and a lot of yourself, passing along what you have learned to future breeders.

Breeders must also be willing to help other breeders with problems. If all breeders could feel free to discuss the problems within their own kennels, knowing that these open talks would be educational, all Westie breeding programs would reap the benefits. Using such information to denigrate the program of another breeder is doing everyone in the breed a disservice. All breeders have problems, some to a greater degree than others, so all breeders can and should share information, help one another, and learn from one another.

These are only a few of the things that a breeder should know. I hope that they have conveyed one message clearly: if you cannot do it right, do not do it. The puppies that are produced will be your creations. True, God makes the puppies, but since you decided to produce a litter and selected the breeding partners, they are your creation, too. The serious breeder wants to take pride in the puppies that he has bred. There is no thrill equal to finishing the champion that you helped to take his first breath. Except one. That is when the buyer of a pet phones or writes to say, "This is the best dog we ever owned."

153

Am. Can. Mex. Ch. Merryhart Paddy Whack, a Best in Show winner, with Neoma Eberhardt.

Ludwig photo

20 The Basics of Breeding

The subject of genetics is so complex that it boggles the mind of most people. It is not a study in which the average breeder of dogs has taken great interest. Still, some simple rules should be followed by every breeder in order to select complementary breeding partners. Whenever dog breeders get together to "talk dogs," the discussion usually turns to inbreeding, linebreeding, and outcrossing. For the novice, these terms must be explained.

Inbreeding involves the breeding of two closely related individuals: father to daughter, mother to son, brother to sister. This type of breeding is not used by most breeders. Certainly it is not a program to be attempted by the novice. In a long-range breeding program, in which the breeder plans to keep many dogs, this method of breeding could be very successful in fixing characteristics, because no new genes are introduced. By selectively breeding only the best offspring from the litter, the breeder could eventually eliminate all of the bad and keep all of the good. A breeder engaged in such a program must be willing to cull the litters and keep only the best specimens. After a few generations, the inbred animals could become a pure strain, rather like a separate breed within a breed. Total outcrossing into such an inbred line could easily produce animals resembling hybrids. Often, the breeder's plans are thwarted when an all-male litter is born and there are no bitches to select for the next generation of planned breeding. Or perhaps the breeder needs a good dog, and the only puppy dog lacks quality.

While inbreeding is a method of fixing the best characteristics, it will also bring out the worst. While the breedings do not result in "monster" puppies, as some people believe, they can and do double the recessive genes. In some cases, this could result in the reduction of fertility in the breeding stock, as well as in a higher death rate in the litters and loss of size in individual dogs. Only the breeder with patience, time, and know-how should attempt inbreeding.

155

Linebreeding is somewhat akin to inbreeding in that related individuals are bred together. Breeders disagree as to where inbreeding ends and linebreeding begins. To many, breeding half-brother to half-sister, cousin to cousin, niece to uncle, nephew to aunt, grandsire to granddaughter, or grandmother to grandson is linebreeding. To many others, this is still inbreeding. For this latter group, linebreeding is the breeding of dogs that are closely related to the same ancestor, thus keeping the breedings in the same "bloodline." After several generations, some of this ancestor's offspring will have to be used in the linebreeding to carry on the strain.

Outcrossing is the breeding of two totally unrelated animals. They have no common ancestors. This method is used in planned breeding programs to bring into a line certain characteristics or to restore vigor to a line by adding new genes. In a planned breeding program, the offspring of such a breeding would be bred back into the line. This is because the breeder knows that succeeding generations of continued outcrossings become heterogeneous, or totally lacking in uniformity.

SELECTING THE BREEDING PARTNERS

Clearly, the best and most predictable breedings are those in which the partners are related to some degree. Every breeder must learn to read and evaluate pedigrees. But combining two pedigrees is only as successful as the quality of the dogs whose names are listed there. Breeding partners must be selected for their compensating physical qualities. This does not mean that a large dog bred to a small bitch will produce medium-size dogs. It means, for example, that a bitch with a small head should be bred to a dog with a perfect head and whose sire and dam both had perfect heads—or that a bitch with a less-than-perfect lay-back of shoulder should be bred to a dog with a perfect shoulder and whose sire and dam both had perfect shoulders. In addition, the two breeding partners should have some mutual ancestors.

Many bitch owners are interested in breeding their bitches to the latest top-winning dog. This is so that the pedigree of the litter will bear the name of that famous champion. No thought is given to the fact that the two breeding partners do not physically compensate each other. A far more sensible approach would be to breed to that top dog's sire, since this is the dog that produced the big winner. Most breeders who rush to form a line to breed their bitch to a top-winning dog do not even wonder about the sire and dam or brothers and sisters of the champion. Some of the top-winning Westies have never produced many winning offspring, even though these dogs are very popular as studs. Such a breeding should only be done if this particular dog and bitch have none of the same faults and have mutual ancestors.

The best Westie breeding programs are those in which the breeding stock has been carefully evaluated for quality and pedigree, staying within the same family "bloodline" or returning to it after an equally well-planned outcross to another linebred family. In this way, the breeder is "purifying" the pedigree by keeping the best of two, or perhaps three, bloodlines which have come from carefully planned breedings. He is getting uniformity in the litters rather than the heterogeneous lot that would result from continued outcrossings and an "open" pedigree. The novice is well-advised to follow his example.

Many good books on the subject of breeding and whelping dogs are available. The casual owner of one bitch may feel that studying the subject is not worth the trouble. On the contrary, the newcomer needs to learn all he can beforehand so that he will start off correctly. He may find, as many people do, that the breeding of dogs is a fascinating hobby, one in which the learning process continues for years. If really good puppies result from the first breeding, the breeder may find that he just has to keep one or two. Soon he is seeking breeding partners for the "keepers." This is the way in which most breeders get "hooked"—by learning and breeding for the best possible dogs.

156

Ch. Hobbit's Sweetheart Patty

Graham photo

Ch. Jolen's I'm A Smarty Pants Too

Graham photo

Ch. Jolen's Heritage O' Simon

Graham photo

Ch. Wishing Well's Gift of Heritage   157

Graham photo

```
                                                                  ┌─ Am. Can. Ch. Royal Tartan
                                                ┌─ Ch. Heritage Farm's    │  Glen o' Red Lodge
                                                │  Ode to Simon  ┤
                                                │                │  Ch. Wishing Well's Betsy
                          ┌─ Am. Can. Ch. Wishing │                └─ o' the Ridge
                          │  Well's Gift o' Heritage┤                  Ch. Kar-ric's Ability Again
                          │  ("Smarty Pants")    │  Heritage Farm's Merry ┤
                          │                       └─ Poppit          └─ Ch. Merryhart Sweet Pea
     Ch. Jolen's I'm a Smarty Pants, Too ┤
          "Tommy"                        │                          ┌─ Int. Ch. Barnstormer of Branston
                                         │        ┌─ Int. Ch. Monsieur aus der ┤
                                         │        │  Flerlage ("Bobby")    └─ Daggi Hallordi (Germany)
                          └─ Heritage Farms Bobby's ┤
                             Imprint      │                          ┌─ Am. Can. Ch. Royal Tartan Glen
                                          │  Ch. Wishing Well's    │  o' Red Lodge
                                          └─ Winnie Pooh  ┤
                                                          └─ Ch. Wishing Well's Quip o'
                                                             Buff Creek
Ch. Jolen's Jolly Jason
Ch. Jolen's I'm a Sissy Pants, Too
Hobbitshire's Bree of Eriador
                                                                  ┌─ Am. Can. Ch. Elfinbrook Simon
                                                ┌─ Am. Can. Ch. Wishing ┤
                                                │  Well's Ulster Patrick └─ Ch. Drumalis Yankee Lass
                          ┌─ Am. Can. Ch. Jolen's ┤
                          │  Heritage o' Simon   │                      ┌─ Am. Can. Ch. Elfinbrook Simon
                          │  ("Patrick")         └─ Ch. Wishing Well's Betsy ┤
                          │                         o' the Ridge        └─ Ch. Wishing Well's Water Baby
     Ch. Hobbit's Sweetheart ┤
     Patti ("Patti")        │                                          ┌─ Am. Can. Ch. Royal Tartan
                            │        ┌─ Jenessy's Dauntless            │  Glen o' Red Lodge
                            │        │  Knight ┤
                            │        │          └─ Ch. Kirkaldy's Roxane
                            └─ Happy's Miss Medora ┤
                                      │                                ┌─ Jenessey's Tuffy of Mac David
                                      └─ White Heather of Douglas ┤
                                                                   └─ Mac David's Bonnie Lassie
```

Ch. Jolen's I'm A Sissy Pants Too
Graham photo

158

Hobbitshire's Bree of Eriador

Ch. Jolen's Jolly Jason

Graham photo

Example of Linebred Pedigree

This family group of Westies is used here to illustrate one of the fine examples of linebreeding from a common ancestor and producing consistently high-quality offspring. The pictured family members are one paternal and one maternal grandsire, the sire and dam, and three puppies. These excellent Westies are owned by Helen and Joe Craigmiles, Jolen's Kennels, Thomasville, Georgia, and Annette Short of the same city, breeder of the litter.

Due to the linebreeding, the pedigree lists the ancestors of all seven of these Westies. This is the "standard" four-generation pedigree (plus the litter). If we were to carry it back two more generations, we would include the fourth-generation ancestors of the two grandsires. Then we would see that, of the sixteen dogs listed in the fourth generation, a total of eight are children or grandchildren of Ch. Elfinbrook Simon, the breed's most prepotent sire.

Reading down the right-hand colum, *Ch. Royal Tartan Glen o' Red Lodge*, appearing three times, was "Simon's" top producing son, the sire of many champions. *Ch. Wishing Well's Betsy o' the Ridge* was a "Simon" daughter. *Ch. Kar-ric's Ability Again* was a "Simon" grandson. *Ch. Wishing Well's Quip o' Buff Creek* was a "Simon" daughter. *Ch. Wishing Well's Water Baby* was a "Simon" granddaughter. *Jenessey's Tuffy of Mac David* was a "Simon" grandson. Since "Simon" himself appears twice in the fourth column, a total of ten of the sixteen dogs are carrying the "Simon" genes.

Also important in the pedigree is one paternal great grandsire, the late great *International Ch. Monsieur aus der Flerlage* an English import, owned by Birgit Coady, "Bobby" was a top winning and top producing dog, with titles in several European countries, England, Canada, Mexico, and the United States. Mrs. Coady and her husband, Clay, are well-known professional handlers, specializing in Terriers.

Equally interesting are the dams in the right-hand column, since four of the eight were noted producers of high-quality puppies and were from top producing dams. Ch. Kar-ric's Gamble was the dam of *Ch. Kar-ric's Ability Again.* She produced four champions. *Ch. Merryhart Sweet Pea* produced, among others, the top winning Westie bitch of all time, Ch. Heritage Farms Jenny Jump Up. "Sweet Pea's" dam, Ch. Kirk o' the Glen Merryhart, also produced champions. *Ch. Wishing Well's Water Baby* was the dam of six champions of eleven puppies. Her dam, Ch. Lawrenton Wee Maggie, was the dam of five champions. *Ch. Kirkaldy's Roxanne*, bred to "Simon," produced a litter of four champions and additional champions from other breedings. She was also the dam of *Jenessey's Tuffy of Mac David.*

Grandsire, *Smarty*, has "Simon" ancestors on both sides of his pedigree, from half brother to half sister breeding in the second generation ("Glen" to "Betsy") and "Ability Again". "Smarty" was a multiple Group winner, Best in Show winner in Canada, and enjoyed Top Ten Terrier recognition during his show career, for three years. Grandsire, *Patrick* was a double "Simon" grandson, the product of half brother to half sister breeding. ("Simon" to "Yankee Lass" and "Simon" to "Water Baby"). "Patrick," too, was a multiple Group winner and "top tenner" for two years while he was being shown. Both of these dogs have sired champion offspring.

Annette Short's bitch, *Ch. Hobbit's Sweetheart Patti*, is similarly linebred from "Simon," with five of her eight ancestors having the "Simon" bloodline. As a stud for "Patti," Annette chose "Tommy," a "Smarty" son and a Group winner. From this breeding, the three pictured Westies were produced. "Jason" and "Sissy" have been shown to their titles by their owners, the Craigmiles. Litter sister, "Bree," is pointed and will soon be finished, shown by her owner, Annette Short.

Producing Westies like all of these dogs is no accident. This is a sample of linebreeding at its best, using the top quality offspring of a top quality sire for consistently top quality Westies. The newcomer to breeding can emulate this example by careful study and planning to get the right bitch to the right dog, wherever he may be, not just to the most convenient stud and not necessarily to the current top winning show dog.

160

American Canadian Ch. Shipmate's Hannibal
(1959-1974)

Hannibal was the foundation Westie stud of the Of The Rouge Kennels. Bred by Mrs. S. J. Navin of Shipmate's Kennels, he was acquired by Mrs. Dorothea Daniell-Jenkins at the age of two. Strongly linebred from Eng. Am. Can. Ch. Cruben Dextor, Hannibal became a dominant sire of many quality sons and daughters, becoming one of the two top producing Canadian dogs as the sire of fifteen champions. He and Ch. Dreamland's Cyclone are tied for the honor of top producing sire of Canada.

Frasie Studio photo

21 What Every Stud Owner Should Know

If your dog has never been shown, and you therefore have no idea about his quality, find someone who knows Westies to evaluate the dog for you. Even though you think that he is a fine specimen, you need an unbiased opinion. The fact that he is the perfect pet and companion does not make him breeding stock. If he has skeletal faults that would make him difficult to finish in the show ring, forget about breeding him and continue enjoying him as a pet. Every dog used for breeding does not require a "Ch." in front of his name, but he should certainly have the potential.

If you own a finished champion dog, owners of bitches will be ringing your telephone to inquire about using your dog to sire litters that they would like to have. You must consider many things before you decide to use your dog as a stud. The most important is the compensating qualities of the two breeding partners. Before agreeing to breed your dog to the bitch, you should see her and make that decision. Remember, you are under no obligation to breed your dog to any bitch just because her owner wants a litter. Many owners who advertise their studs include the words "To approved bitches only." I have seen one ad that I like even better. It reads, "At stud to champion or pointed bitches only." That certainly clarifies the stud owner's breeding policy. A champion or pointed bitch has been seen by dog show judges who have given their opinion of her quality. Further, this stud owner knows that the bitch owner is sincerely interested in breeding for the betterment of Westies. Let us hope that every stud owner has done much reading on breeding better dogs, has studied pedigrees, and knows the value of a good bitch in a breeding program. He should also know a good bitch when he sees one.

Some owners of stud dogs feel that if an owner is absolutely determined to breed an inferior bitch and will only look elsewhere for another, perhaps inferior, stud, breeding the bitch to their better dog will improve the litter. They should remember that their stud's name will be on the pedigree of the puppies. If the puppies resemble their dam, the stud dog will be blamed for every poor-quality puppy in the litter. People who insist that they must have a litter from their pet-quality bitch are rank amateurs in dogs. As the owner of the stud, you will have no control over the disposition of the litter. If the bitch owner is overly anxious to sell the puppies, he will not be too fussy about where and to whom he sells your stud's offspring.

Most stud owners are reluctant to tell a bitch owner that the bitch is unfit to be bred. Some resort to quoting an exorbitant stud fee to discourage the breeding. One breeder whom I know accepts the bitch to be bred but does not breed her. The owner is then told that the dog did not get a good tie and that the bitch may not be pregnant. Therefore, no stud fee is accepted "until we see if she has puppies." I must admit that this is an effective ploy in keeping inferior bitches from being bred to any stud.

But I cannot understand what is wrong with telling the bitch owner the truth. Surely the knowledgeable Westie owner is passing up an opportunity to educate the bitch owner in the fine points of the breed. It can be done with kindness. The bitch owner should be helped to understand that his lovely pet should not be bred and be given the reasons. The stud owner should suggest that the bitch be spayed and that her owner buy a quality bitch for breeding.

Before you agree to breed your dog to any

Ch. Royal Tartan Glen o' Red Lodge
"Glen" is the most prolific son of Ch. Elfinbrook Simon. At this writing he is sixteen years old. During his outstanding career as a stud dog, he produced twenty-five American champions plus several in Canada. He is owned by Richard Hilliker, Glenwood, New York.

photo by Norton of Kent

162

Ch. Whitebriar Jervish 1972-1979
"Jamie" was bred in England by Mrs. J. E. Beer and imported and co-owned by Jodine Vertuno, Naperville, Illinois, and Betsy Finley, New Brighton, Minnesota. At this writing, he is the sire of seventeen champion offspring, winning the 1980 Kennel Review top producer award.

Francis photo

Am. Can. Mex. Ch. Merryhart Happy Hobo

Another of the fine dogs bred at Merryhart by Neoma and Jim Eberhardt, Hobo presently is owned by Betsy Finley, New Brighton, Minnesota. Currently he is the sire of thirteen champions, with more on their way in the show ring.

Ludwig photo

Am. Mex. Ch. Merryhart Honest John

Born in 1973, John had an outstanding show career. To date, he is the sire of twelve champions. His children have also made some exciting wins in the show ring. One daughter, Am. Mex. Can. Ch. Merryhart Love Child, was Best of Winners at the Montgomery Specialty at the age of ten months. He was bred and is owned by the Eberhardts of Merryhart Kennels, Santa Ana, California.

Ludwig photo

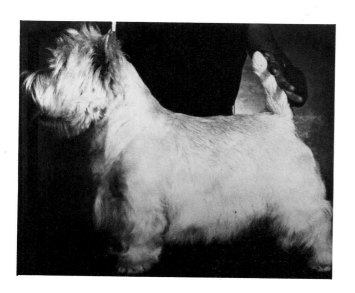

Ch. Laird Brig-A-Doon MacDuff

Brig was born in 1969 and was bred and is owned by Mr. and Mrs. J. W. Williams, Jr. (Betty) of Jeffersontown, Kentucky. He finished in five shows with four majors, twice going Best of Breed over specials, always owner-handled and conditioned. In very limited showing as a special, Brig won several Group placements. He is the sire of ten champions to date.

bitch, you should require her owner to produce proof of her AKC registration. Many owners never bother to register their pet, and at this point, the owner may no longer know what he did with the application. He may never have gotten a pedigree from the breeder at the time of purchase and may no longer have the name and address. This could make the registration of the bitch very difficult, if not impossible. Unless the dam is registered, the litter is not eligible for registration.

You should also require the bitch to have a thorough checkup by a veterinarian before being bred. She should be checked both for skin problems and worms which she could pass on to her litter. She should have a digital examination of her vagina to be certain that she has no obstruction that would discourage the dog and prevent a successful breeding. She should have a blood test for canine brucellosis. This disease is on the rise and can cause aborted fetuses as well as sterility in your stud, since it is passed along in breeding. All of this should be done before the bitch is brought to the stud.

THE STUD AGREEMENT

Written stud agreements are standard practice so that both owners know what to expect. The stud owner agrees to breed the stud to the bitch but does not promise a litter, since he has no way of knowing if the bitch will conceive. If the bitch does not have a litter, the stud owner agrees to a second stud service at her next season, and it is well to state "at her next season only." If the bitch owner were to find it inconvenient to breed the bitch again for a year or more, the stud owner would not be required to service the bitch again at her owner's convenience, but only at her next heat. If a stud fee is charged, no refund will be given, regardless of the outcome.

Often, novices ask the stud owner to accept a puppy in exchange for the stud's service. They feel that in this way they will not be out of pocket should no litter result. Many owners prefer to breed their stud for a puppy, too. However, it should be understood by both parties that complications can result. If only one puppy survives, this must constitute a litter, and the puppy

would go to the stud owner. Also, the stud owner may want as "the pick of the litter" the very puppy that the bitch owner adores. A time limit regarding the age at which the stud owner must select his puppy must be set. Otherwise, the bitch owner will not be able to sell the puppies until the stud owner has made his choice.

If no puppies survive to the age of selection, then the stud owner merely postpones his choice of pick of the litter. He should agree to breed his stud to the bitch again, for no compensation, if that is his wish, and select a puppy from the next litter. This could be a year or more hence if the bitch had problems in the whelping and is not in condition to be bred again at her next season. If the same situation should develop at the next breeding, then both parties should end the agreement. Also, the stud owner's right to a puppy should be honored, even if the bitch changes owners. If this has occurred, the stud owner should have the right to decide if he still wants to breed his stud to the bitch or forfeit his right to a puppy. If the stud should be ill or dead by the time of the second breeding, the stud owner should have the right to use another stud of his choosing.

The bitch owner should be required to notify the stud owner that the bitch is not pregnant at the end of fifty days after the breeding. This is two weeks before the litter is due. Unless the bitch owner so advises the stud owner, a return stud service must be forfeited.

CONSUMMATING THE BREEDING

The breeding of short-legged, deep-chested dogs is not easy. It should be understood that the owner of the stud will have to have help to accomplish it. Just closing your dog in the garage with the bitch will not result in a litter, unless your dog is an old experienced dog and the bitch is equally experienced and eager to be bred. The breeding requires one person to restrain the bitch and one person to assist the dog. Many stud owners place the bitch on a table, while the dog is assisted in mounting. This is successful if the dog has been trained to breed the bitch in this manner. It is more natural—if less dignified for the two handlers—to breed the two dogs on the floor so that the dogs can run about, flirt, and play before the breeding takes place.

This requires monitoring of the breeding pair and great patience. When the dog is earnestly trying to penetrate, the bitch must be firmly held. A dog could be severely injured by a flighty bitch should she decide to bolt when the dog is tied to her and cannot get free. Such an injury could ruin your dog for the rest of his life, because he would not be anxious to become injured again. Virgin bitches are most often the problem. Be certain that the bitch is wearing a collar for ease of restraint and that one handler is holding her head so that she cannot turn around and bite your dog. While the dog is tied to the bitch, be certain that she stands quietly.

If you have never bred dogs, try to get someone who has to come and help. I go to my veterinarian for help. At first, I detected reluctance on his part, and I presume that he felt such an activity did not fall under the heading of "professional services." When I explained that I could not very well call in the garden club ladies to help me breed dogs, he understood. The two of us and the two Westies get on the carpeted floor of an examining room, where I restrain the bitch and he assists the dog. At the instant that the dog's penis is at the bitch's vulva, the veterinarian places his large palm under the dog's tail, pushing firmly and lifting upward so that the dog can penetrate the bitch. This lifts the dog's deep chest onto the bitch and raises the dog's back feet off the floor. When the tie is accomplished, the dog is allowed to dismount, his forelegs to one side of the bitch. One of his hind legs can then be lifted over the bitch's back to the same side as the forelegs. This way the pair can stand comfortably, tail to tail, while the tie subsides.

Ch. Loch Ness MacTavish C.D.

This dog is a "triple threat" great. MacTavish is a conformation champion, has a Companion Dog degree in Obedience, and is a top producing sire. Born in 1969 and bred by Kenneth Lutes, he has produced twelve champions to date. He is owned by Rita MacDonald, Hingham, Massachusetts.

165

My own method of accepting bitches early for breeding may be the same one used by many other stud owners. For "us," it has resulted in 100 percent pregnancies. I have the bitch brought to my home at the fifth or sixth day of her season. I am very fortunate in having a sophisticated stud who knows, almost to the hour, when a bitch is in ovulation. Until this time, he is friendly but not seriously interested in breeding the bitch. When he lets me know, by his ardent actions, that the bitch is ready, we drive to the veterinarian's office for help. We return to the veterinarian two days later for an "insurance" breeding. Actually, one breeding at the right moment is all that is needed, but most breeders breed twice to be sure.

Certainly it is more trouble for the bitch to be brought early because she will have to be boarded for several days. But if the owner brings her for the day, the breeder must rely on the owner's observation of his bitch and on the owner's determination that the time is right. While the traditional time is the twelfth and fourteenth days, this can vary widely from bitch to bitch. Variances can also occur if the bitch owner failed to notice for two or three days that the season had started. I prefer to rely on my dog's unerring nose. Once the different scent of ovulation is present, a dog will be willing to breed the bitch until the end of her season days later, long after ovulation has passed. Since the stud agreement commits me to a second stud service if the bitch fails to conceive a litter, I prefer to do everything possible to insure a pregnancy the first time. This way I send a bitch in whelp home to her pleased owner, and I do not have to concern myself with a repeat breeding.

In the best interest of breeding better Westies, every stud dog owner must consider the compensating characteristics of his dog and any bitch being brought to him for breeding. The stud owner must also consider the two pedigrees. If another dog would seem to be a better choice of breeding partner for the bitch, both in conformation and pedigree, the breeder who is really dedicated to Westies will not hesitate in recommending that the other dog be used instead of his own.

Ch. Kirkaldy's Roxanne (1961-1971)

Roxanne was the dam of 8 champions and one of the top producing bitches of all time. Bred to her uncle, Ch. Elfinbrook Simon, she produced a litter of seven, four of whom finished their titles. A second breeding to Simon resulted in one more champion. Her third breeding to Ch. Dreamland's Happy Mick resulted in two more champions. Another champion was from a litter sired by her cousin, Ch. Royal Tartan Glen o' Red Lodge. This dominant bitch consistently produced excellence bred to three different studs. Roxanne was bred by the late Jean Goddard and was owned by Ronald M. Davis, Wayne, Pennsylvania.

Francis photo

22 Breeding Your Bitch

In the chapter on selecting a puppy, the reader who wishes to become a breeder was advised to buy the best bitch that anyone was willing to sell. That means both pedigree-wise and conformation-wise. She should be a top-quality, carefully bred bitch. The daughter of a top-producing dam would be an excellent choice. A premium price will be asked for such a bitch, and rightly so. Chances are good that her grandmother was also a top producer.

These bitches have dominant characteristics. The offspring may not closely resemble the mother, but they will strongly resemble one another, regardless of the sire. A stud dog, depending on his popularity, may sire one hundred puppies or more. A Westie bitch will probably never have more than fifteen puppies in a lifetime, which limits the number of champions she can produce. A dominant bitch will consistently produce good puppies.

Unfortunately, the demand for such bitches far exceeds the supply. Still, this should not deter the serious breeder from buying the best quality bitch he can find. This will be the foundation of the breeding stock. It is well to remember that weeds beget weeds, and no one needs to study genetics to know that.

When your bitch reaches six months of age, you should begin to check her daily for signs that she has come into season. On a white Westie, you may see dark stains on her tail. However, some bitches keep themselves very clean, and you should not rely on visible signs. It is easy to check her every morning by gently wiping the fold of her vulva with a piece of white tissue. That way you will be one of the first to know that your bitch is in season. In a notebook or on a calendar, jot down the date. You may think that you can rely on your memory, but written records are better.

Your bitch's season will last for twenty-one days, and you must see to it that she is protected from dogs and her own instincts. If you have children, they must be instructed in the importance of keeping the bitch confined.

It is best to keep the bitch indoors, if possible, for this period of time. If you must walk her on a leash, to relieve herself, carry her away from the house. Put her down and allow her to relieve herself. Then pick her up and carry her home. This is so that dogs happening along and smelling her urine will be unable to track her back to your door. Make certain that you do not step in the urine yourself and get it on the soles of your shoes. A dog will usually scratch his feet in the urine of a bitch in season and follow her paw prints. Other dogs come along and follow the first dog's tracks. Soon, several dogs could be baying at your door. You can avoid this by simply carrying the bitch a good distance from home or by keeping her inside. If she was paper trained as a puppy, she will return to using her papers with your encouragement.

Make a note in the book or calendar when the next six-month period will be. Once again, check your bitch daily. Your bitch may have her first season at seven months of age or older. Her second season may also occur at a longer interval than six months. However, because she could be on a six-month cycle, it is best to begin checking her then. Each time she comes in season, record the date so that you will know when to expect the next season.

When you have decided that you wish to breed the bitch, begin considering stud dogs. This should be done months in advance—a good time being at your bitch's first season. If she seems mature enough to mother a litter and be bred at her second season, you will have done your homework in plenty of time. Some Westie bitches are still in the tomboy stage at the second season, so you may wish to defer breeding her until the third season, at which time she will be nearly two years old.

Information on locating a complementary breeding partner should be sought from the breeder who sold you the bitch. This person should know Westie family groups and be able to refer you to the owner of a stud with a "matching" pedigree. If this breeder shows Westies on a regular basis, he may have seen the dog or dogs that he can recommend and may know the dog's good qualities from personal observation. If the breeder of your bitch is unavailable for some reason, another source of information would be the owner of your bitch's sire.

If you have a subscription to *Terrier Type*,

168

Ch. Rannoch-Dune Delia

Delia is the dam of six champions. Four of these were an entire litter of puppies. One was the only puppy in another litter, and one was from a third litter. She was bred by Clare Brumby and is owned by Dorthea Robinson, DVM, Mickthea Kennels, College Station, Texas.

you will find the pedigrees of champion stud dogs listed in the back each month. These are the newly finished dogs. The October issue of the magazine is the Terrier Stud Dog Register, and many owners of Westie studs submit photos and pedigrees of their dogs with the owner's name and address. Studying these can be a great help in selecting the right dog for your bitch. If you decide to inquire about stud fees and the dog's availability, send his owner a copy of your bitch's pedigree, a good photo of your bitch taken in the "show stack" (if you have one), and a self-addressed, stamped envelope so that the owner of the stud can reply. State the estimated date when you believe that your bitch will be ready to be bred. All of these items sent with the inquiry will indicate your sincere interest in the services of the stud dog.

If the dog is a long distance from you, you will need to get your bitch to the dog either by air or car. Shipping a bitch requires an airline crate and a health certificate from your veterinarian. You will want to have the bitch checked by your veterinarian before breeding her anyway, as described in the advice to the stud owner. If she is due for booster shots, she should have those before she is bred. It should be obvious that the decision to breed your bitch cannot be made on the first day that you notice she is in season, or worse yet, the day you think she should be bred. If she is overweight, you may wish to diet her down before she is bred. This could take up to six months, depending on how much she needs to lose.

The most important factor in getting a bitch in whelp is to get her to the stud dog at the right time. Remember that the sperm cells live for seven days, but the eggs of the bitch live only about two days. The largest percentage of missed pregnancies occur because the bitch arrives too late. If the owner of the stud will accept your bitch early and board her until the time is right for her to conceive, so much the better. If she will stand for the dog, and he will breed her early, this breeding is more likely to succeed than one that is late, even by one day. Your bitch may

169

The value of a good bitch in a breeding program cannot be overemphasized. Ch. Bonnie Brier She's Groovin' ("Dulcey") is one excellent example. Bred and owned by Christine Swingle, Bonnie Brier Westies, North Canton, Connecticut, "Dulcey" is the dam of six champions.

be gone a little longer, but she will have a better chance of returning to you in whelp. Arriving a few days early helps the bitch to "settle down" and get "settled in" before she is bred.

If you ship the bitch, the weather must be taken into account. In midsummer, the baggage compartment of a plane can be very hot if the plane must land and be on the ground for a time. Try to make nonstop flight arrangements if possible. Airlines will not accept dogs for shipping if the temperature is above eighty-five degrees. In the winter months, airlines will not ship dogs if the temperature at the destination is below forty-five degrees unless the dog owner has a certificate from a USDA-accredited veterinarian stating that the dog has been acclimated to lower temperatures. In addition to the usual shipping labels on the outside of the crate, tape another paper with all of the information inside the crate. This should list your name, address, and phone number and the name, address, and phone number of the person to whom the dog is being shipped. Many bitch owners accompany the bitch as passengers in the plane. Be certain that the crate has identification, even though it is going with you as excess baggage.

Phone the stud owner to verify that the bitch has been boarded on the agreed flight so that she will be promptly claimed at her destination or can be traced if she fails to arrive as scheduled. Ask the stud owner to phone you when the bitch has been boarded for her return flight so that you will know exactly when she will arrive.

Bitches that have been bred must be carefully guarded from all other dogs until the season is over. During her season, a bitch can be bred by more than one dog and conceive puppies by each, which would make for an unwanted mixed litter if the other dog were not a Westie. Even if he were a Westie, the litter would have two different sires. The old wive's tale that such an accidental breeding would make your bitch unfit for producing purebred puppies is totally untrue. Even so, keep your bitch away from other dogs so that your carefully laid plans do not go awry.

Owners of bitches often ask how often the bitch should be bred. No bitch of any breed should be bred until she has reached maturity. In Westies, this could be at her second season, when she will be fourteen to fifteen months old. With some individuals, it is better to await the third heat, since a bitch needs to be "settled" before she takes on motherhood. One can only wait and decide if the bitch seems ready when the time comes.

After having a litter, the bitch's next season will begin six or seven months after the previous season. Allowing for two months of pregnancy, that would be only four to five months after whelping. A judgement as to whether or not the bitch should be bred in the next season must be left to her owner, who surely has her best interests at heart. If she is a "free whelper," delivering puppies with little trouble, a breeding at her next season could be considered. Then she would not be bred again until her second season after that, which would be her third litter.

Surely three litters in her lifetime is enough for any owner to expect from a bitch, unless you are one of those people who only cares about this bitch paying you back for her purchase price and her keep. Most Westie owners do not breed any bitch that is past six years of age. Owners who care about their bitches feel that this is a good age for "retirement" from motherhood and its responsibilities.

If your bitch had a difficult labor with the whelping of her first litter, it would be best to wait and allow her to pass her next season. You should ask the advice of your veterinarian, who will be better able to evaluate the bitch's condition before the bitch who had great difficulty in whelping her puppies is bred again.

23 Waiting for the Litter

A litter normally requires nine weeks, or sixty-three days, to develop. However, if the litter is large, or if it is the bitch's first litter, plan on the whelping at any time after the fifty-eighth day. During this time, prepare to care for the dam and the puppies. For the first four weeks, your bitch should be on her regular diet with her normal amount of food. She should be taken for a walk every day, in addition to her regular exercise. Just because you have a huge fenced yard, do not assume that she is getting her daily exercise. She may just be moving from the shade of one tree to another and chasing an occasional squirrel. There is nothing like regular roadwork to build stamina and muscles, both of which will be needed at whelping time. These should be brisk and fairly lengthy walks, started as soon as she has been bred.

I like to take my bitches to the veterinarian on the twenty-eighth to thirtieth day after being bred to have them palpated for puppies. Before the twenty-eighth day, there is some danger of injury to the fetuses. At this stage of development, the fetuses are like small, hard marbles or beads lying in the horns of the uterus. After the thirtieth day, the sac of amniotic fluid forms, so the softer lumps are more difficult to feel and identify. I am very lucky to have a veterinarian who has sensitive fingers that can feel the tiny whelps. He does no probing, only palpating of the bitch's abdomen to verify that there is at least one puppy. Now we know that we can definitely plan for a litter.

If your veterinarian is not blessed with sensitive fingers, one good indication that the bitch is in whelp is that her vulva will not return to its original position. Before a bitch comes in season, her vulva is high and tight against her body. As the season progresses, the area around the vulva enlarges, softens, and drops downward. As the bitch comes into ovulation, the vulva appears to tip to the rear, where its position makes it accessible to the dog. After breeding, the vulva area will remain enlarged and soft, continuing in its lower position if the bitch is pregnant. The bitch owner who is familiar with the normal condition of the vulva area can easily recognize the continuing enlargement and the lower position of the vulva. At whelping, the vulva area would certainly need to enlarge and drop, so it is rather as if the vulva knew this and decided to stay dropped.

Another indication that often accompanies pregnancy is a sticky discharge from the vulva. This is clear and odorless. It is rather like uncooked egg white. When it has dried, it has a shiny look, and if hairs are around the vulva, they will become stiffly glued to each other and to the vulva. This discharge should be removed daily with warm, soapy water. It may develop at about the fourth week. Any other type of discharge should be investigated by your veterinarian.

During the second half of the pregnancy, all forms of strenuous exercise should be discouraged. By "strenuous" I mean jumping down from the grooming table or the easy chair, or leaping skyward as the dinner dish is filled. Daily walks should continue but at a more leisurely pace, and perhaps should be divided into two shorter walks. By the seventh week, your veterinarian should examine the bitch to see that all is well or to determine that she is pregnant, if this is still in doubt. You will want to notify the stud owner of your veterinarian's findings. Having X-rays done is not a good idea unless the pictures are needed as a diagnostic tool, because the radiation could harm the puppies.

This will be a good time to trim all of the hair from the bitch's belly to make the teats accessible to the puppies as they nurse. This can be done with the snub-nosed scissors, and the hair should be trimmed very close. The hair

around the vulva and from the inside of the back legs should also be trimmed. After whelping, the bitch will have a discharge for several days, and shorter hair will be easier to keep clean. Remember that leg furnishings grow very slowly, so confine the trimming to the hair *between* the legs.

FEEDING YOUR PREGNANT BITCH

If you have followed the advice in the chapter on nutrition, you are already feeding your bitch a dog food on which protocol studies have been done for growth, maintenance, and lactation. This is all she needs to be fed for the first four weeks of her pregnancy, especially if you are adding brewer's yeast, kelp for hormonal balance, vitamin E to help prevent reproductive failure, vitamin C for the immune system and stress, plus the addition of high-quality protein to a dry food. Vitamin A is heavily supplied in a quality dog food, and none should be added. In "Feeding for Breeding," an article by Dr. David Kronfeld, it is noted that vitamin A fed in doses that are too large during the seventeenth to twenty-second days of gestation has been found to induce bone fractures, hemorrhages, and cleft palate in puppies. Since the vitamin A content of liver can vary so widely depending on the age of the animal from which the liver comes, I would avoid adding liver to the diet on these five days of the pregnancy.

If you are feeding a dry food, remember that these foods are heavily supplemented with calcium, so none should be added to the diet of your bitch. For this reason, vitamin D should not be added either, since it increases the absorption of calcium. This would decrease the absorption of all the other needed minerals. Dr. Kronfeld also says that feeding excess calcium during the last twenty days of pregnancy could make the bitch more likely to have eclampsia.

If you have dieted your bitch prior to breeding her, she should be returned to her maintenance amount of food after being bred. For the early part of her pregnancy, she should not have her meals increased. If you have been feeding her once a day, halve her meal and feed her twice a day. As the fetuses displace room in her abdomen, two smaller meals will keep her more com-

172

fortable as well as provide slower and better digestion. Just after breeding, in the early part of pregnancy, some bitches exhibit disinclination to eat, especially in the mornings. This is rather like "morning sickness" in women. Of course, refusing food for several days is not normal and should be investigated by your veterinarian.

Many breeders increase the amount of food after the fourth or fifth week of pregnancy. If you follow this course, remember that Westie litters are usually small and that you do not want an overweight bitch trying to whelp fat puppies. My own method is to increase the *quality* of the diet by increasing the canned meat products, which have some cereal, and decreasing the dry food. Egg yolks, chicken, liver, or other meat can be added for variety. If the bitch tolerates milk well, it can be added as well. Some dogs cannot digest milk after they have not had it for a long time, so a small amount should be introduced at a time.

You should record your bitch's weight as soon as she is bred. After that, weigh her weekly. My own records indicate that my bitches gain from three to three and one-half pounds during pregnancy. Puppies weigh an average of five and one-half to six ounces at birth. I had one as small as three ounces that did not survive, two that weighed three and one-half ounces that did live, and some as large as six and one-half ounces. I

have had very "good luck" with normal whelpings out of bitches that were well-exercised, well-fed, and not fat. Neither were the puppies overlarge and difficult to expel. The smallest puppy at birth may be the largest dog at maturity.

PREPARATION FOR THE WHELPING

As soon as it has been determined that your bitch is in whelp, you should decide where the whelping will take place. This should be a room that is easy to keep at about eighty degrees, day and night, for the first week after the puppies are born. It should have a floor that can be mopped, and it should be in a quiet area of the house, where the bitch will have seclusion from children and outsiders. All she will need is her trusted owner to assist. The area should be large enough to accommodate a whelping box, with room on all sides for the assistant to monitor the whelping. Humidity in the area should be fairly low, since high humidity encourages the growth of bacteria. Needless to say, if you have other pets, the whelping area must be off-limits to them. Everything should be done to make the bitch feel comfortable and secure.

You will need a whelping box large enough for the bitch to lie comfortably at almost any angle. A box that is thirty by thirty inches is a nice "Westie" size. It may seem large for the first few days, but three or four growing puppies, plus mother, will soon fill it up. A square of plywood can be used for the floor. Strips of wood one by one inch or one by two inches underneath the floor on two sides will provide circulation and warmth. Walls eleven or twelve inches high can be made for three sides of the box, and the corners can be reinforced with L-shaped molding. The fourth side of the box will be open so that the dam can get in and out. It must also have some sort of closure to keep the puppies in the box and to prevent drafts. A board the same height as the walls can be hinged to the floor, and hooks can be placed on the side of the box to fasten the "door" up in place. Or a slot can be made at each side of the front opening with two narrow strips of wood. A fourth wall can then be cut to slip down into the slots, and it can be

173

Star Dust's Ave Maria approves of the thirty-by-thirty-inch whelping box provided by her owners. "Puddin" belongs to Mr. and Mrs. Ed Chappell, Jr., Signal Mountain, Tennessee.

removed to give the dam access to the box. If this fourth wall is made of two pieces, each piece half the height of the other walls, one can be used to form a low barrier while the puppies are tiny. This allows the dam to step easily in and out of the box. As the puppies get larger, the second strip can be added to keep them in the whelping box.

During the actual whelping, the floor of the box should be thickly layered with newspapers so that the top, soiled layers can be removed as needed to provide a clean surface. After the whelping, some kind of surefooted surface to cover the newspapers must be provided for the puppies. The material should be heavy enough so that the bitch cannot scratch it up easily and smother a puppy, and it should be washable or disposable so that the interior of the box can be kept scrupulously clean. Thirty-inch squares of old mattress pads, cut to size and stitched around the cut edges, make excellent covers. These have enough body to lie flat and can be tossed into the washer with some *Clorox,*® then into the dryer. They are nearly lint-free and provide good traction for crawling puppies. Heavy bath towels or scatter rugs are another good choice if puppy toenails are kept short enough so as not to catch in the terry loops. Old blankets are fine if they are not linty. Fine lint may irritate newly opened puppy eyes and collect on tiny feet and claws. Squares of carpet, unless washable, would need to be thrown away daily.

I have seen pictures of whelping boxes that have a cover and completely close in the bitch. I do not like this, because I am shut out of the box! Also, some bitches are pacers during whelping, seeming to find that walking about assists with delivery of the puppies. These boxes were evidently designed with the thought that the bitch is a descendant of cave dwellers and that she will like a closed in place in which to have her litter. I provide a similar atmosphere by setting up my grooming table over the whelping box. This serves a double purpose in providing a handy place for the whelping supplies.

I set up this arrangement at about the fiftieth day of the pregnancy. This gives the bitch an early introduction to the whelping box, well in advance of the time when she will use it. At this time, I begin to take her temperature twice a day, morning and evening, and record it. This is done while she is "at rest," not immediately after a

174

Future Ch. Fairtee Simon-pure Pippin, center, and his two brothers, Dickens and Angus, age four weeks, like the low barrier that allows them to view their surroundings.

walk or other exercise. A distinct drop in temperature will occur just prior to whelping, which is why it should be monitored. The temperature will fluctuate, dropping below one hundred degrees, then coming back up to near normal. At the fifty-fifth day, I begin taking the temperature every four hours. If the temperature returns to normal at any time in a twenty-four hour period, whelping is not imminent, but if the temperature drops and stays down, the bitch is due to whelp. Some breeders advocate taking the temperature every two hours around the clock. If this is done, there will be noted a steep drop, to as low as ninety-six degrees. When the temperature returns to ninety-nine degrees, whelping is ready to begin. This temperature drop is said to be nature's way of getting the puppies accustomed to the much cooler temperature of their new environment. A drop in temperature below one hundred degrees that continues for more than forty-eight hours could mean the first sign of trouble, and if your bitch shows no sign of whelping, your veterinarian should be notified. This could mean some obstruction to delivery and permit an early cesarean section to be performed before further complications develop.

In addition to that handy thermometer, other items to assist in the whelping should be accumulated on the table or on a tray. You should have a stack of washcloths or small hand towels, about one dozen or more. These will be needed for drying puppies and perhaps for turning puppies or otherwise assisting them into the world. You should have a pair of scissors for cutting cords, if this becomes necessary. A spool of thread may be required for tying cords, if one should begin to bleed. A bottle of nail polish should be available for marking the puppies as they are born. You will want your notebook or calendar for recording birth weights, sex, and time of birth. A clock for timing the onset of contractions should be on the table or in some other place where it is easy to see. You will need a scale that weighs grams or ounces for weighing puppies as they are born and for monitoring their gains in the first three weeks.

You should also have a box or deep dishpan about the size of a heating pad. This will serve as a temporary nursery for the newborn puppies if needed. The most important thing that a new-born puppy needs is warmth. Puppies are born wet into a very chilly atmosphere. They must be dried and kept warm. For the first few hours, this is more important than food. A badly chilled puppy will probably never recover from the shock and will die. The box can be warmed by a heating pad with a folded terry towel over it, by a chicken brooder lamp suspended above the box, or even by an infrared heat lamp. If you use either lamp, keep a room thermometer in the box to be certain that the box does not get too hot. You want to keep the puppies warm, but you do not want to cook them. You will also need a large trash bag or container for the soiled newspapers from the whelping box. A small stool or low chair will make the assistant's waiting more comfortable. From your veterinarian you should buy a can of *Esbilac®* and a tube of *Nutri-cal.® Esbilac®* is replacement bitch's milk and comes in liquid and powder. The liquid must be used in forty-eight hours or poured out, so the powder, which can be mixed with water as needed, is the better choice. The small can should be more than enough. If all goes well, you will not need any at all. *Nutri-cal®* is a very high-caloric, high-nutrient "goo" in a tube. It is usually recommended for stimulating the appetite of dogs that have been ill or have had surgery. It is completely digestible. It is not often thought of in relation to newborn puppies but it can be an invaluable aid in saving a weak puppy. I like to have these items on hand just in case they might be needed. I like to be prepared for emergencies. A bit of brandy is often useful. One drop of it from an eye dropper can act as a stimulant for a puppy that is having a difficult time beginning to breathe. You should also have a clean eye dropper in the supplies.

The breeding program of Jim and Neoma Eberhardt, Merryhart Kennels, Santa Ana, California, is currently one of the best in the United States. It clearly shows what can be done, with dedication, thought, and planning, not to mention hard work. The Merryhart Westies are nearly all owner bred and nearly always owner handled to their titles. The Eberhardts have finished thirty-six champions bearing their own kennel name, and four from other kennels. In addition, their dogs have been shown to eleven Canadian titles and twelve in Mexico. These wins include three Best in Show awards, eight Sweepstakes wins, and two Specialty wins, both by Merryhart bitches. Pictured here is Am. Mex. Ch. Merryhart Tattletale, with Mrs. Eberhardt. "Tattle" is a classic example of a beautiful Westie bitch.

Ludwig photo

24 The Whelping of Puppies

When I had my first Westie bitch bred, I took her to my veterinarian at the twenty-eighth day to have her palpated for puppies. When her pregnancy was confirmed, I voiced my trepidation at the coming event of whelping. "Oh," my veterinarian said, "Westies don't usually have much problem. They just have nice, square little puppies." He butted his thumbs together and extended his forefingers to illustrate the nice, square puppies I could expect. I think that I envisioned the puppies emerging in their little wrappers, like so many loaves of freshly wrapped bread emerging from the assembly line at the bakery.

As he had recommended, I was then reading every book I could find on the subject of dogs in general, and more specifically on the subject of breeding and whelping. I made a list of every book that the library owned, from the card files. Those that were not on the shelves could be requested at the desk. By filling out a postcard, I would be notified when a book was returned so that I could be next to borrow the book. On that particular day, I had not yet read any books that had pictures of puppies being born. When the time came for my bitch to have her litter, I was very glad that I had taken that advice and the time to read all I could find beforehand.

Now that I have experienced the actual process, I know that there is probably no such thing as a "standard" whelping. Every bitch is different, and every litter is different. Assisting the bitch requires patience and fortitude. Watching and waiting while this beloved family member endures the often painful birth process can be difficult for the owner, who may wish that he could turn a switch to reverse the whole process. Remember that your calm presence is absolutely essential. I have read many books that advise the owner not to worry. They claim that centuries of domestication of the dog have not dimmed the natural instincts of the bitch. Do not count on it. With a first litter, the bitch may seem to have no idea whatsoever of what is going on.

The first indication of impending whelping is the continued low temperature of the bitch. If it is daytime, she may refuse food and not want to go for her daily walk. She may seem restless and anxious, pacing the floor and whining gently. She may get into the whelping box and make confetti of the carefully layered inch of newspapers, digging with her feet and even using her teeth to aid in the shredding. She will pant and perhaps shiver. She may decide to lie in the whelping box, or she may not. If you have not already alerted your veterinarian that you have a bitch ready to whelp, now would be a good time to call him. That way you will know where to reach him in case of an emergency.

The first puppy will be preceded by a water bag. If the bitch happens to be sitting as it is passed, you may not see the bag, only a spreading puddle. The first puppy should follow the expulsion of the water bag within four hours. If after four hours there are no visible contractions indicating that a puppy is about to be born, call your veterinarian. If the bitch has shredded the papers in her whelping box, try to replace them with several fresh layers so that the surface of the floor is smooth, making it easier for you to watch for the emerging puppies. Not all bitches like to lie at rest on one side while whelping. Some bitches prefer to squat or to stand in order to make the whelping easier. First-time whelpers often want to be let out, thinking that they have to relieve themselves. Some bitches prefer to pace and may leave the prepared area entirely, if not watched, to seek out the sofa cushions on which to whelp the puppies. I remember hearing about a Boxer bitch that had her puppies, one after the other, at various spots on the living room and dining room carpet.

THE ONSET OF LABOR

The actual labor is usually obvious, although I have talked with breeders who said that no contractions were seen. Be alert for the hard inward pulling of the abdominal muscles. When you notice the first one, look at the clock and write down the time. If these hard contractions continue for more than two hours without producing a puppy, call your veterinarian. Usually, the puppy will be expelled in ten to twenty minutes. After the first puppy is born, the hard contractions will begin anew to signal the impending birth of the next puppy. In most cases, the second puppy will be born in thirty to forty minutes, but there is no set "standard." Two to three hours could elapse between puppies. Each time the hard contractions begin again, the time should be recorded so that if the labor for any puppy is overly long, you can call your veterinarian. If such lengthy labor is observed early in the whelping, it means that a puppy is for some reason unable to be expelled. If this puppy is in trouble, then all of the others are in trouble, too.

Patience to let nature take its course is hard to muster. If your bitch is able to deliver the litter normally, this is the best course. Remember that the bitch that must be loaded into the car to drive to the veterinarian's office will be upset at this turn of events and may cease all contractions. Watching the labor and the clock will help you to tell your veterinarian exactly what has taken place and when, so that he can advise you if your bitch needs his help.

THE PRESENTATION OF THE PUPPIES

In the normal delivery, each puppy will be preceded by hard contractions. In a short time, the puppy will be presented, headfirst in his sac, surrounded with fluid. The puppy-filled sac will be followed by the cord and the placenta, all as one unit. The sac must be removed from the puppy so that he can begin to breathe. A bitch that knows what this is all about will break the sac with her teeth, lick and tumble the puppy until he squeals and cries, bite the cord to separate the puppy from the placenta, and eat the placenta. If the puppy is close to the dam, he may make his own way to a teat and begin to suckle. If not, the dam will help the puppy find his way. The dam will do a considerable amount of licking to stimulate the puppy. This will assist him to have his first bowel movement, which is black. It is important that the puppy should empty this "meconium" from his bowel so that he can digest the food that he is about to get from his mother.

But puppies are often presented feet first

178

rather than headfirst. Sometimes the sac ruptures during the passage down the birth canal; sometimes the cord breaks off from the placenta; sometimes the puppy has no sac and is stained with blood or may be stained green. This puppy has been under stress for some undetermined length of time and must be made to breathe as soon as possible. A puppy that is presented feet first may create difficulty if his broader shoulders are hung up inside the bitch. Any or all of these problems must be handled by the breeder rather than being left up to the dam, especially if this is a first litter.

The first puppy is often the largest and can cause the bitch much pain. She might turn and bite this thing that has hurt so much. You must be alert to prevent it from happening. A bite that goes through the puppy will kill it. Some bitches will be more interested in the placenta than the puppy and may bite the cord, perhaps too close, in an eagerness to consume the placenta. If the contractions for the next puppy commence as soon as the first puppy is expelled, the bitch may be more concerned with her labor than with the newborn puppy.

Breeders of quality purebred dogs want to be present at whelping. I find that my bitches are willing and grateful to have my help. They seem to regard it as a joint effort. As the puppies are born, I break the bag covering the nose and mouth so that the puppy will breathe air, not fluid. If the placenta is attached, I use my fingers to compress the cord, "milking" the bloody fluid in the cord toward the puppy's abdomen. This gives the puppy this last bit of nourishment. Often the cord has a weak spot and will break readily. I compress it about one inch from the puppy and in another spot about one-half inch further from the puppy, tearing the cord with my thumbnails. If it is a very tough cord, scissors may be needed, but I avoid using them if I can. Tearing the cord after squeezing it causes the blood vessels to close, so usually no hemorrhaging occurs. However, watch for any sign of bleeding, and, if necessary, tie the end of the cord with a piece of thread from the spool that you have on the table. Sometimes the cord already will have broken away from the placenta and may be very short. You will need to tie this cord, too.

*All placentas must be accounted for during whelp-*ing. One must be expelled with every puppy or along with the next puppy. A retained placenta can cause a very serious infection. Opinions differ as to whether or not the bitch should be allowed to eat the placentas. Most breeders feel that eating the first two is very good for the bitch. Placentas are full of nutrients and hormones, which have collected during pregnancy. The hormones are believed to be beneficial in stimulating the whelping process and "keeping things going." Some veterinarians say that the placentas will cause the bitch to have diarrhea and recommend that the bitch not be allowed to consume any of them. Certainly all of the placentas from a large litter of puppies will cause voluminous and foul-smelling stools. Some bitches are not interested in eating the placentas, but others are willing to fight for one. Whatever happens, just make certain that all placentas are counted so that you will know if one has been retained.

If you are assisting the bitch, your next act, after separating the puppy from the placenta, is to get the puppy to breathe. Lift the puppy with one of the washcloths wrapped around him for warmth. Turn the head downward but be certain that you are supporting the puppy's neck. Give a sharp shake to rid the air passages of fluid. Then rub the puppy vigorously with the rough surface of the washcloth. This will stimulate him to breathe, just as his dam's rough tongue would do, and will also dry him. Rubbing the hair on the neck the wrong way acts as a stimulant. Continue to rub briskly until he gives some squeals and cries of protest.

If this does not start the puppy's breathing, clasp him in both hands and turn him feet up. Then, alternately, turn him head up. As he is swung head down, his stomach will push into the chest cavity, compressing the lungs. As he is swung head up, the lung pressure will relax. This works rather like chest massage, forcing the lungs to expand and contract. Do this rhythmically, about twenty to thirty times per minute. Many breeders use mouth-to-mouth resuscitation, which should really be mouth-to-nose so as not to blow air into the puppy's stomach. Sometimes one drop of brandy on the puppy's tongue will help if other measures fail. If rubbing causes hair to fall out, this puppy has been dead for a long time, and if a puppy is so premature that it has little or no hair coat, it will usually not survive.

Sometimes a puppy can look very white or even blue and appear to be dead. But do not discard a puppy as beyond hope until you have worked on him about fifteen minutes. In Mrs. Pacey's book, *West Highland White Terriers*, she tells a story of a litter that was born prematurely in the barn during the night. A kennel man had decided that two of the puppies were dead and had tossed them into the rubbish. Mrs. Pacey retrieved the two puppies and took them to the house to work on them. One of them revived and grew up to be Champion Wolvey Patrician, which Mrs. Pacey believed was the best Westie she had ever owned.

Once the puppy is giving lusty squeals, you will know that all is well. Be sure that he is dry. Then quickly weigh the puppy and record his weight, and sex, and time of birth in your notebook. Next, mark the puppy with nail polish. My system is to mark the left front toes of the first puppy and the right front toes of the second one. Third and fourth are marked on the left and right rear toes. If a fifth one appears, you can mark it on the tip of the tail. Number six can have no marking at all. If the litter is larger than that, which is most unusual, you will have to hunt up a different color of polish.

Marking the puppies is very important to monitor their progress. Westie puppies will be like so many peas in a pod. Without identification, in a day or two you will only be able to sort out males from females. I know breeders who use food coloring to mark the tails. I find that this, or different colors of felt-tipped pen markings, will quickly disappear, since the dam does so much licking and cleaning. Nail polish on the toes will remain for several days, usually never disappearing without trimming off the hair.

If the dam is not having the contractions that indicate the arrival of another puppy, put the first puppy on a clean washcloth and place him at a teat to nurse. You may need to express a drop or two of milk from the teat to get the puppy started. Nursing will stimulate the contractions of the bitch's uterus, aiding in the delivery of the rest of the litter. Getting this first meal is important for the puppy, too. If the whelping should become protracted, it could be a long time before all of the puppies are born and can be nursed as a group. You will have to play it by ear. If the bitch is in the throes of having the next puppy, place the dried and weighed puppy in the warm box or pan that you have provided. Then try to get this one and the new arrival to nurse at the first possible moment.

Between deliveries, remove the top layer of newspapers so that the box will have a clean surface to receive the next puppy and the attendant mess of the next delivery. These soiled papers can be put into the trash bag that you have handy. Be sure to note if you discard a placenta, if the bitch eats a placenta, or if no placenta accompanies a puppy. If the latter occurs, it probably means that the placenta is still in the birth canal and will be expelled with the next puppy. If only one placenta comes with the next puppy, you will know that one is still missing and must be accounted as still retained. Or, you can accumulate all of the placentas in a throwaway container and count them after the whelping is completed.

A feet-first presentation is about as common as a headfirst presentation but may require your

180

Westie puppies will be like so many peas in a pod. These four "peas" are all males and, without markings, would be almost impossible to identify. This litter was sired by Ch. Jenessey Sir Scott x Fairtee Platinum Piper. The puppies are two days old.

assistance. If the bitch is having a problem, grasp the emerging hindquarters of the puppy with a washcloth to prevent slippage, and at the next contraction, tug slowly and steadily. The broader shoulders may be hung up inside the bitch. If this is the case, swing the hindquarters to the left and give a small tug to loosen one shoulder. Then swing the puppy to the right, giving a steady tug to loosen the other shoulder. One more steady tug should release the whole puppy, as you pull it between the bitch's back legs in the direction of her nose. If you have to assist with the removal of any puppy, always tug toward the bitch's nose, which is the direction in which it would be expelled naturally.

Remember that whelping is hard and often painful work for your bitch. During the whelping, offer her a small bowl of milk, or milk and egg yolk, or chicken or beef broth. Offer her a drink of water between puppies. She may or may not want anything until the whelping is completed, but offer it to her anyway.

Make certain that all of the puppies nurse as soon as possible. This first milk is "colostrum" and is high in antibodies which help to protect the puppies from disease, particularly distemper. This is true whether the puppies were delivered normally or by cesarean section. It is also important that each puppy have his first bowel movement. If you are the assistant, watch for this black material to be passed from each puppy. Either the bitch's licking of the genital area or your own stimulation of the puppy should cause the puppy to urinate and defecate. Puppies must have this stimulation, since their reflexes are not operative at birth. You may need to wet a corner of a washcloth with hot water to warm it, and wipe the genital area to stimulate the puppy to relieve himself. While the puppies are still nursing, the bitch will perform this task many times a day, and she will eat all of the stools. This is the bitch's instinctual way of keeping her nest clean, dating from the dogs in the wild, who did not have assistance in this matter.

Most newcomers to breeding wonder how they will know when the whelping is over, since it is impossible to know beforehand how many puppies to expect. Most often, a definite change occurs in the attitude of the bitch. Her anxiety will dissipate, and she will seem to relax, resting contentedly as she nurses her new family and nuzzles them to clean and stimulate them. If she has refused food and drink, she will now usually accept a light meal of broth or milk. However, I had two bitches that appeared to be finished with whelping, then delivered another puppy. You should palpate the bitch's abdomen carefully to see if you can feel another unborn whelp. In one instance, I did this and knew that there was another puppy, yet the bitch ate the meal that I offered her with great relish. In the other case, the bitch ate well, too, and seemed completely relaxed. I felt safe to leave the room for about two minutes. When I returned, I nearly stepped on a puppy. The bitch had gotten out of the box to get a drink, which I had failed to offer her. Evidently the puppy had been in the birth canal, and neither of us knew that it was there. I quickly worked on the puppy to get him breathing and was glad that I had not been gone for more than two minutes.

Once the whelping is over, the whole area should be an island of contentment, completely surrounded by quiet. Warm and well-fed puppies are content to sleep quietly until the next meal. The whelping box should be cleaned of soiled newspaper. A heavy layer of clean newspaper should remain in the box with a clean pad or towel to cover it and provide easy traction for the crawling puppies.

AFTER THE WHELPING

"Postparturition" is the correct name for the next care that must be provided. How quickly it must be given depends on whether any placentas have not been accounted for during whelping. If all of the placentas have been expelled by the bitch, it will probably be safe to wait twenty-four hours before taking her to the veterinarian. In one case, I had a bitch that had retained a placenta. She had had her litter on a weekend, and the clinic was closed. Before twenty-four hours had elapsed, she passed the placenta. Some breeders say that they will never remove a bitch from her litter for the first twenty-four hours, regardless. Others insist that a retained placenta means a trip to the veterinarian about four hours after the whelping. I suggest that you ask your own veterinarian and follow his advice. Retained placentas, as well as retained membranes from the puppies, can cause metritis, a very serious infection. For this reason, the bitch should be seen by your veterinarian shortly after whelping for a shot of oxytocin. This is needed to clear the debris from the uterus and prevent infection.

This one shot is all I ever give my bitches. I do not want "routine" shots of antibiotics, which some veterinarians like to give as an additional protection against infection. If an infection were actually proven to exist, I would certainly want my bitch to have the necessary antibiotic. But the bitch that is promptly taken to the veterinarian for postparturition care will not have time to develop infection. Dosing the bitch with an antibiotic has been known to create problems in the puppies, since they ingest some of the drug as they nurse. The kidneys of neonatal puppies are underdeveloped in their ability to excrete antibiotics until the puppies are about eight weeks of age. In some cases, an antibiotic administered to the dam has been known to kill all of the "good" bacteria in the puppies' digestive tract, leading to colicky and bloated puppies.

FEEDING THE LACTATING BITCH

Your bitch's appetite may lag for the first few days after whelping, and she may have a slightly elevated temperature—just about 102 degrees. As long as it is no higher than that, you have no cause to worry, but you should take her temperature at least twice a day for the first week. In about three or four days, it should be the normal 101.5 degrees. I treat my bitches as I would any other member of the family—by serving food that will tempt the appetite. For my bitches, this is cooked chicken. I have never met a dog that was feeling puny that would not eat cooked chicken. In fact, all chicken and no cereal is a fine diet for a few days. Chicken has more calcium than beef, making it a good food for the lactating bitch. After about three days, I begin adding my regular kibble to the ration, gradually increasing it until the bitch is eating about three-fourths kibble.

Between meals, I mix a favorite "milk shake," which consists of a beaten egg yolk mixed with a small amount of milk and a teaspoon of honey. My "girls" love this and have it twice a day. I also feed cottage cheese for extra complete protein and natural calcium, and to add variety to the dry food diet. A lactating bitch needs plenty of protein to produce milk for her litter. I return the brewer's yeast, kelp, vitamin E, and vitamin C to the daily ration. And, once again, I begin to add canned meat with some cereal to the diet.

The bitch's need for food will depend on the size of the litter. Her appetite will also increase as the puppies grow and require increasingly more milk. I put my bitches on a self-feeding program, making sure that food is always available. If she is not on a self-feeding program, she should be fed three or four times a day. She could never supply her needs in one meal. For the first week, she will need about one and one-half times her usual ration. By the third week, this should be increased to about three times her usual amount. If you do not wish to use the self-feeding plan, prepare her three or four meals a day, always offering more food if she eats all of the serving. Before going to bed, I leave food in case the new mother is hungry during the night.

Your bitch may be quite reluctant for the first few days to leave her new babies to go out to relieve herself. You will have to carry her, if necessary, to get her out to perform these important functions. Take her to a clean area, where she will not drag her full teats and pick up dirt. If this is not possible, wash and dry her well before returning her to the whelping box and her litter.

You will also want to wash her hindquarters and tail daily. Mix a pan of water and shampoo, as described in the grooming chapter. Because of the bloody stains, the water should not be hot, only tepid. This helps to remove the stains without "setting" them, as hot water does with any bloodstain. Use an old washcloth to apply the lather to the soiled areas. Then rinse with fresh, clean water. Dry the coat with a terry towel before putting the bitch back with her puppies.

THE CESAREAN SECTION

This is one situation which I have never experienced, so my information is secondhand. In some circumstances, the bitch is unable to normally whelp her puppies. To be expelled, the puppies must travel upward through the neck of the uterus, through the pelvis, and downward through the birth canal. The very short-coupled Westie bitch may lack the space required for this maneuvering. The puppies may be overly large, or one puppy may be lying across the opening to the birth canal. There also may be uterine inertia, in which one or both horns of the uterus fail to contract and expel the puppies. The bitch that has expelled a water bag and failed to begin contractions after four hours, or the bitch that has been laboring over the birth of a puppy for longer than two hours should be seen by your veterinarian. A "C-section" may be needed to save her life and that of the puppies.

Your veterinarian will give her some anesthetic, open her abdomen, and remove the puppies. The puppies, as well as the mother, will probably be groggy from the anesthetic. The bitch will wake up almost as soon as the surgery is complete, but she will be groggy for several hours. You should have a box or crate for her trip home and a separate box for the puppies, taking care that plenty of warmth is provided. Once the bitch is settled at home, she should be given the puppies to nurse one at a time to make certain that she is ready to accept the new family. She will still be groggy and may not know what the puppies are, especially if this is a first litter.

Keep the puppies warm, and supplementally feed them if necessary. If the dam readily accepts the litter, no lengthy period of feeding by the breeder will be necessary, of course. For the first four days, it is important that the puppies get the colostrum from their dam. Also, the nursing causes the uterus to contract, which is good for the bitch. One at a time, try to get the puppies to nurse.

You may wish to get instructions and equipment for tube feeding the puppies while you are at the veterinarian's office, just in case you need to tube feed. This is the fastest way to feed puppies that have been refused by the dam. Supplemental feeding with an eye dropper can be done if the Esbilac® is given to the puppy one careful drop at a time. An eye dropper full of milk looks like a lot, but if measured into a teaspoon it will only be about one-half teaspoon. Many breeders feed milk to rejected or orphan puppies in small baby bottles with nipples used for feeding premature infants.

For a large litter, tube feeding is certainly faster. But to the bottle advocates, tube feeding does not develop the jaw muscles or satisfy the puppies' need to suck. With a little practice, two puppies can be bottle-fed at the same time, with a bottle for each. If you need to tube feed puppies, you also need to be sure that they do not suck on each other's feet and genitals. If this happens, you will have to hunt up some boxes to separate the puppies, keeping the puppies warm at the same time.

If separate boxes are necessary, each one should have a folded towel or diaper in the bottom. This covering should be checked often for puppy stool. Each puppy will need stimulation to help him relieve himself for the first week. You will need to use a warm, damp washcloth to rub the puppies in the genital area, just as the dam would do with her warm, wet tongue.

"C-sections" are performed often on all breeds of dogs. Many times the bitch can have a second litter and normally deliver the puppies. You should ask your veterinarian why the surgery is necessary so that you will know whether it is caused by a pelvic malformation which would prohibit breeding the bitch again. Follow your veterinarian's advice, and be sure to get instructions for postoperative care of the bitch. No C-section should be taken lightly. This surgery is done in a life-threatening situation for both the dam and the puppies. Many breeders who have seen a bitch through such surgery and the recuperation have vowed never again to breed a bitch. Careful monitoring of your bitch during the whelping and seeking help the moment it is needed can make all the difference between a successful C-section, with uneventful recovery of the bitch, and severe complications. Remember that the best veterinarian in the world cannot help your bitch if you bring her to the clinic too late.

POST-WHELPING COMPLICATIONS

Problems after whelping are uncommon in the bitch that has had the proper care, nutrition,

183

and veterinary care. However, it is only prudent to learn what the problems and their symptoms are so that help can be sought if needed.

Eclampsia

Eclampsia is a disease in lactating bitches and results from a lowered level of calcium. It is most often seen in the Toy Group and in bitches that are nursing large litters. It usually occurs about three to four weeks after the puppies are born, but it may occur before they are born, during whelping, or even as late as weaning. Early signs can be panting and restlessness, anxiety, drooling, and chomping of the jaws. Later, the bitch's gait becomes stiff. She may stagger, collapse with the inability to rise, and have spasms of muscle groups. The bitch needs early veterinarian attention in the form of intravenous calcium gluconate, which will relieve the symptoms immediately. She may also need an intramuscular shot of calcium solution and/or calcium gluconate to be given orally. A bitch with this problem should be well nurtured during her pregnancy if she is ever bred again.

Mastitis

Mastitis is an inflammation of the mammary glands and may be acute or chronic. It can be caused by injury to the gland or by failure of the glands to empty following weaning of the litter.

It can also accompany acute metritis, an infection of the uterus. Infection with streptococci or staphylococci may be involved. The first signs are swelling of the glands involved, with discoloration and perhaps abscessing. Fever, lethargy, and dehydration follow. The involved glands may form cysts in the chronic form of mastitis. If the puppies are still nursing, they should be weaned from the dam and hand-fed, or they may die. The bitch will require antibiotic treatment by your veterinarian and the lancing of any abscesses. If the condition is caused by failure of the glands to empty, using a breast pump three times a day may help, as well as hot compresses followed by cold compresses two or three times a day. If the condition is chronic, the breast cysts may need to be surgically removed, or the bitch may need to be spayed.

Metritis

Metritis is an acute inflammation of the uterus. It occurs as a result of retained membranes or placentas, which provide a breeding ground for bacteria that can enter through the open cervix after whelping. Infection can also be caused by the careless use of non-sterile instruments or be introduced by the stud dog at breeding. Dilating a small vagina prior to breeding is another possible source of infection. Bacteria of the kind found in feces may be present, plus streptococci

184

Glinda at age six weeks. Owned by Tom and Lois Drexler, North Huntington, Pennsylvania.

or staphylococci. The acute form will require antibiotic treatment, possibly combined with estrogen. In this form, the bitch will have a fever, be depressed, and may vomit. A discharge of bloody mucous from the uterus may be present. A history of abortion or resorbed fetuses may accompany the acute form. Metritis can also be a secondary infection resulting from mastitis. In the chronic form, intermittent uterine discharge may be seen as well as prolonged bleeding during the bitch's season. Failure to conceive when bred or the whelping of dead or weak puppies suggests the chronic form of metritis. This form, too, requires lengthy treatment with antibiotics but without the use of hormones. If the inflammation does not improve with treatment, the bitch should be spayed.

Pyometra

Pyometra is an accumulation of pus in the uterus. In metritis, bacterial infection is present, while pyometra appears to be of endocrine origin. Lack of appetite, together with much consumption of water and vomiting of the water, are early signs. Renal failure may accompany the dis-

ease. Diarrhea or a discharge from the vulva that has a "sickly sweet" odor may be present. High fever is usually followed by a subnormal temperature as the disease progresses. The bitch will become increasingly weak and be unable to stand. The uterine horns, which will be distended, can be detected by palpation. The affected bitch will exhibit signs of pain. The symptoms, together with a history of nonpregnancy and/or false pregnancy, confirm the diagnosis. The bitch will need treatment for dehydration before spaying, and careful monitoring for signs of renal failure after the surgery.

Early treatment by your veterinarian at the first signs of illness is essential. New treatments are being tried which could prevent the spaying of a bitch with pyometra. Any owner of a valuable show-quality bitch will wish to avoid spaying if treatment can prevent it. This is a serious disease, often causing death if treatment is delayed.

Since pyometra is frequently seen with a false pregnancy and at two to eight weeks after the bitch's season, it has been included with "post-whelping" for the benefit of the owner who expected a litter that did not materialize.

186

This puppy, about five weeks old, was bred by Christine Swingle of North Canton, Connecticut.

25 Care of Neonatal Puppies

If friends and neighbor children know that you have new puppies at your house, they may come calling to see the little newcomers. It may be necessary to hang a "Do Not Disturb" sign on your door or disconnect the doorbell. Just tell them that the puppies look like white rats and invite them to return in six weeks. The last thing that a bitch with a new litter needs is visitors. Even with the most amenable and calm bitch, you are risking disease being tracked into the nursery on strange shoes. If someone simply cannot be turned away, have the visitor remove his shoes at the front door and wash up before entering the puppies' quarters.

THE FIRST THREE WEEKS

Neonatal puppies are rather like premature babies. You know how carefully these babies are protected at the hospital. It is very important for the breeder to understand the fragility of neonatal puppies. About 75 percent of the deaths in newborn puppies occur in the first eighteen days of life. It is estimated that about 60 percent of these deaths could have been avoided with the proper care and help from the breeder. Puppies have few reflexes when they are born. Tests done in the 1950s at Hamilton Station, Bar Harbor, Maine, the results of which are written up in *The New Knowledge of Dog Behavior* by Clarence Pfaffenberger, indicated that the brain waves of neonatal puppies are nearly flat. Puppies cannot control their own body temperatures and are unable to shiver, which is the body's way of creating warmth. This reflex will not be fully operative and effective until the puppies are three weeks old. Puppies cannot urinate and defecate without stimulus of the genital area by the licking of their dam, or a substitute mother should the need arise. This reflex will not be present until they are one week old. The puppies' eyes are sealed shut because they are not fully developed at birth. The eyes will open at ten to fifteen days of age. The ears are also sealed, so the puppies are deaf as well as blind. The ears will open at fifteen to nineteen days of age. The sucking reflex is present, and the puppies are able to move to their dam if placed near her.

The newborn puppy's body temperature for the first week of life is 94 to 97 degrees. Since the normal temperature for an adult dog is 101.5 degrees, this very low temperature in the puppy makes him very susceptible to rapid chilling. The most important thing that the puppy needs is warmth. Ideally, this would be 80 to 85 degrees in the whelping box, or wherever the puppy is kept. The wall thermometer is not a good guide, since the box is on the floor. What feels comfortable to you may be too cold for the puppy. In the second week of the puppy's life, the room temperature can be a little lower. By this time the puppy's temperature will have risen to about 97 to 99 degrees. By the fourth week, his temperature will be about the same as that of an adult dog.

Humidity is also important. It should be between 40 and 60 percent. The puppy's water turnover is three times that of an adult dog, so humidity that is too low will quickly bring on dehydration. Humidity that is too high in a warm, ambient temperature will decrease heat loss and increase body temperature. This will bring about the same result as an overheated room. High humidity in the room will also promote the growth of bacteria.

If the warmth and humidity are comfortable, the puppy will be relaxed and undisturbed, sleeping 90 percent of the time. The puppy is born with very little reserve subcutaneous fat and stored glycogen (carbohydrates). If the ambient temperature and/or the humidity are too low or high, the puppy will be alert, restless, and crying. Using the extra energy required for these activities will deplete the small reserves that the puppy has at birth. If the puppy becomes chilled so that the body temperature drops below ninety-four degrees, the digestive system becomes paralyzed. Nursing is then ineffectual, and the lowered intake of food, combined with the already low energy, will cause the puppy to die.

For the first three weeks, the dam will decide that it is time to feed her litter and will waken the sleeping puppies with her licking and nuzzling. Puppies seem to have no favorite teat but will move to the nearest one that they find and suck vigorously. Puppies must be weighed at birth and every eight hours for the first twenty-four hours, and the weights should be recorded. A normal, healthy puppy will maintain his birth weight and begin to gain immediately. Occasionally, a puppy will lose a small amount, which should never be more than 10 percent of his birth weight, in the first day. This loss should be followed by steady gains. A larger weight loss or a failure to gain indicates the first sign of a problem. A loss of a fraction of an ounce, or the failure to gain, is not visible to the eye, but the scale shows it. As the puppies grow and gain, the scale will be your security blanket, telling you that the puppies are thriving. This is why it is so important to mark the puppies at birth.

Removal of Dewclaws

If all is well with the puppies, it is a good idea to take them to the veterinarian for dewclaw removal at about three days of age, or as soon as possible in the first week. The veterinarian will remove the claws with sterile scissors and will cauterize the wounds. If it is the dead of winter, all precautions must be taken to keep the puppies

188

Stardust's Ave Maria, owned by Mr. and Mrs. Ed Chappell, Jr., is available for lunch to one of her litter of two puppy dogs. Little brother is invisible under his mother.

warm going from and coming home. I use a Styrofoam® ice chest preheated with the heating pad to transport the litter. The lid is left ajar, of course, for air circulation. Line the bottom of the chest with old terry towels. See that the car is warm before returning home. No puppy that is having a struggle to survive should be taken along, since he does not need any extra trauma. Since the extra claws are not needed, it is good to have them removed to avoid problems later, but not if the puppies are not thriving.

Westies are not a common breed, and often office personnel have never seen the dogs. When a friend of mine took her two puppies for dewclaw removal, the office assistant spoke aloud as she wrote instructions: "Now, let's see. Removal of dewclaws and tails docked." My friend nearly fainted before she was able to cry out, "Oh, NO! Not the tails!" We wonder what would have happened if the girl had not been talking to herself.

I use this office visit to have all of the puppies thoroughly checked, and I do it as soon as I can see that the puppies are gaining and doing well. I take the dam along, since she is happier that way.

The Healthy Puppy

The breeder needs to recognize the visible signs of both healthy and problem puppies. The healthy puppy is warm and plump, round and firm, with good muscle tone and pink skin underneath his white coat. His gums and other mucous membranes are reddish-pink. His coat feels sleek and dry to the touch. Rubbing the puppy's back brings forth high-pitched squeaks and squeals and vigorous movements. Warm and fed, the puppy lies on his side or on his back, limbs and muscles twitching and jerking now and then as he gets his "puppy exercise" in his sleep. The healthy and warm puppy is a quiet puppy. If he is strongly sucking, he makes no sound. The dam's teat is firmly pressed between his tongue and the roof of his mouth. The only visible sign of his nursing are his sides gently moving in and out as he ingests the milk. Tummy full, he will go to sleep until his dam awakes him with her nose and tongue, to tell him that it is time to eat again. A warm and well-fed puppy is a creature of total bliss.

He breathes about 20 times per minute. His tiny heart beats about 150 times per minute at birth, increasing and leveling off at about 200 beats per minute for the first month. A physiologically mature puppy has no "soft spot" on the top of his head, as human babies do. At two to three days of age, the dried cord will drop off. The puppy's steady weight gain will result in the doubling of birth weight at nine to twelve days of

189

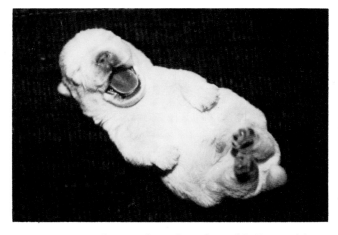

This lovely fellow is about four days old. His cord has dried and fallen off. He is flexing his legs as he exercises. He appears to be full of milk and ready to nap. He fits that description, "a nice square little puppy." This one was bred by Christine Swingle, North Canton, Connecticut.

These puppies have just opened their eyes in the last day or so, before this picture was taken. You can see that the ears are not fully open yet. This litter was bred by Catherine Wilson, Amherst, Massachusetts.

age. The Westie puppy has good substance, making him fit that description illustrated by my veterinarian: "a nice, square little puppy."

The Fading Puppy

This term is used to describe a puppy that is not thriving for some reason or reasons. The condition is often called "fading puppy syndrome," because a group of signs and symptoms occur together to indicate disease. The first sign is a weight loss in excess of 10 percent in the first twenty-four hours of life. The puppy has slowed breathing and poor reflexes when stimulated. He does not move to the bitch and suck with vigor. When he sucks, he makes a smacking or munching noise, which indicates that he is not firmly latched onto the teat. He has a tendency to lie on his chest, or he may be alert, crawling about and crying until he tires and falls asleep. His coat feels rough and may be damp to the touch. His muscle tone is poor, and he feels limp and cool. Because he feels cool, his dam may push him aside, sensing that he is going to die. The puppy may have a potbelly, even though he is obviously not nursing strongly. The mucous membranes may appear purplish, rather than the healthy reddish-pink of the puppy's littermates.

This puppy needs help at once. Many people feel that a weak puppy should be allowed to die or be euthanized because he will never be a healthy dog. This is not necessarily true. I know some fine champions that had a real struggle in the first few days of life. One puppy could have a more difficult time in being born and be weakened by the struggle. I simply cannot go away and silently say, "Okay, sink or swim," to any puppy that is still breathing. I use the "where there's life, there's hope" approach. Unless the puppy has a cleft palate or some other obvious deformity (and I have been lucky enough not to have had any deformed puppies), I must try to save him. Sometimes, I have been a red-eyed zombie, not knowing what day it was, before I won or death won. But, I *have* to try. It is interesting that those puppies I have helped to survive the first few days have grown up to be as healthy and sound as their littermates. The two that I eventually lost may have had physical problems that were not visible.

Helping the Fading Puppy

It must be presumed that the puppy with a problem is being kept with the rest of the litter and therefore is not suffering from the cold. He must be helped to nurse so that his small store of fat and glycogen can be replaced. Two drops of honey from the end of an eye dropper gives an instant source of soluble carbohydrate. If the puppy is not nursing strongly, bracing him underneath the rump and pushing him gently toward the teat will often help him to suck more strongly. If the puppy is still not able to nurse, mix some powdered *Esbilac®* in a custard cup, according to package directions, and feed him. If you do not have equipment for tube feeding or a baby bottle, use an eye dropper. This is not a good method for feeding orphan puppies, but for supplementing a weak puppy, it will work fine. You must be careful to feed the puppy slowly so that you will not give too much too fast and get the formula into the puppy's lungs.

Heat the mixed formula in the custard cup in a pan of water to about your body temperature. A puppy will not accept cold food. The eye dropper will take up only about enough liquid to half fill the glass tube. This is about one-quarter teaspoon. Try to get the puppy to take at least twice that amount, and more if you can. A four-ounce puppy, if fed entirely on *Esbilac,®* should be fed two tablespoons of the mixed formula. If that amount were divided into twelve feedings per day, or one every two hours, the puppy would be fed one-half teaspoon of formula each time. Two half-droppers of formula is not very much. The idea is to get the puppy strong enough to nurse his dam so that he can get the colostrum.

A definite relationship exists between low birth weight and survival. The undersize puppy may be very premature. Since the liver grows to its proper size very late in the development of the fetus, the small puppy may have a liver that is too small for his brain size. Since the brain depends on glucose manufactured by the liver, the small puppy may quickly use up his small store of glycogen and lapse into hypoglycemia (low blood sugar). He should be kept at about ninety degrees ambient temperature. If he is unable to nurse, he should be supplemented with

Esbilac® and given 5 percent glucose by your veterinarian, or a drop or two of honey every three hours. A dab of *Nutri-cal®* will supply the essential amino acids as well as glucose. The small liver may make the puppy bruise and bleed easily, which could be a real problem if he were subjected to injury by the dam.

Some breeders advocate the feeding of blood from beef liver, or pureed beef liver (in the blender) to puppies that are not thriving. These foods would be uncooked, of course, and would be brought to room temperature, then placed in a warmed cup (warm the cup, not the raw liver or the blood). A few drops of the blood or a small dab of the pureed liver on the tip of a finger or spoon is said to work wonders. Pork liver could contain trichinosis and is not recommended. However, beef liver and blood from it could be contaminated. Having read Dr. Kronfeld's series of articles in the *American Kennel Gazette* on "Home Cooking For Dogs," I would never feed raw meat to my dogs, especially to newborn puppies. A later article in the Vizsla column of the *American Kennel Gazette* written by May Carpenter* describes a puzzling case of toxoplasmosis which caused the loss of an entire litter and motor damage to the dam before the diagnosis

was confirmed. Consumption of raw or undercooked meat is now recognized as a principal culprit in this disease, which causes damage to the central nervous system.

A safer booster for the puppy is *Nutri-cal®*. This is very high in calories and nutrients. A ten-pound dog would need only one tablespoon per day as the entire ration if he were eating no other food. *Nutri-cal* contains carbohydrates, fats, protein, and all of the vitamins and minerals in a highly concentrated form that will not burden the digestive tract. One-eighth teaspoon per day with two tablespoons of water to prevent dehydration would keep a four-ounce puppy alive. Thus, a tiny dab of this "goo" will give the puppy the energy he lacks, and he will soon have the strength to nurse his dam, which is exactly what he needs to do. Oversupplementation of unthrifty puppies has been known to cause diarrhea, but *Nutri-cal* will cause no digestive problems if fed in the recommended amounts.

I recently read about a bitch that was so full of puppies that she had no room for food. The litter was not due for two weeks and the bitch refused food. Her owner fed her nothing but *Nutri-cal* until the litter was born. One of my bitches began to behave peculiarly one Fourth of

*November, 1979

191

These three boys at age five weeks are learning to eat from separate dishes. Larger litters are impossible to feed this way and are much easier to feed from a community dish.

July, when her litter was about three weeks old. The bitch would not eat and had very shallow respiration, and her temperature dropped to 98.4 degrees. I gave her one teaspoon of *Nutri-cal,* and in half an hour she drank a "milk shake." In two hours her temperature was normal. She was eating her normal food shortly after the "milk shake." The following day I asked my veterinarian what could have been the trouble. He said that it sounded like a sudden drop in blood sugar, reason unexplained. I was happy that I had *Nutri-cal* on hand that holiday, when all the vets were closed. I have given away more tubes than I have used, to friends with puppies in trouble. Everyone has reported the same excellent results that I have had. I always keep a tube on hand, in case it might be needed for my own dogs or for the dog or puppies of a friend.

I prefer to regard the newborn litter with a degree of pessimism concerning survival. In this way, I avoid over-optimism, which could lead to relaxation of vigilance. If one puppy is not gaining, help him at once, rather than wait to see if he will lose the acceptable 10 percent, then begin to gain. Puppies can go downhill very rapidly. I lost one puppy from the first litter that I assisted, because I did not know that it was important to monitor weight. I will always feel that I might have saved him had I known that he was not gaining. I lost one puppy that weighed only three ounces at birth. I did not know about *Nutri-cal* in those days. It might have saved his life.

Antibiotics for the Bitch

A veterinarian may have a good reason to give an antibiotic to a bitch. Certainly, in the event of C-section, the dam is given something to prevent infection. Breeders feel that this can cause diarrhea in puppies, because the friendly bacteria in the puppies' intestines are destroyed by the antibiotic in the bitch's milk. Highly recommended by breeders as a supplement for the puppies are the friendly bacteria found in lactobacillus acidophilus. This can be found at the drugstore as *Lactinex®,* in powder and capsule form. This same bacteria is found in yogurt. If the bitch has had an antibiotic, ask your veterinarian about feeding this bacteria to the litter and/or the dam. The puppies should be started on it immediately

and fed the bacteria until one week after the dam's last dosage of antibiotic or until weaning, whichever comes first.

In an article by Paddy Magnason, a discussion appears regarding tests that were conducted on sixty-six patients, half of which were fed the bacteria and half of which were not. After various antibiotics were administered for infections, all of the patients had a buildup of staph germs in the intestine at beginning of treatment. Those patients on the antibiotics alone showed a continuing increase in staph, whereas those given the bacteria showed a pronounced drop.*

In the January 1980 issue of *Dog World,* an interesting article by Patricia N. McNab sings the praises of *Lactinex®* as a treatment for a bitch with a history of "acid milk." The bitch was given a packet of the powder daily on her food for one week before whelping, as well as for the first ten days after the puppies were born. In addition, the powder was dissolved along with *Esbilac®* and fed to the puppies. For the first time, the bitch had no problem with the "acid" milk. The article continues to say that *Lactinex®* has great curative powers for fever blisters and canker sores. These ailments are known to be caused by herpesvirus, a form of which is often fatal to neonatal puppies.

In Paddy Magnason's article, a study on newborn piglets is described. It was found that lactobacillus acidophilus created a natural barrier against E. coli bacteria in piglets, which causes diarrhea and death of piglets. Of course, since pigs are important commercial animals, more research is done for them, to help the farmers produce more pigs for pork. It is suggested that newborn puppies be given the bacteria for the first two days of life, as is recommended for the piglets. Ask your veterinarian about this when you take your bitch in for her seven-week checkup, before the litter is born.

Toxic Milk Syndrome

This condition is usually seen in puppies at four days to two weeks of age. The puppies cry

---

*Paddy Magnason, "Great Dane Breed Column," *American Kennel Gazette,* December 1979.

192

and bloat, rather like colicky babies. The rectum of the puppies may look red and swollen. This can be caused by the failure of the bitch's uterus to return to its normal size and condition (subinvolution of the uterus). This condition should be differentiated from uterine infection, although both problems may cause toxic milk. The puppies must be taken away from the dam and kept warm. They should be given 5 percent glucose solution until the bloating has been cleared up, then hand-fed with *Esbilac.*

Canine Herpesvirus

This disease is not seen too often, but there is no cure. A bitch can have the disease and show very few symptoms, since adult dogs do not die from it. Any nasal discharge, or vaginal discharge during the last three weeks of pregnancy should be investigated by your veterinarian. The bitch is thought to transmit the virus to the puppies as they travel down the birth canal. It is not transmitted to the bitch by the stud dog in breeding. Some bitches may lose an entire litter the first time, followed by normal and healthy litters afterward. Some bitches may be carriers and may never be able to have a healthy litter.

Puppies appear to be normal for the first few days of life. The usual age for the puppies to be affected is between eight days and three weeks. The low body temperature of the neonate helps the virus to multiply. The puppies will suddenly be unwilling to nurse, will cry, and will have a yellowish-green diarrhea. Death comes in twelve to twenty-four hours after onset of the diarrhea. The disease is 100 percent fatal to puppies under two weeks of age.

The first puppy to die should be autopsied by your veterinarian. The puppy's kidneys will have red, hemorrhagic speckles on a pale background. This condition differentiates herpesvirus from any other disease. Treatment can then be tried for the rest of the litter in the form of high environmental temperature of 100 degrees for short periods of time, with water and tube feeding and therapy with vitamin K, all administered by your veterinarian. Although success is not always possible, treatment should be attempted.

Puppy Septicemia

Several different forms of bacteria can cause severe diarrhea and other kinds of abdominal distress in the litter. These bacteria will cause low blood sugar, distension of the abdomen, rapid breathing, crying, and low body temperature. The puppies should be kept warm and fed fluids. A culture should be run to determine the type of infection so that an antibiotic can be given. It is true that the kidneys of young puppies do not excrete antibiotics well until the puppies are about eight weeks old, but it is better to risk an antibiotic than to let the puppies die without help. I know one puppy, the only survivor of a C-section, that lived for about three weeks on one-eighth teaspoon of *Nurti-cal,®* mixed with two tablespoons of sterile water. This ration was tube-fed to him in small amounts every two hours. The veterinarian had given up on the puppy. Finally, the puppy lived to be old enough to risk giving him some liquid penicillin. In six hours, all the crying and bloat was gone, and he is currently a beloved family member. The veterinarian calls him "Wonder Dog." You can see that there are many "red eyed zombies" among breeders who refuse to give up as long as the puppy is breathing.

Twenty-One Days and All's Well

193

Neurologically, the puppy's immaturity during these first three weeks causes him to be insulated from his surroundings. He needs the tender loving care of his dam, as represented by her massaging, warmth, and milk. The problem puppy also needs the help of the breeder and perhaps the veterinarian. I never "count puppies" until this critical period has passed.

The puppies will open their eyes at ten to fifteen days of age. The lids open gradually, beginning with slits at the inside corners of the eyes. If the eyes are not open by the sixteenth day, talk to your veterinarian to be sure there is no problem. The blinking reflex will still not be present. Vision is very blurry, and the puppy may do some backing away from his first sight of a human.

Ears will open at fifteen to nineteen days of

age. By this time the puppy will be making some tentative motions at walking. The sight of a littermate may encourage a spark of interest in this fellow creature. Now the puppies will begin to play with each other, gnawing, growling, and tumbling about in the whelping box.

THE FOURTH WEEK

This is a very important time in the life of the puppy. During the first three weeks, the brain has been developing slowly, but now it will begin to take on its adult form. It is as if the puppy were a little machine in which all the wires were not completely connected at birth. However, at twenty-one days of age, all the connections have been made, and the little machine is ready for the trial run of all the systems. Now the puppy is ready to walk on all fours. By the seventh week, the puppy will have an adult-size brain, with all systems "Go!"

Tests indicate that very rapid development occurs in the crucial fourth week. Now the puppy is aware of his dam and his surroundings. No attempt to wean the puppy by taking him away from his mother entirely should be made at this time. He needs his mother. Until now, the dam has been making the overtures at feeding time. For the next ten days or so, the puppy will initiate the action of nursing, and the dam will make herself available, whether inside or outside the whelping box.

Because the puppy is now aware of his surroundings, this is the time to open the whelping box. Do this as soon as the puppy awakens, so that he can exercise his natural instinct to keep his bed clean. If papers are spread in front of the box, the puppy will walk to them and relieve himself. I set up a portable puppy pen around the box and keep the front of the box open so that the puppies can get in and out. I like to watch them waken, yawn, and stretch, then walk to the papers and squat to urinate. This simple act is the first visible sign of the rapid development that is now taking place in the puppies. From being near-vegetables, crawling, and responding only to reflex and the creature comforts supplied by the dam, this represents the beginning of their future independence. If one puppy is slow to realize that the box is open, he can be gently encouraged to follow suit. As a breeder, it is important to me to see that the puppies, which I plan to place in other homes, are learning clean habits from the beginning. The papers feel slick under the puppies' pads, but the puppies will show great determination in learning to cope with this new surface. I keep the hair of the pads well trimmed to allow for better traction. If such arrangements are made, the puppies will paper train themselves.

Teaching the puppies to eat from a dish can be started as a supplement to mother's milk. The puppies will need plenty of protein for the next six weeks. They can be started on very small amounts of canned puppy food, just a taste in the beginning. Some people start the puppies on baby oatmeal mixed into a gruel with *Esbilac.*® A raw egg yolk can be added for extra protein.

Starting any new food can cause diarrhea at any age; therefore, any new food should be given in very small quantities and be increased gradually. Puppy chows are available in bags, but the pieces are too large and hard for the weanling. If you wish to start with one of these, put the dry puppy chow in the blender, a small amount at a time, and chop it into a meal. I make a large jarful each time so that I have a quantity on hand. With hot water added, this makes a lovely gruel. As was noted in the chapter on nutrition, the animal proteins in dry dog foods are sprayed on the surface for palatibility, so this gruel is rather like meaty gravy for the puppies.

The dam at this time still needs to nurse the puppies. I put my bitches into the pen with the puppies throughout the day, so that there can be plenty of interaction between dam and puppies. This allows the puppies to play with the dam and be subjected to her discipline, as well as to seek her for nursing. During this time, I gradually feed the puppies more from the dish, beginning with small feedings twice a day and increasing the quantity and frequency to four times a day over the next ten days.

After about thirty days, the dam will make herself less available for nursing, often lying on her teats or going somewhere else. This will be a gradual process until weaning is completed. I like to leave the puppies with their dam for most of the time until they are seven weeks old.

THE FIFTH AND SIXTH WEEKS

At the end of the fourth week, all of the puppies should be taken to the veterinarian for worm checks and to make certain that they are problem-free. Now that they are nursing less, they should be offered water regularly after eating. Canine teeth will be cutting through at this time, and all of the puppies should be watched to see how their mouths are developing. I record the eruption of teeth on every puppy.

I also introduce toys to the puppy pen at this stage. An old sock tied with several knots makes a soft tug or toss toy. A small ball makes a nice challenge to roll about and chase. A *Rawbone*® provides a chewable item to help cut teeth. Now, with the whelping box removed from the puppy pen, more room is available for active play. I replace it with a crate and put a folded mattress pad into the pan. I tie open the door so that the

puppies can have access to the crate. They like to take naps in it. I keep the floor covered with newspapers, cleaning up the soiled ones as quickly as possible. Before retiring for the night, I remove the toys and lay fresh papers. Often by morning the puppy pen looks as if a small whirlwind had touched down. With the toys removed, clean-up is easier, and there is no possibility of accidentally throwing away a ball or Rawbone.

At the beginning of the sixth week, I begin individual play periods daily. I take each puppy away from the litter to a different room. I allow a fifteen-minute session (by the clock so that no one gets cheated of his time) of investigation and play. In one or two days, I put a small show lead on the puppy for about five minutes and persuade him to come to me or with me. I enjoy these play periods as much as they do. When they are aware that I am ready to play with them, the clamoring to be next becomes very

These handsome puppies, about five weeks of age, were bred by Christine Swingle, North Canton, Connecticut.

195

loud. These times alone help each puppy to realize that he is an individual and that it is fun to become the "only child" for a while. This also provides new sights, sounds, scents, and floor surfaces to experience. This may be the reason why buyers of my puppies say that the puppies do not cry at night or show other signs of the trauma of leaving their litter.

THE SEVENTH AND EIGHTH WEEKS

At the end of the sixth week, I take my puppies for their first immunization shot—the measles vaccine. You should check with your veterinarian to see when he likes to begin the immunizations. My veterinarian gives one at six weeks, one at ten weeks, and the "permanent" shot at fourteen weeks of age. Puppy dogs

should also be checked for the location of the testicles at this time. The testicles are very small, and I do not have the "talented" fingers to find them, so I must rely on my veterinarian for this examination. The vital importance of finding these "family jewels" is discussed in the chapter on congenital defects under "Cryptorchidism."

Meals are increased so that the puppies are fed all that they want at each of the four meals—breakfast, lunch, dinner, and bedtime. They still seek out the dam's teats, often being warned off with a growl and a soft bite. When they are seven weeks old, I remove the dam from them entirely, taking her off food for a twenty-four hour period. This slow process of weaning has always resulted in the natural drying up of the milk as the puppies nurse less and less. Taking the dam off food for a full day has always completed the process. I have one bitch that needs to

196

I put a little show lead on the puppy at the age of five weeks.

When they are aware that I am ready to play with them, the clamoring to be next becomes very loud.

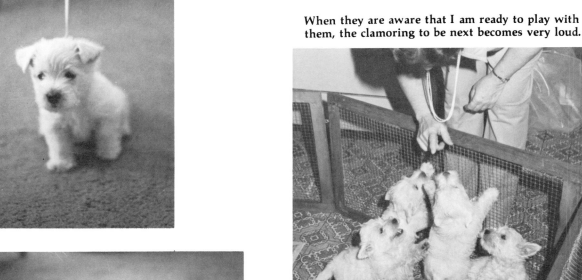

This puppy takes time to check out the interesting bristles on a brush.

be watched, because after weaning she still wants to feed her puppies and regurgitates her food for them, in the manner of bitches in the wild. I have to keep her away from the litter for four hours following her meals.

The puppies now begin three or four daily play periods outside of the puppy pen. I keep them in the kitchen, where they can romp and investigate. I stand with a plastic flyswatter in hand and, along with a stern "No!" give a light tap on the rump of a puppy that chews on any object. I keep a section of the floor covered with newspapers and love to watch them suddenly stop chewing on brother to seek the papers and urinate there. Backsliders are gently corrected. It is amazing how early they learn this, if given the opportunity. This early paper training will be appreciated when the puppies go to new homes.

Weather permitting, they are introduced to the outdoor puppy run once the first immuniza-tion shot has been given. I keep puppies separated from the adult dogs. Being outdoors is another new adventure, so the learning process continues. I also invite the neighbor children to play with the puppies, and everyone gets down on the floor or the ground for the play period. The puppies are also introduced to new noises like the banging of pans and the sound of the vacuum cleaner.

Along with the leash training at an early age, the puppy should have training in being groomed early in his life. What the puppy learns in these early weeks of his life, he will never forget. Not one precious moment should be wasted by the breeder who is interested in turning out well-adjusted pets. There is more to raising good dogs than simply having a pen full of puppies. When short periods of training can help the puppy real-ize his full potential, what a shame it is for any dog to miss this opportunity.

197

Neighbor children do not need much persuasion to come and play with the puppies.

Ch. Merryhart Adam Act Up, always owner handled to his title, pictured here at the age of two, having completed his title with two Best of Breed wins over Specials. Bred by Jim and Neoma Eberhardt, Merryhart Kennels, Santa Ana, California.

Ludwig photo

26 Selling the Litter

Every Westie breeder must decide for himself when to sell the puppies. When the puppies are seven weeks of age, the weaning process is accomplished; therefore, this is a good time for the puppy to break his ties with the litter and go to a new home. If puppies are taken from the litter before the age of seven weeks, they miss socialization with other dogs. Dogs that are taken away from their dam too soon miss the discipline that she gives and may develop into aggressive dogs. Puppies taken away from the dam at the crucial fourth week and given much attention by the buyer become very well adjusted to humans but often care nothing about other dogs.

The choice of most Westie breeders is to keep the puppies until they are about three months old. This gives the breeder the opportunity to watch the development. It also allows time to get the soft coats plucked, if this is necessary. Heads are formed, teeth are erupted, and male testicles are descended into the scrotum at three months of age. The person who is going to be associated with the puppy during this most important period of development needs to fully understand the puppy's needs.

The personal attention that the puppy receives as an individual, along with a little simple training on a regular basis beginning as early as five weeks of age, offsets the puppy's dominance relationship with his littermates, yet he learns to get along with other dogs. From the age of seven to twelve weeks, the puppy needs much individual attention, since this is the time when he learns to become a co-worker with people. This cultivates the "pack instinct" as he works with his master, and his permanent attitudes toward humans, learning, and direction are formed.

Now real learning begins. The puppy must learn that people are to love. He must be trained with no harsh discipline, only mild correction, and he must be praised for his accomplishments. Only the prospective buyer who understands that he is shaping the dog's character during these weeks should be allowed to take the puppy home at the age of seven weeks.

CONTACTS AND ADVERTISING

When the litter is born, advise the owner of the stud dog that the puppies are safely into the world, and tell him how many puppies of each sex were born. This person will probably have inquiries about puppies and can refer people to you. If other Westie breeders live in your area,

let them know that you have a litter. These people get frequent inquiries for puppies, often at a time when they have none to sell. They are usually glad to know where puppies are going to be available. If your local kennel club has a puppy referral service, make certain that they know about your litter. If you have become a member of the parent club, for a nominal fee you can have a litter listing published in the next newsletter.

Advertising in the "Pets" column of the classified section of your local paper should not be placed until the puppies have been given their first immunization shots, since you will not want strangers visiting the puppies. You can run an ad earlier with a clause stating that you are taking "reservations" for the puppies. You may wish to advertise in the newspapers of nearby cities as well.

A lovely, large litter of Westie babies gets plenty of attention from breeder, Mrs. J. H. Baldwin (Pat), who understands the need for the early socialization of puppies.

200

REGISTERING THE LITTER WITH THE AKC

When the litter is born, write to the American Kennel Club and request a form for registration of a litter. When this arrives, read it carefully, then fill in all the spaces intended for the use of the litter owner. Take or mail the form to the owner of the stud dog so that he can fill in his part and sign the form. It will save time if you give or send the stud owner a stamped, legal-size envelope addressed to the American Kennel Club along with your check, payable to the American Kennel Club, for the litter registration fee. That way the stud owner can forward it to the AKC rather than mail it back to you.

In a short time, you will receive individual applications for the registration of the puppies. There should be one slip for each puppy. Read one of the slips carefully (they should all be identical) to be sure that all of the information is correct. If there should be an error, the applications will have to be returned for correction. When the puppies are sold, one of these slips should be given to each buyer so that he can register the dog in his name. The AKC requires that a dog seller keep records of every dog sold for a period of five years. The record must show the sire and dam, date of whelping, name and address of the buyer, or the disposition of each puppy, i.e., sold, died, or given away. The AKC prints and sells, for a nominal amount, a record book with spaces for all of the information that the dog seller is required to keep.

If for any reason the applications for registration are delayed, give the buyer a bill of sale that shows the registered name and number of the sire and dam and the number of the litter registration if you have it. If you have the individual applications at the time of the sale, fill in all the information on the back, i.e., your name and address and the name and address of the buyer. On the front of the application, you must list the sex. A space must also be filled in for color. It would seem obvious that the dog being sold as a West Highland White Terrier is a white dog. Nevertheless, you must write "White" in the space, or the application will be returned to you.

If you sell a puppy that you know is not breeding stock, you have the right to withhold the registration application from the buyer. The fact that the puppy is not to be bred must be discussed with the buyer so that it is mutually understood at the time of purchase. In addition, you must have an agreement in writing and in duplicate for both you and the buyer to sign. This states that you are withholding the registration application and gives the reason why. If the buyer should later decide to breed the puppy, he could attempt to register the puppy with the AKC claiming that you had refused to give him the registration application at the time of sale. Only an agreement in writing, and signed by both parties, will be honored by the AKC. File your copy in a safe place, along with the other records that you are required to keep.

As the breeder, you are entitled to select the registered names of the puppies and to register them as individuals. You may prefer to do this to assure yourself that the puppies will be assigned appropriate names. You will receive the individual registration slips. When the puppies are sold, each one can be transferred to the new owner by filling out the back of the registration slips and mailing them to the AKC with the transfer fee.

SCREENING PUPPY BUYERS

It is very important that you know something about the people who want to buy your puppies. You should also know about the type of living quarters of the prospective buyers so that you can evaluate the home. Many people are impulse buyers of dogs and may not have the best housing and care in mind. Remember that these are *your* puppies and that you are under no obligation to sell them to the first people who come with cash in hand—unless you are interested in nothing but the money.

It is important that all members of the family want the puppy. If the puppy is to be purchased as a pet for a child, make certain that the mother wants the puppy. Eventually, most of the work of caring for and cleaning up after the puppy will fall to her. Buying a puppy to teach the child responsibility is wishful thinking. Once the "new" wears off, the mother will be feeding and caring for the puppy. Young children need training in being gentle with a pet, and the mother must be willing to give such training to the children. I once had a woman tell me that her family had had a Toy breed. But she had decided to make a Westie their next family dog, "so the children will have a dog that they can throw around." I silently said, "Not from me, you don't!"

You must ask enough questions to ascertain why the people want a pet and a Westie in particular. If they have only seen photographs and know nothing about the breed, it is up to you to educate them. Sincerely interested buyers are grateful for the help that the breeder is willing to give. It may be that a bouncing and investigative breed like a Westie is not the best choice for their life-style. Perhaps no dog is, and they should consider a gerbil or a parakeet as a pet.

I will not sell a puppy to home owners who do not have a fenced yard or run for the dog. One man wanted a puppy bitch so that his Westie dog would have a "sex life." No sale. One woman wanted a dog and a bitch from a litter, to be used for breeding. No sale. She was ready and willing, cash for two puppies in hand, and most annoyed that I would not take it. She lived in a nearby county, and a long distance call to the only veterinarian in the area gained the information that the woman had just moved into the area and was starting a "puppy mill"—breeding small dogs that did not require much food, to be sold to pet shops. You cannot be too careful.

The most satisfactory homes that I have found for my puppies have been those where the buyers have been willing to wait to get a Westie puppy. These are the people who have given some real thought to dog ownership and have made arrangements for the care of the puppy. One of these was an apartment dweller who had never owned a dog. She was interested in two or three breeds and asked to see my Westies in the flesh. I loaned her books from my "library" so that she could read about dogs and their care. Eventually, my bitch had a litter, and the woman bought a male puppy. She has been the most satisfactory dog owner anyone could hope to find.

Some breeders are annoyed when a prospective buyer asks the price of the puppies as one of the first questions. "If they have to ask the price, they cannot afford the dog," is their attitude. This could be a person who has never owned a purebred dog or has not purchased a dog in a long time. The caller may have no idea about the fair price for a quality Westie. One breeder told me that if a person could afford to buy a Westie, he could afford to take care of it! To me, "care" consists of many things, not just the money for food and booster shots. If my puppies cannot go to homes with responsible dog owners, they can stay right here with me.

When the new owner of one of your puppies leaves your house, make certain that you send along an immunization record and a copy of the puppy's pedigree. If you are paid by check, you may wish to keep the registration application until the check has cleared. This is standard practice, and most people understand that the few dishonest people in the world make such precautions necessary. You can write out a bill of sale, if the buyer wishes one. It is nice to give the buyer a bag of the food that the puppy has been eating, along with the name of the food and a feeding schedule. You should make it clear that you are always available for "consultation" in case of problems, and for the lifetime of the dog. Insist that the puppy be taken to a veterinarian so that the buyer will feel sure that you have sold him a healthy puppy. And, lastly, make it clear that you will always be interested in the puppy and that if for any reason the buyer does not want or cannot keep the dog, you wish to be the first person to know so that you can take the dog back.

Now we have gone in a full circle, from the puppy bitch that you acquired from another breeder to the sale of her offspring. In rearing the litter, you learned all about what went into that lovely puppy that you brought home from her breeder—the loss of sleep, the hours of time, the checks written to the veterinarian and the grocer, the floor mopping—along with the joy of watching the little miracles grow and develop into individual personalities.

Now it is your turn to answer the question, "How can you bear to let them go?" You have taken the trouble to produce the best litter possible and have helped each puppy realize his best potential with early training. Some buyers may have been waiting for months to welcome that bouncing bundle with the fast pink tongue and the dark, hazel eyes. Now it gives you great pleasure to know that these puppies will go to the carefully chosen new homes.

27 Your "Seasoned" Citizen

Westies do not exhibit some of the visible signs of aging that are obvious in other breeds. For example, the breeds with color in the coat, especially black dogs, will begin to look a little grizzled about the muzzle often by the time they are six years of age. This is roughly equivalent to forty years in human terms. Your white Westie does not get grey, and if you have been keeping the beard white, your Westie's face will not show much sign of aging.

Just like people, dogs are prone to the problems associated with growing older. Some age in different ways and at different stages in life. Westies, with their dominant gene for white coat color, do not suffer the loss of sight and hearing that is associated with the breeds that are bred to white through a recessive gene. In fact, one of the charms of the breed is that the well-nurtured and exercised Westie grows older with grace. Six-month checkups by your veterinarian for your older Westie will pay big dividends in early care for any health problems that may develop.

At home, daily care remains important. Cleaning of the ears, eyes, and teeth should never be neglected. Systemic problems can often be detected in foul or urine-scented breath. A dog can have no more valuable friend than an observant owner who watches for changes in the dog's condition and habits.

FEEDING YOUR OLDER DOG

Overweight is to be avoided in the older dog, just as it is in the older human. It is easy to be "kind" to your older pet, telling yourself that just one extra treat cannot possibly hurt. You are being kind to *yourself*, not to your dog. As your dog becomes less active, the added pounds will creep on, unnoticed, unless you weigh the dog monthly.

The older dog needs less carbohydrate in the diet and more protein. The persistent rumor that a high-protein diet for the older dog will cause kidney problems has been in circulation for a long time. This is only rumor and has absolutely no basis in clinical fact. Quite the contrary is true. Studies show that dogs on low-protein diets improve all renal functions when the protein is increased. Studies in large numbers of rats show that more protein is needed to keep the kidneys in good working order.

In Dr. Kronfeld's series of articles, "Home Cooking for Dogs,"* a study by Dr. Kenneth C. Bovee is cited in which some dogs had 75 percent of the kidney tissue removed in order to speed up the aging process of the kidneys. The dogs fed 54 percent protein after surgery did much better than dogs fed 29 percent protein, and much better than dogs fed 19 percent protein, for a period of four years. If kidney failure develops, a very low-protein diet has been found to lessen the symptoms but not prolong the life of the dog. Therefore, commercial dog foods that advertise a low-protein diet for the older dog, in order to protect his kidney function, promote the old rumor, but have no basis in fact.

Actually, your dog's changing dietary needs should be met on an individual basis. If the dog is less active and requires smaller portions of food, ask your veterinarian about a vitamin-mineral supplement for the dog. If your dog has signs of congestive heart failure, the diet may require less salt intake. If your dog shows signs of becoming incontinent in his old age, especially suddenly, this may indicate a kidney problem and the dog should be seen by your veterinarian. Dogs that need to urinate frequently require an uptake in fluids, which can be supplied with water on the food or with broths. If the dog seems less interested in his food, it may be that the senses of smell and taste have diminished. Heating the food will make it more appealing, heightening the scent and flavor. Do not promote finicky eating habits by substituting fun food. Rather, have the dog checked by your veterinarian to see why the dog is not interested in food.

204

---

*AKC Gazette, June 1978, p. 65. In May 1980, Dr. Bovee was honored for these studies as a recipient of one of the Ralston-Purina Research Awards (AKC Gazette, October 1980, p. 28).

QUARTERING THE OLDER DOG

The older dog may appreciate comforts that he shunned in his youth. A soft pillow or two can feel very good underneath old bones. Arthritic dogs appreciate warmth and should have a comfortably warm bed, so moving the dog's sleeping spot nearer to a source of heat in the winter may be a good idea. Elderly dogs should not be left outdoors during the winter except for the hours of sunshine. Neither should these dogs be subjected to the heat of summer for long periods. Put the dog out early in the morning or in the cool of the evening. During the heat of the day, indoors in the air-conditioning is the best place for the dog.

As the dog ages, he likes changes less and less, even as you and I. Some dogs may seem less responsive to commands and may appear to be stubborn. This could be due to a loss of hearing rather than willful disobedience. Your dog needs you during the September of his years. He wants only your familiar hands to brush and check him over, only your familiar hands to fill his dinner dish and place it in the usual spot. Finding "a good home" for the older dog is an act of utter callousness. His love and loyalty to his family should be rewarded with daily care, exercise to match his abilities, games to stimulate his brain, and his master's voice to cheer him. All of these things, along with good nutrition and the care of your veterinarian, will help you and your Westie to enjoy a long and happy life together.

Ch. Briarwood Bonnet, age sixteen, shows her great-great-great-grandson, Joey, the way to a favorite spot. "Bonnie," who died in 1979, was the foundation bitch of the Bonnie Brier Westies, belonging to Christine Swingle, North Canton, Connecticut.

28 Congenital Defects in Westies

Just like people, all breeds of dogs are subject to defects and medical problems, some known to be inherited and some believed to be inherited. All are termed "congenital," meaning that the defect is there at birth, having occurred sometime during the development of the fetus. While much medical research on dogs has been conducted for the benefit of humans, relatively little has been done *for* dogs. Dog research is usually funded only by groups that are interested in dogs and their welfare. If a problem is widespread, like hip dysplasia in the large breeds, research is well funded, but if a problem is rare or is seen in only one or two breeds, research is seldom done. Research money is scarce, and it must be used to benefit the greatest number of dogs.

It is interesting to read lists of these defects as they are attributed to the various breeds. The purebred dogs that appear to have the fewest problems are the rarest breeds. The most defects are seen in the more popular breeds. This would seem to indicate that when a breed becomes very popular over a period of years, the indiscriminate breeding that takes place tends to multiply the congenital defects. Many breeds of dogs have medical problems associated with their development by man. In his interest to create something new, man has crossbred two or three different breeds, inbred indiscriminately, reduced size, increased size, lengthened backs, shortened backs, bred for very short forefaces and popped eyes, bred for long forefaces, cropped ears and docked tails.

Westies—thank goodness—are not one of the popular breeds. The Westie has been left in his natural state. Only the white coat color was used in developing the breed, and it results from a dominant gene. Other than sometimes being minus some of his premolars, a lack of which creates no medical problems, the Westie has no other defects due to the development of the breed.

The few defects in Westies are *rarely* found. In fact, they are so seldom seen that some Westie owners feel that there is no real need to mention possible defects for fear of giving the entire breed a "bad name." My own feeling is that any new person coming into the breed needs to know the possible problems so that Westies can remain the wonderful breed that they are—hardy and healthy.

GLOBOID CELL LEUKODYSTROPHY

This is a disease that causes degeneration of the central nervous system. It is due to the lack of an enzyme, galactocerebromide b-galactosidase. This results in a metabolic defect in the systems necessary for the synthesis of myelin, a white, fatty substance that forms a sheath around the axis cylinders of the nerves. Early symptoms, appearing at two to seven months of age, may seem to mimic distemper, with weakness in the hindquarters and tremors. Some dogs may develop severe paralysis in the hindquarters during the course of the disease, at three to six months of age. Some dogs may develop a hopping front gait, with the inability to judge distances or to recognize objects or people. Death usually occurs in two to three months. Only your veterinarian can make the proper diagnosis.

This disease is *very rare*, but research seems to indicate that the disease is due to a recessive pair of genes. It may run in families, skipping one generation, with puppies of normal parents being affected. The disease has been found in Westies, Cairns, Miniature Poodles, Beagles, and in some cats. It is seen, also rarely, in humans, where it is called Krabbe's disease, after the doctor who found it in two sister infants in 1916. The number of people and dogs affected is so small that little research has been done. The dogs could serve as experimental animals to study, if sufficient research were possible.

CRANIOMANDIBULAR OSTEOPATHY (CMO)

This is a disease of young dogs and is usually seen between four and seven months of age. It is a *rare* disease, and the cause is unknown. Since it is found in Westies, Cairns, and Scotties, all of which were probably once found in the same litters, it would appear to be inherited, but no mode of transmission has been established. So few cases are seen that no research has been conducted.

The disease affects the lower jawbones (the mandibles) and the adjoining skull bones in the puppy. It usually affects both sides of the jaws and head. The disease is a proliferation of growth in the bones and is sometimes called "lion jaw." The bone cells multiply, although the disease is not cancer of the bone. The thickening of the bone occurs in stages, with some periods of resorption of the excess cells. Studies of the bones involved show blue lines, indicating that the disease goes into a resting stage, then begins to proliferate again.

The puppy exhibits signs of pain in the lower jaw when it is palpated, and he has a difficult time in opening his mouth and chewing. Reduced food intake will result in malnutrition unless a highly nutritious diet is fed. The disease progresses until eleven to thirteen months of age and may stop or regress. Once mastication is impaired, however, the disease is not likely to recede.

Treatment consists of aspirin for pain and cortisone therapy, administered by a veterinarian. There is no specific treatment, nor a cure.

INGUINAL HERNIA

High risk for this condition was found to exist in Basset Hounds, Basenjis, Cairns, Pekingese, and Westies. My own veterinarian says that he sees the condition more in Miniature Poodles and Chihuahuas than in any other breeds. Similar to the opening for the umbilical cord, the inguinal canals, on each side of the belly, are slit-like openings to allow passage from the body cavity of the spermatic cord in the male and the round ligament in the female. Failure of this slit to correctly close may allow a fold of lining (omentum) or a loop of the intestine to protrude into the canal. The presence of the hernia is detectable as a soft, fluctuating enlargement on one side of the dog's penis or on the side of the bitch's belly. Replacement of the protrusion is sometimes possible by palpation, by a veterinarian, or by holding the animal up by the hind legs.

If these methods fail, surgery is required to repair the hernia.

CLEFT PALATE

This condition can be found in many breeds of dogs, and it is seen in newborn puppies. The bony roof of the mouth, which separates the mouth from the nasal passages, fails to close. This is sometimes accompanied by a hair lip. The breeder or veterinarian can recognize the defect when ingested milk runs back out of the nasal passages instead of being swallowed. Most puppies with this condition will die of starvation or from pneumonia caused by ingestion of fluid or food into the lungs. If the condition is not severe, tube feeding of the puppy can be tried and surgical correction attempted.

It is not known whether this is a genetic defect. In humans, it is considered a birth defect, caused by improper development of the fetus during the period when the lips and mouth are being formed. In dogs, high dosages of vitamin A given to the bitch during the seventeenth to twenty-second days of pregnancy have been found to cause cleft palate.

CRYPTORCHIDISM

This word is from the Greek, and it translates to "hidden testicle." The dog with no testicles properly descended into the scrotum is called a bilateral (both sides) cryptorchid, or "anorchid." This total lack of testicles is very rare. Very common in all purebred dogs and in crossbreds is the dog with only one testicle properly descended into the scrotum. These dogs are called unilateral (one side) cryptorchids, commonly, if incorrectly, known as "monorchids."

The testicles are formed inside the body and are attached to the spermatic cord. Under normal conditions, the testicles leave the body cavity through the inguinal canal and pass through the inguinal "ring." These "rings," or slits, are located at the flank on the dog's belly in about the same location as the ovaries of the human female. Once through the "rings," they travel diagonally through a canal, which lies just underneath the skin, and down to the scrotum. Ideally, the two testicles will be completely descended into the scrotum at birth.

Testicles are located outside the body cavity in the scrotum, where their important sex hormones are not subjected to the internal heat of the body. If one or both are retained within the abdominal cavity, they are thought to be a health hazard. Often, a retained testicle has been found to grow very large and create intestinal problems. One school of thought is that the retained testicle may become malignant, while another theory claims that the incidence of malignancy is no higher in these dogs than in the average dog.

A testicle may fail to pass through the inguinal canal if inguinal hernia is involved. If the abdominal lining and/or a loop of intestine were to protrude into the open canal, the testicle would be blocked from leaving the body cavity.

A testicle may pass through the inguinal canal and through the second "ring" but have a spermatic cord which is too short to allow full descent to the scrotum. In this case, the testicle will remain in the canal just underneath the skin of the belly. This is seen more often on the right side than on the left side, in a ratio of almost two to one. During fetal development, the kidneys are located on the right side so that the right testicle has a longer distance to travel to the scrotum, causing the spermatic cord to be too short. Many breeders believe that maintaining puppy dogs on the slender side, with no fatty deposit on the belly, helps to insure fully descended testicles. This condition will probably never cause the dog any problem, since the testicle is located outside the abdominal cavity and is not subjected to internal body heat.

The undescended testicle in humans is considered a birth defect and is not thought to be inherited. Male humans are given shots of chorionic gonadotropin in the sometimes successful attempt to cause the testicle to fully descend. If this is not successful, surgery is performed to correct the condition. In dogs, the undescended testicle is believed to be inherited, although the mode of transmission has not been established. One theory purports that the condition is caused by a sex-linked characteristic and is passed along by the dam to her sons, while another theory claims that the sire passes the fault on to his sons. In either case, dog breeders are told that the "monorchid" dog should not be used for breeding. Many veterinarians do not believe in

207

the use of chorionic gonadotropin, and surgical correction of the condition is considered unethical.

Monorchids in the Show Ring

About 1950, the American Kennel Club decided that a monorchid dog was not "entire" and therefore was ineligible to be shown in the conformation ring. Similarly, spayed bitches are disqualified from the Conformation ring. No one questions the good intentions of the American Kennel Club in disqualifying these dogs. The objective is to eliminate monorchid dogs from breeding programs, thus eliminating the fault.

This is sad for breeders, since the most handsome dog in the litter invariably seems to be the one that fails to have two descended testicles. Thus far, no studies have been done on the subject, but the numbers of monorchid dogs being produced does not seem to have declined. Prior to the ruling by the American Kennel Club, the monorchid dogs were shown and used as stud dogs. While no studies were done at that time either, these dogs apparently produced no higher numbers of monorchid sons than dogs that were entire.

The English Kennel Club also decided, and at about the same time, to disqualify monorchid dogs from the Conformation ring. After several years, they studied the records of the number of monorchids still being produced, and this led them to rescind the disqualification of monorchids. The English are more interested in producing good animals of correct type than they are in simply showing dogs. They concluded that they were eliminating their best dogs from breeding programs while failing to reduce the number of monorchids being produced.

An article in *Dog World*, February 1980, under the "Then and Now" heading, written by Vincent G. Perry, is subtitled "A Disqualifying Fault." Mr. Perry is a highly respected all-breed judge of dogs and a "dog man" of many, many years. In his article, he covers the subject in depth, in his usual thought-provoking style. He makes the valid point that if a bitch is missing some part of her reproductive organs, she is not disqualified from showing, and that the number of barren bitches is equal to the number of monorchid dogs. Mr. Perry advocates that a study like the one conducted in England be done by the American Kennel Club, and the policy of disqualifying monorchid dogs be reconsidered.

The breeder who has a monorchid puppy dog to sell should discover exactly where the "hidden testicle" is located. A young puppy that has one testicle not fully descended has every chance of becoming "entire" if the testicle is out of the body and in the canal. This puppy dog should be sold to owners who will not wish to show the dog in the event that the cord is too short for full descent into the scrotum. If the testicle is retained inside the body, the buyer of such a puppy should be told that the dog must be subjected to surgery at maturity to locate and remove the testicle. At this time, the attending surgeon will remove the other testicle, neutering the dog. This will in no way make the dog less desirable as a family pet.

LEGG-CALVE' - PERTHES DISEASE

This is another ailment that affects people as well as dogs. It was first diagnosed in humans by three different researchers almost at the same time—hence, the long name. It is seen in young children and in young dogs. No evidence that the condition is hereditary has been established, although it has sometimes been found in sibling children. For some unknown reason, the blood supply to the head of the femur (upper thighbone) is restricted or completely cut off. This causes necrosis (death) of the bone where the femur fastens into the pelvis. In children, the treatment consists of putting the child into an A-frame brace to prevent pressure on the affected bone. In dogs, surgery is possible to remove the dead bone. The muscles take over the job of supporting the leg, the bone recalcifies, and in a few weeks the dog is moving about on all four legs again. It has been suggested that the condition in dogs is caused by an injury to the affected leg. No evidence to dispute this has been discovered in children. Many of the small breeds of dogs are included in the list of those that have been known to be affected.

DERMATITIS

This is a complex subject, since the causes of skin problems are both varied and many. Skin problems affect many breeds of dogs, the Terrier group among them. In the training of veterinarians, very little time is spent on the subject of allergies in the dog. In the past ten years, the veterinary profession has come to realize the importance of this kind of problem and the great expense that the owner of an allergic dog often must bear. In the field of human medicine, the allergist is a relative newcomer. In dogs, research funds being what they are, very little research has been underway until recently. Hope lies ahead, with new groups and facilities now being developed for the study of skin problems in dogs. In the past few years, the veterinary allergist has appeared on the scene, and science is understanding the events that lead to allergic attacks.

For a dog to exhibit an allergic response, a foreign substance and a specific antibody manufactured by the dog's body must be present. "Antigen" is the word used to define the foreign substance, a combination of two words, "antibody" and "generating." "Allergen" is also a combination of two words, "allergy" and "generating," made up to refer to an antigen that causes an allergic response. Not all antigens are harmful. All vaccines are antigens, developed to stimulate the body's white cells to manufacture the correct antibody to resist an infection before it can cause illness.

The dog manufactures four kinds of antibodies, but only one, Immunoglobulin E (IGE), is involved in allergies. When the dog first comes in contact with an antigen, the white cells will fight it off with the correct antibody. Then, depending on the number of allergens involved, the dog's body releases chemicals that bring on an allergic attack. Allergies can be "idiopathic," which means that the allergy is peculiar to one individual dog, and of unknown origin. Allergies can, on occasion, be "atopic" (a-toe-pick), which means that the dog has an inherited predisposition to be allergic. This dog may have a dam that was allergic to pollen and a sire that was allergic to mold, while the offspring is allergic to feathers. In other words, the dog inherits only the ability to become allergic, not an allergy to a specific substance. This inherited predisposition may be due to a defect in the immune system.

The Control of Dermatitis

The best ally that a dog with dermatitis can have is an observant owner. So many things can cause the dog to itch. The most frequent problem is fleas and/or allergy to flea saliva. Help for fleas is discussed in the chapter on housing and care. If the dog is flea-free, he will not have a flea saliva allergy. In Westies, a common cause of itchiness is a lack of care, like daily brushing and the removal of dead coat. Also, the Westie whose owner just feels he *must* bathe the dog frequently (usually because previously owned breeds were bathed regularly) will often be itchy from his dried skin.

One of the most common allergens in dogs is pollen. Pollens vary from one part of the country to another and with the seasons. Molds are also culprits. These are multitude in type and are essential in nature. Molds are found in compost piles, in flower bed mulches, in raked leaves in the fall, in house dust, in the drip pans of self-defrosting refrigerators and freezers, in air filters and humidifiers, underneath the sink, and on fresh melons and fruits—and mushrooms, toadstools, and green growth on cement are molds. Fortunately, only a few molds affect dogs adversely. Then there are feathers and kapok in pillows, horse and cattle hair in furniture upholstery, and man-made fibers in carpet and furniture covers. Chemical pollutants in the air can be irritants. Bacteria, especially staphylococci and streptococci, can be skin irritants as well as cause other infections. Food allergies can also be exhibited by some dogs.

Adding to the problems in dermatitis is the fact that the dog scratches and/or chews the itchy spots. A dog that is intensely itching can multiply the problem by breaking the skin, sometimes bringing on secondary infection. So the owner of a dog that is scratching with a chronic form of itchiness must never ignore the condition. Many other conditions can seem to be caused by allergy. Beside fleas, the itching could be caused by one of the mange mites, by seborrheic dermatitis, or by the dog having made contact with some irritant. Before any diagnosis of allergy can be made, all other possibilities must be ruled out.

The owner of an itchy dog must exercise common sense. Where I live, our weather reports give the pollen and particulate count every day. For example, one day the report will say that the pine pollen count is very heavy. If it rains the next day, the evening weather report will say that the air is pollen-free. But where is the pollen? On the wet grass in the yard. I advise the owners of all short-legged dogs to keep their dogs out of the wet grass; dew-wet grass in the early morning, dew-wet grass in the late evening, rain-wet grass, and freshly mowed grass. I follow my own advice, and my dogs never have skin problems. I feed brewer's yeast, which fights bacterial infection; I feed kelp, which keeps the thyroid in healthy balance and makes for healthy skin; and I brush my dogs regularly and keep their coats free of dead hair. We never have fleas, and my dogs do not have any skin problems.

However, an occasional dog has atopic dermatitis. This dog will not be helped with simple preventative measures. All owners of dogs with chronic dermatitis should have the advice of a veterinarian. Along with an observant owner, this dog needs a veterinarian that is patient and a detective. With your careful observance and note-taking, you can be a great help in assisting with the diagnosis. Besides contact dermatitis, there is Allergic Inhalant Dermatitis (A.I.D.). Remember that the dog is like a little vacuum cleaner, sniffing into everything. The atopic dog will probably not develop his allergy until he is between one and three years of age. Skin problems will begin as seasonal, but will eventually become perennial. This dog can be helped by skin tests, the same type of tests that are done on people, with antigens being injected underneath the skin. Testing can determine the allergens that are causing the problems, and desensitization treatment can be given. At this writing, research is underway for more help for this atopic dog. Projects are directed toward the development of a blood test to identify the atopic dogs and to try to confirm if this predisposition toward allergic response is inherited.

210

The author with Ch. Fairtee Simon-pure Pippin.

About the Author

One late, snowy February evening in 1962, Ruth Faherty flipped on the television set and happened upon the broadcast of the Group and Best in Show judging from the Westminster Kennel Club show in Madison Square Garden. Ruth had never been to a dog show, so she was fascinated if not altogether certain about ring procedures. Not that it mattered. From the moment the Best in Show judging began, her focus was riveted on the cutest dog she had ever seen, the Terrier Group winner Ch. Elfinbrook Simon.

Simon sold himself to everyone in the Garden that night, and in only eighteen minutes was declared Best in Show by judge Haywood Hartley. Ruth had never seen such self-assurance in a dog. As if to emphasize it, when the big "Number 1" was moved in front of Simon, he walked up to it with the greatest aplomb and marked it as his by lifting his leg. The explosion of laughter from the spectators nearly brought down the rafters.

Ruth never forgot the little white dog, and decided on the spot that she would someday own a Westie. Nine years later the dream came true. In 1971 she received a Westie puppy as a birthday gift from her daughter. "Duffy" had every fault in the book, but a lovely disposition. "Owning him was," she says, "rather like eating one peanut."

In due time she was looking for a bitch for breeding and show. Meanwhile, she trained Duffy in obedience and began reading everything that she could find about Westies and dogs in general. She was fortunate to find a Westie breeder nearby who owned a grooming parlor and who taught Ruth a great deal about grooming. She attended shows and visited breeders and soon learned how to recognize a good Westie. Both Ruth and her husband became active in the local kennel club and their regional Westie club.

Eventually she found a bitch, and soon a litter of puppies sired by a Simon son were on the way. One of them, Ch. Fairtee Simon Pure Pippin, went on to become many time Best of Breed winner and won a Group first.

Ruth has an insatiable curiosity and desire to learn, and the knowledge she gained soon earned her the role of teacher, especially when it comes to grooming. She has given many, many lessons to beginning Westie owners. Out of this experience came Ruth's interest in sharing her knowledge still further by writing a book. At first it was to cover only grooming, but the staff at Alpine convinced her to share even more. Thus, *Westies from Head to Tail* was conceived.

While there are many breeders with more experience, or more champions to their credit, they do not always have the time or the willingness to write. For Ruth, sharing and teaching are truly a way of life.

Although her showing activities were greatly curtailed after the death of her husband, Lou, in 1976, Ruth remains an active breeder. She is a member of the West Highland White Terrier Club of America, the West Highland White Terrier Club of England, the American Dog Owners Association, the West Highland White Terrier Club of Western Pennsylvania, and the local Chattanooga Kennel Club. Although Ruth calls herself a "hobby breeder," her attitude and knowledge purely proclaim her a professional.

212

Alverson photo

Other Sources of Information

BOOKS ON THE BREED

Dennis D. Mary. *The West Highland White Terrier.* London: Popular Dogs Publishing Company Limited, 1970.

Hands, Barbara. *The West Highland White Terrier.* London: John Bartholomew and Sons Limited, 1977.

Marvin, John. *The Complete West Highland White Terrier. New York, New York: Howell Book House, Inc., 4th Edition, 1977.*

Pacey, May. *West Highland White Terriers.* Trowbridge, Wiltshire, England: Redwood Press Limited, 1973.

Sherman, Florence. *How to Raise and Train A West Highland White Terrier.* Neptune, New Jersey: T.F.H. Publications, 1964.

BOOKS ON BREEDING

Battaglio, Dr. Carmello. *Dog Genetics, How to Breed Better Dogs.* Neptune, New Jersey: T.F.H. Publications, 1978.

Frankling, Eleanor. *Practical Dog Breeding and Genetics.* New York, New York: Arco Publications, 1977.

Harmar, Hilary. *Dogs and How to Breed Them.* London: John Gifford Limited, 1974.

Richards, Dr. Herbert. *Dog Breeding for Professionals.* Neptune, New Jersey: T.F.H. Publications, 1978.

BOOKS ON TRAINING AND SHOWING

Cross, Jeanette, and Saunders, Blanche. *New Standard Book of Dog Care and Training.* New York, New York: Hawthorne Books, Inc., 1962.

Davis, L. W. *Go Find! Training Your Dog to Track.* New York, New York: Howell Book House, Inc., 1974.

Forsyth, Robert and Jane. *Successful Dog Showing.* New York, New York: Howell Book House, Inc., 1975.

Lent, Patricia. *Sport with Terriers.* Westmoreland, New York: Arner Publishers, 1973.

Lydecker, Beatrice. *What the Animals Tell Me.* New York, New York: Harper and Row, 1977.

Nichols, Virginia Tuck. *How to Show Your Own Dog.* Neptune, New Jersey: T.F.H. Publications, 1969.

Siegal, Mordecai, and Margolis, Matthew. *Good Dog, Bad Dog.* New York, New York: New America Library, 1973.

BOOKS ON NUTRITION

Agriculture Handbook #8. *Composition of Foods.* Washington, D.C.: United States Department of Agriculture, 1963.

Davis, Adele. *Let's Eat Right to Keep Fit.* New York, New York: New America Library, 1970.

The Merck's Veterinary Manual, Fifth Edition. Rahway, New Jersey: Merck and Company Inc., 1979.

Morris, Dr. Mark L. *Canine Dietetics.* Topeka, Kansas: Mark Morris Associates, 1979.

BOOKS OF GENERAL INTEREST

The American Kennel Club Complete Dog Book. New York, New York: Howell Book House, Inc., 1978.

Elliot, Rachel Page. *Dog Steps.* New York, New York: Howell Book House, Inc., 1973.

Pfaffenberger, Clarence. *The New Knowledge of Dog Behavior.* New York, New York: Howell Book House, Inc., 11th Printing, 1974.

Vine, Dr. Louis. *Your Dog, His Health and Happiness.* New York, New York: Arco Publications, 1977.

ARTICLES ON FEEDING

Kronfeld, Dr. David. *Feeding for Breeding.* Pure-bred Dogs American Kennel Gazette. New York, New York, July, 1977.

Kronfeld, Dr. David. *Home Cooking for Dogs,* in eleven chapters. Pure-bred Dogs American Kennel, Gazette, New York, New York, February, March, April, May, June, July, August, September, November, 1978 and January, February, 1979.

Magnuson, Mrs. Paddy. *Assure Healthy Pups.* Great Dane Breed Column. Pure-bred Dogs American Kennel Gazette, New York, New York, December, 1979.

McClennon. *Where Healthy Puppies Begin.* Welsh Terrier Breed Column. Pure-bred Dogs American Kennel Gazette. New York, New York, November, 1979.

McNab, Patricia. *Care of Dam and Puppy.* Dog World, Westchester, Illinois, January, 1980.

OTHER ARTICLES OF INTEREST

Kalstone, Lawrence M. *Soundness in the Dog and How to Recognize It.* Pure-bred Dogs American Kennel Gazette, New York, New York, November, 1979.

Perry, Vincent G. *A Disqualifying Fault.* Then and Now Column. Dog World, Westchester, Illinois, February, 1980.

Small, Dr. Edward. *The First Eighteen Days.* Dog World, Westchester, Illinois, March, 1978.

Reports on the Annual Symposium of the University of Pennsylvania. *Internal Parasites, Plague of the Dog Owner.* Pure-bred Dogs American Kennel Gazette, New York, New York, April, May, 1976.

Report on the Annual Symposium of the University of Pennsylvania. *Planning Your Breeding Program.* Pure-bred Dogs American Kennel Gazette, New York, New York, April, 1977.

VETERINARY MEDICINE REFERENCES

Baker, Edward, V.M.D. *Allergy and the Dog.* Pure-bred Dogs American Kennel Gazette, New York, New York, March, 1978.

Ettinger, Stephen J. *Text Book of Veterinary Medicine.* Philadelphia, Pennsylvania: W. B. Saunders Company, 1975.

Foley, C. W., Lasley, J. F., and Osweiler, G. D. *Abnormalities of Companion Animals.* Ames, Iowa: Iowa University Press, 1980.

Hirth, R. S., and Nielsen, S. W. Jr. *A Familial Canine Globoid Cell Leukodystrophy (Krabbe Type).* Great Britian: Pergason Press Limited. Article in Small Animal Practice, Vol. 8, 1967.

Miller, Dr. Malcolm E., Christenson, Dr. George, and Evans, Dr. Howard E. *Anatomy of the Dog.* Philadelphia, Pennsylvania: W. B. Saunders Company, 1964.

Reedy, Lloyd M., D.V.M. *Canine Atopy.* Compendium of Continuing Education for the Small Animal Practitioner. Veterinary Learning Systems, Inc., Lawrenceville, New Jersey, July, 1979.

ADDRESSES

American Kennel Club, 51 Madison Avenue, New York, New York 10010.

American Kennel Gazette (Pure-bred Dogs American Kennel Gazette), same as above.

Dog World Magazine, 10060 West Roosevelt Road, Westchester, Illinois 60153.

National Research Council, 2101 Constitution Avenue, Washington, D.C. 20037.

Terrier Type Magazine, published in 11 issues annually by Dan Kiedrowski, P.O. Drawer A, La Honda, California 94020.

Working Terrier Trials, Mrs. Patricia Lent, Dogwood Cottage, R.D. 2 38A, Franklinton, North Carolina 27525.

Index

216